INDIANAPOLIS

LEADING THE WAY

URBAN TAPESTRY SERIES

TOWERY
PUBLISHING, INC.

By Nelson Price   Art Direction by Jonathan Postal

INDIANAPOLIS

LEADING THE WAY

Sponsored by the Indianapolis Chamber of Commerce

By Nelson Price

**S**OMETIMES I THINK MY HOMETOWN AND I GREW UP TOGETHER. Almost simultaneously, we grappled with our awkward stages, then reached maturity, and eventually, at least in the case of Indianapolis, attained vitality and radiance. ▨ Here's the deal: During my childhood in the mid- and late 1960s, I considered myself a "boy of the burbs"—even though I was growing up well within Marion County and what's now urban Indianapolis. Castleton may have been a cornfield and Carmel a cow town, but suburban life—culs-de-sac, pizza parlors, shopping malls, and all—flourished in the townships that hugged the county borders. Among the townships are Washington, Wayne, Pike, Perry, and the township that included my family's *Leave It to Beaver*-style house, Warren Township. Our neighborhoods and townships had hearts, but our city did not—because there was no pulsating center.

Trips to Downtown, at least for many suburban township kids, were so rare they had the allure of expeditions to an Amazon rain forest. For my brothers and me, the occasion usually was a Saturday morning visit to my dad's law office on Monument Circle. I would play "grown-up," lugging his briefcase or yellow legal pads as I stared at the skyscrapers and gaped at the vacant asphalt lots and deteriorating housing.

"Wow," I remember telling myself. "Real, live slums."

I like to think that, as my height increased, so did my compassion. I wouldn't dream of using the word "slums" to describe Downtown housing today, and not just because of cultural or economic sensitivity.

Slums is a laughably inappropriate term for the diverse, charming, and historic residential urban neighborhoods such as Lockerbie, Chatham Arch, and the Old Northside. In fact, in one of many ironies, I now live in one of these thriving, revitalized Downtown neighborhoods. More about that in a bit.

Back to my dad's law firm on Monument Circle. His office was on the fifth floor of the Circle Tower Building just a few yards from the Soldiers and Sailors Monument, our city's eternal symbol. The towering monument is an Indianapolis

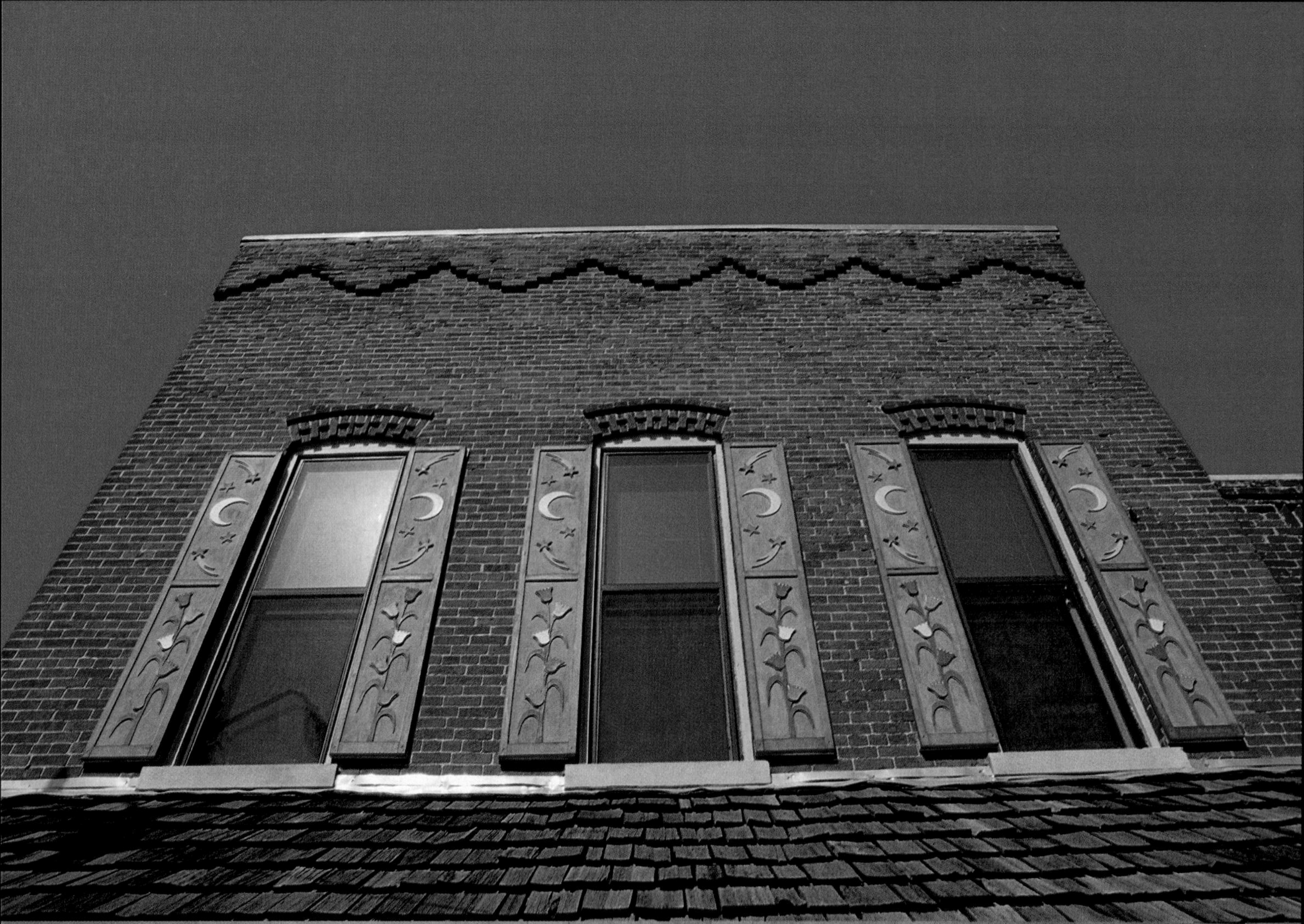

© CURTIS B. STAHR

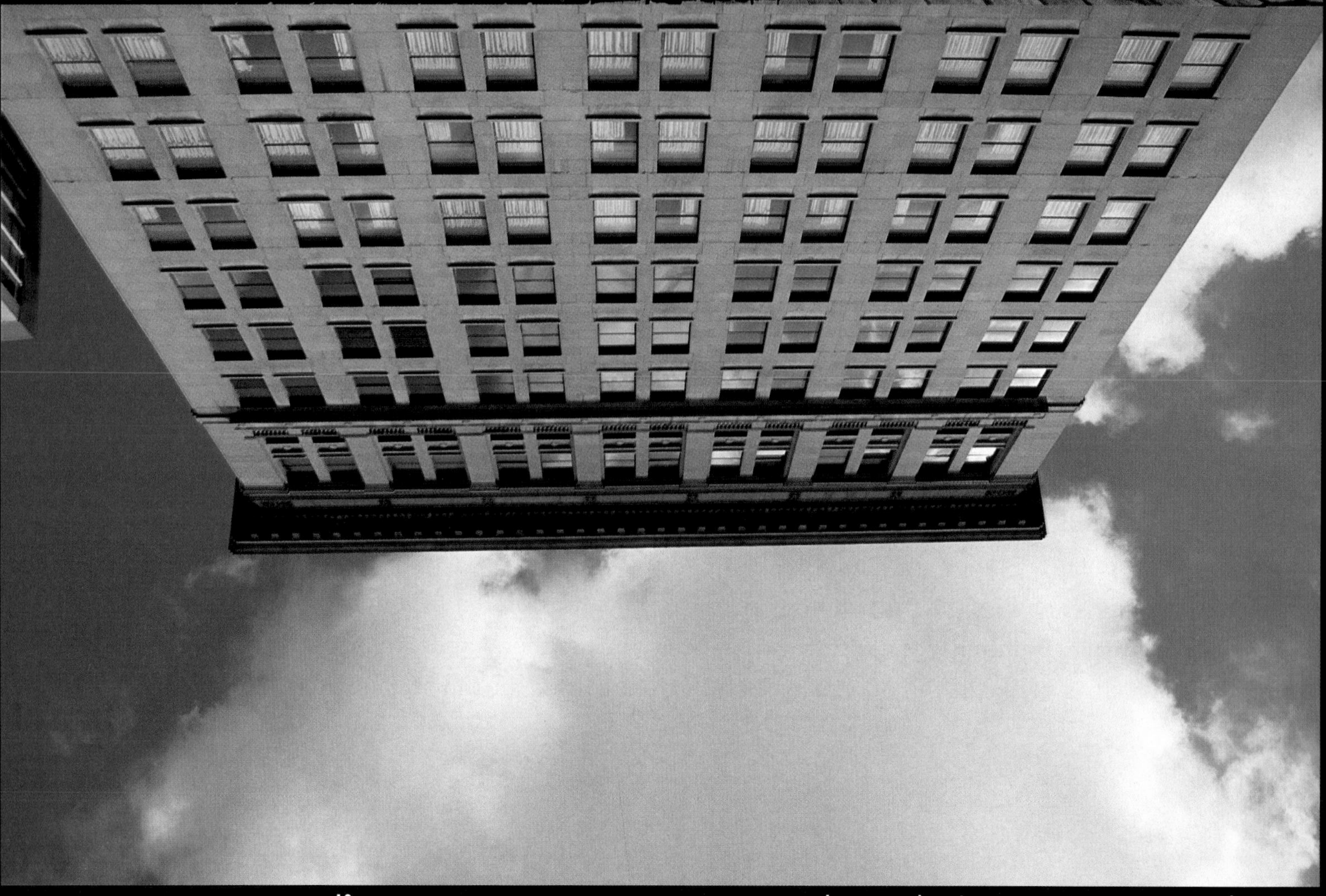

▼ © JONATHAN POSTAL / TOWERY PUBLISHING INC.

landmark that, in the early 1970s, became part of pop folklore when an irreverent young radio broadcaster and Channel 13 weekend weatherman named David Letterman announced that the distinctive memorial to war veterans had been acquired by foreign investors and would be painted green as a colossal tribute to the asparagus.

That never happened—He was joking! He was joking!—but Letterman, Broad Ripple High School's most famous alum (class of '65), told me years later that the incident taught him a sobering lesson. "A lesson I've had to learn over and over in my life, I'm sorry to say, is that just because I may think something is funny doesn't mean it's funny to everyone else," he said. "People called the radio station [WIBC-AM, still going strong] very upset because their relatives had given their lives in battle for this country. To them, the Soldiers and Sailors Monument had sincere, symbolic significance."

Precisely. But it was so darn tempting to poke fun at the Downtown of "India-NO-PLACE" or "Naptown" then. To be fair, there were bursts of vigor and warmth even in the absence of a real city heart, particularly during holiday seasons. Aside from trips with Dad on Saturdays, my journeys Downtown were on birthdays or during the Christmas season.

Holding my grandmother's hand, I would ride the bus to shop at department stores and, like generations of Hoosier kids, visit Santa at L.S. Ayres and eat lunch at the legendary Ayres Tea Room. Has chicken velvet soup ever tasted better than at that magical place, where it was served piping hot by matronly, white-haired waitresses who called you "hon," ruffled your hair, and slipped you a sugary treat?

Nothing, of course, lasts forever. Not the tea room, which closed amid much public outcry in the early 1990s (one of the few disappointments during Downtown's glorious renaissance), nor my boyhood. In the mid-1970s, Downtown and I went through our awkward phases. As a teenager, I ignored the urban area we natives refer to as "the Mile Square."

(Quick history lesson: The city was planned in 1821 by the same folks who designed Washington, D.C. That means the Mile Square's thousands of daily pedestrians and motorists travel around a square grid of streets with diagonal arteries—and with Monument Circle as the center or heart.)

Once, when I was about 14, my best buddy and I begged our parents to let us take our first jaunt Downtown unaccompanied by an adult. We caught a matinee movie at the tarnished Circle Theatre; its stunning restoration as the concert hall of the Indianapolis Symphony Orchestra was still about 10 years away.

Other than trips like that—treasured more for the chance to roam free rather than for any appealing destination Downtown—we teens of the burbs didn't venture to the city's center. Who did?

My pals and I hung out at a pizza parlor or at the Steak 'n Shake near Franklin Road and Washington Street. (I'm delighted to report the Steak 'n Shake is still there at the Far-Eastside corner, continuing to serve those distinctive, skinny french fries and creamy milk shakes.) Sometimes we entertained ourselves at malls like Glendale or Eastgate. Or at each other's homes. Any place but Downtown.

"You could fire a cannon there on evenings and weekends," people would say, "and not hit anyone or anything but pigeons."

Hello, 21st century—and overwhelming changes. So much has been spectacularly transformed about our heart that I want to mention a few places that have remained intact, thankfully.

Remember the Circle Tower Building where I played grown-up with Dad's yellow legal pads? It's still there on Monument Circle in all its art deco grandeur, including the building's dazzling, gold-leaf, caged elevators.

Also still standing is a saloon south of Monument Circle on Meridian Street that's been a hopping nightspot from the horse-and-buggy era clear through the Jazz Age and the millennium countdown: the legendary Slippery Noodle Inn. ☞

Dating to the 1850s and claiming to be Indianapolis' oldest tavern, the Slippery Noodle was the hangout of public enemy number one during the Great Depression. As locals enjoy telling visitors, charismatic bank robber John Dillinger and his gang frequently patronized the Noodle, which today is a nationally known venue for blues music.

Another popular nightspot—at least for journalists, poets, politicians, and assorted groupies—is the Chatterbox, a bar in the 400 block of Massachusetts Avenue. The Chatterbox is known for jazz music (clarinetist Frank Glover has legions of fans and plays a heartbreaking version of "Have Yourself a Merry Little Christmas"), Jamaican patties (careful, they're really spicy), and a decor that features year-round Christmas lights.

Talk about ambience and character. When it comes to Downtown, including Monument Circle, my attitude has come—no pun intended—full circle.

I've gone from being a boy of the burbs filled with awe at the urban landscape . . . to a teenage critic who knocked Downtown as much as any other local during the "awkward" era . . . to a guy who risks being accused of nonstop boosterism. In 1989, this former burb boy even moved Downtown to one of the revitalized historic neighborhoods.

About six months later, a superstar moved next door. Reggie Miller became my neighbor shortly after being drafted by the Indiana Pacers. In addition to being a swell neighbor, Reggie pulled off what some cynics considered a miracle. He ignited the Pacers, leading the team to its first-ever victories in the second round of the NBA play-offs in 1994. Reggie got richer, got married, and moved to one of the sprawling homes built during the 1980s and 1990s in the Geist Reservoir area.

Eventually, Reggie was coached by a former superstar player who returned to his Hoosier roots—Larry Bird, of course. Reggie and his teammates also enjoy a new stadium. Conseco Fieldhouse opened in fall 1999, the latest in a seemingly never-ending series of whopping additions to Downtown. ☞

Indianapolis

Who would have thought 20 years ago that among Downtown's jewels would be a nationally lauded museum with rare collections of Native American and western paintings and artifacts? Yet the Eiteljorg Museum of American Indians and Western Art opened here as one of the first steps in the astonishing overhaul of the White River State Park area.

The Eiteljorg added a rich dimension to our cultural scene, which has been blessed for generations with the Children's Museum and, since 1988, the relocated, expanded, and lavishly upgraded Indianapolis Zoo.

Who would have thought 20 years ago that the city whose claim to fame hinged on one major sporting event, the Indianapolis 500, would become known as the country's amateur athletics capital?

Yet our résumé includes not only hosting the 1987 Pan American Games, but also becoming the new headquarters for dozens of athletic organizations and governing bodies. They range from USA Gymnastics, USA Track & Field, and the National Collegiate Athletic Association (its headquarters opened in fall 1999 on a campus in White River State Park) to U.S. Rowing. Yes, voyagers, U.S. Rowing chose landlocked Indianapolis for its headquarters.

Don't get me started on the spectacular sports facilities that have become part of our urban postcard. Suffice it to say that my blessings include living in a city where I can swim laps daily at the world-league Indiana University Natatorium, site of every Olympic Swimming Trials since its opening in 1982. Tell skeptics that the greatest diver in history, Olympic gold medalist Greg Louganis, identified the natatorium as his favorite facility.

My favorite views of the city's skyline, by the way, are from vantage points at our sports facilities. Highly recommended: a leisurely gaze east from the Indianapolis Tennis Center, site of the always-thrilling RCA Championships. (Also highly recommended: the international tennis tournament itself. By arranging my summer schedule around the tournament dates, I've been able to attend every Sunday

finals match since the courts were converted from clay to a hard-court surface in 1988—a move that resulted in the influx of top players like Pete Sampras and Andre Agassi.)

The view of Downtown from the stands at the tennis center—with the leafy, towering trees of Military Park in between spectators and the multicolored office buildings—is lush and stirring. Word has quickly spread, of course, that our shiny, new baseball stadium—Victory Field, home of the Indianapolis Indians—also offers spectacular vantage points for admiring the Indianapolis skyline, particularly at dusk.

What sparked all of the revitalization? In my analysis, our Indy pride was jumpstarted (or place-kicked) in 1984 with the arrival of the Indianapolis Colts at our newly opened, domed stadium. Finally, we were entering the major leagues, citywise. Civic pride has been spiraling ever since, what with annual advances like the opening in 1995 of Circle Centre, the Downtown shopping and entertainment complex that captivates so many visitors.

Action isn't confined to Downtown, of course. Restaurants, art galleries, antique shops, and nightspots in Broad Ripple long ago deserved to be called something other than "trendy." Popular for more than 25 years and enhanced by natural delights like a canal, Monon Trail (almost always bursting with bicyclers and joggers), and, of course, the dozens of squawking ducks that enchant children, Broad Ripple obviously isn't faddish. The Northside neighborhood is a classic. Timeless, not trendy.

Even the facility that's the home of the world's largest single-day sporting event has evolved in big ways. (Can any crowd this side of the Super Bowl rival the quarter-million spectators at the Indianapolis 500 for sheer color and pageantry?) Pause, fasten your seat belt, and consider how the Indianapolis Motor Speedway has roared off on exciting, unexpected paths. Most notably, there's NASCAR's Brickyard 400. This enormously popular annual race, along with the astonishing success of former central Indiana resident Jeff Gordon on the NASCAR circuit, has

turned Indy into a city of stock car enthusiasts. And how could a Hollywood screenplay outdo the inaugural Brickyard in 1994, which Gordon won, making him an instant hometown favorite. Gordon is young, handsome, clean-cut, and married to a model, and he grew up just 15 minutes away from the track—well, this is the stuff of dreams.

I'm grateful that, as we roar toward our dreams, we haven't left the glory of our past in the dust. In fact, our past is a vibrant part of our present. Take, for example, the historic Madame Walker Theatre on Indiana Avenue, the thoroughfare that played such a vital role— probably THE vital role—in the flourishing of our city's jazz scene after World War II.

Today, Hoosiers and our guests have continual opportunities to admire the Walker Theatre's decor, which includes intricate carvings celebrating African folklore and culture. To appreciate all of this, you simply attend one of the dozens of cultural and civic events at the Walker, which reopened in 1988 after a stunning renovation.

Just a few blocks away is a new home from the past that's practically incandescent: the $36 million headquarters of the Indiana Historical Society. Since the unveiling of the historical society's neoclassic home in July 1999, visitors have been tempted just to stand on the marble floor in its great hall and ogle the split staircase. Gawkers do themselves a disservice, though, if they don't visit galleries and rooms that celebrate our rich heritage, including the Cole Porter Room (where the Hoosier composer's music, such as "Night and Day," "You're the Top," and "In the Still of the Night," is played) and the Stardust Terrace, named for an immortal tune created by another legendary Hoosier, Hoagy Carmichael.

If Hoagy were alive, I have no doubt he'd be composing a song about rejuvenated Indianapolis, the city where he spent much of his adolescence and was influenced by his first mentor, local ragtime piano player Reggie DuValle.

How could Hoagy resist setting this city's transformation to music? Our growth is on display everywhere from Downtown on the Canal Walk—on sunny weekends, it becomes a tapestry of diverse Hoosiers, including parents pushing baby strollers,

fitness enthusiasts, and skateboarders—to Castleton, one of the most bustling commercial centers in the state. Just across the county line, Carmel is anything but a cow town; it's the site of some of the state's most expensive residential real estate.

We don't have every possible blessing, of course. Our winters last longer than many of us would prefer. And if I were creating our landscape, I'd give Indy an ocean and some beaches.

Fortunately, so much goes on here, more than I can ever cram in on weekends—from stimulating plays at theaters such as the Indiana Repertory Theatre and Phoenix Theatre to literary festivals at Butler University and art fairs on the lush grounds of the Indianapolis Museum of Art—that I forget about gifts Mother Nature may have withheld. This place percolates.

Speaking of the art museum: It's always seemed appropriate to me that this city, known for its Hoosier hospitality and heartland values (we even toss an annual Heartland Film Festival that's become nationally prominent), is the home of the famous *LOVE* painting and statue. Located near the entrance to the art museum, the *LOVE* statue—as well as the painting and other, similar images—were inspired, of course, by a Hoosier artist. The talents of painter Robert Clark—who became internationally acclaimed as Robert Indiana—first were apparent at Tech High School in the 1940s.

Indiana left to study art in Chicago and England, although opportunities abound here these days. The growth of Indiana University-Purdue University Indianapolis (IUPUI) has been explosive. And even though I'm a proud Indiana University grad who spent four years on the Bloomington campus, I have a particular fondness for—or owe a certain debt to—Butler University. Without the scenic, Northside university, I wouldn't exist. You see, my mom and dad met on a blind date while they were Butler students in the 1950s.

When I flip through our family photo albums from my boyhood in Naptown, then fling open a window of my Downtown home and hear the hum of bustling street life, I'm tempted to ask, "Is this really the same place?"

One of the few hassles about Downtown life is finding a parking space on evenings and weekends; many other American cities, of course, would plead for such a problem.

But, you know something? Proud as we have become about our city, Indianapolis residents still seem to suffer from a certain syndrome. It's an inferiority complex.

Part of the explanation for this, I think, is an endearing aspect of the Hoosier character. Unlike, say, Texans, we're not braggarts. We're a humble, hardworking bunch.

When I travel around Indy to talk to civic groups about the 160 influential Americans profiled in my book, *Indiana Legends: Famous Hoosiers from Johnny Appleseed to David Letterman*, I sense some surprise. We don't think of ourselves as the stuff of legends. Never mind that Indianapolis has produced famous Americans ranging from astronauts, athletes, and novelists to artists, musicians, and TV stars.

We don't regard ourselves—or our place on Earth—as better than anyone or anyplace else. Who can fault such modesty? Sometimes, though, it means that while other folks are calling attention to themselves, our accomplishments are overlooked.

But we don't have to go against our nature and tout our city. Not anymore.

All we have to do is extend invitations to visit. These days, Indianapolis—glistening, rejuvenated, and cultured—speaks for itself. 🖋

WITH ITS REGAL COLUMNS, central rotunda, and marble interiors, the four-story, limestone Indiana State Capitol Building commands an intimidating presence. Equally impressive, Veteran's Memorial Plaza (PAGE 28) and the Indiana World War Memorial (PAGE 29) dominate the five-block setting of War Memorial Plaza, an area dedicated to Hoosiers killed in foreign conflicts.

POSING IN SILENT VIGIL, MAJESTIC animals guard the city's many well-known sights, from the Indiana World War Memorial (OPPOSITE), to the Indiana State Museum (ABOVE), to Crown Hill Cemetery (PAGES 32 AND 33).

SOLDIERS AND SAILORS Monument, a tribute to the courage of Indianans who served in the Civil War, is the centerpiece of the city of Indianapolis—literally. The avenues of downtown radiate outward from the 284-foot, limestone monument, which also houses a museum and a glass-enclosed observation deck.

Indianapolis

DePew Fountain, located in University Park, was designed by sculptor Karl Bitter. Both fountain and park are part of the Indiana War Memorial Plaza, a series of memorials that sprawl across five blocks, honoring soldiers killed during World Wars I and II, as well as the Korean and Vietnam wars.

THE INTRICATE DETAILS OF Indianapolis' public art and sculpture are evident throughout the city, especially in the beautiful doors of the Indiana World War Memorial (OPPOSITE TOP).

A compelling piece of architecture in its own right, Union Station (PAGES 40 AND 41) has been revitalized into a multimillion-dollar festival marketplace, including eight full-service restaurants, three nightclubs, and more than 45 specialty shops. A Romanesque Revival-style building, the station greets visitors with barrel-vaulted ceilings and stained glass windows.

LIGHT

TRUTH

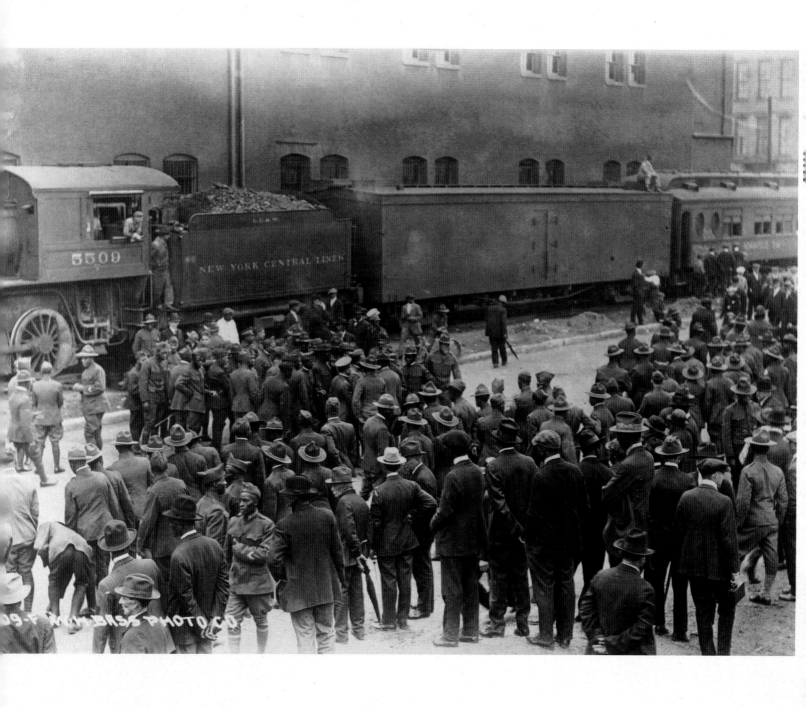

N THE LATTER PART OF THE 19TH century, Indianapolis emerged as a major stockyard and railroad hub, earning the nickname Crossroads of America.

Indianapolis

THE 12TH-LARGEST CITY IN the nation, metropolitan Indianapolis includes a nine-county area with a combined population of more than a million people.

F OOD CRITIC REID DUFFY
(OPPOSITE) ensures that chefs
in Indianapolis—including
Scott Brittingham of the Hyatt
Regency (ABOVE)—cater to the
city's sophisticated palate.

W ITH 18 COMMERCIAL PAS-
senger airlines, Indianapolis
International Airport serves
more than 7 million people annually.

GASOLINE ALLEY

THE INDIANAPOLIS 500, HELD annually at the Indianapolis Motor Speedway originated in 1911. The race has continually attracted legions of exuberant fans on the lookout for that checkered flag.

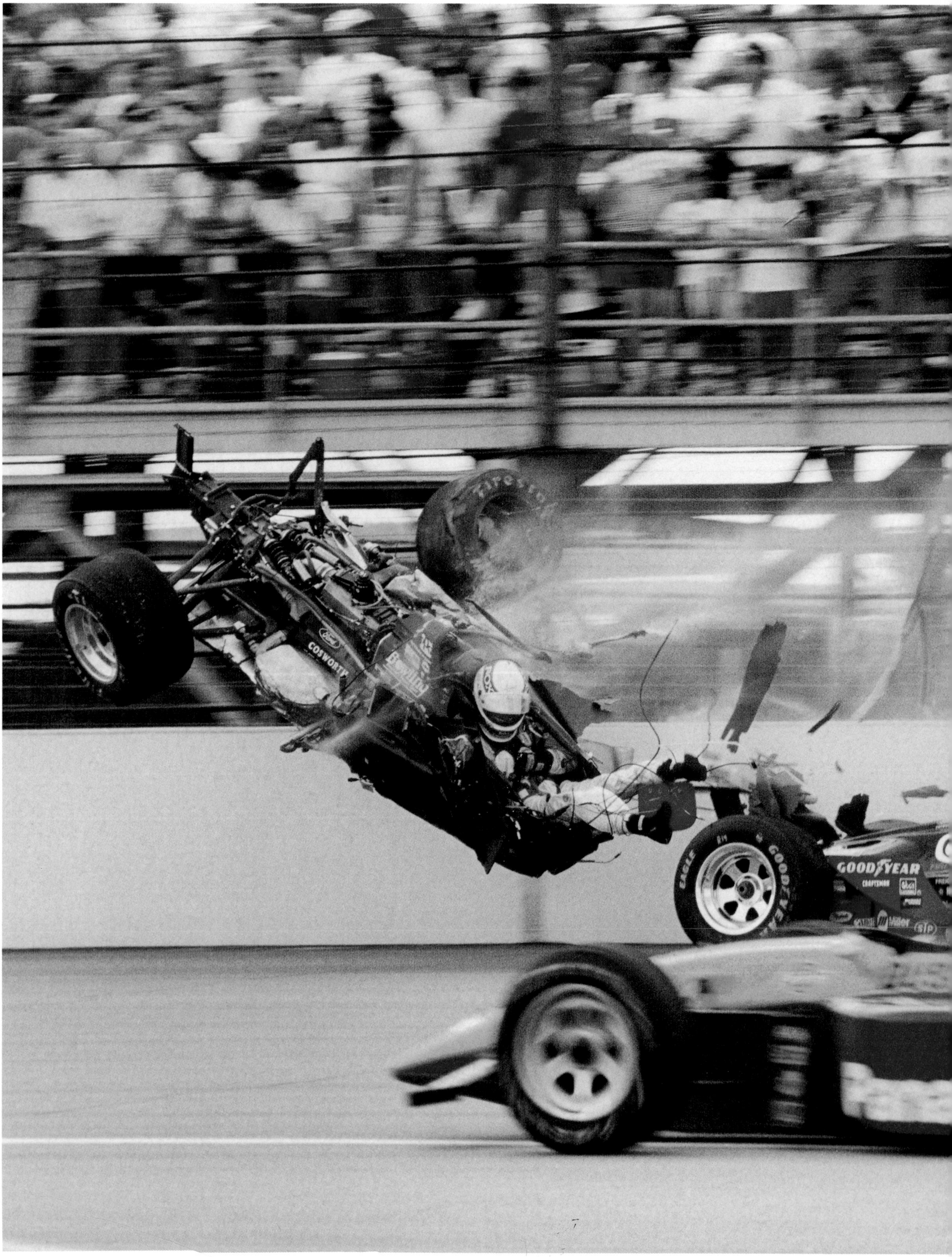

▲ © PHOTOS COURTESY INDIANAPOLIS MOTOR SPEEDWAY

CLOSE TO HALF A MILLION PEOPLE attend the Indianapolis 500 every May, making the illustrious race the world's largest single-day sporting event (PAGES 54 AND 55). But life in the fast lane isn't always a smooth ride, as driver Stan Fox realized in the 1995 Indy 500 (LEFT). Fox received no broken bones, but sustained a head injury that ended his racing career.

MINOR-LEAGUE BASEBALL'S Triple-A Indianapolis Indians owe much of their popularity to fan-friendly Victory Field. Since the ballpark's opening in 1996, the Indians have held a second-place ranking in attendance in all of minor-league baseball. But not even Victory Field can outshine such local stars as pitcher John Riedling (TOP LEFT), whose presence inspires even the youngest of players to root, root, root for the home team.

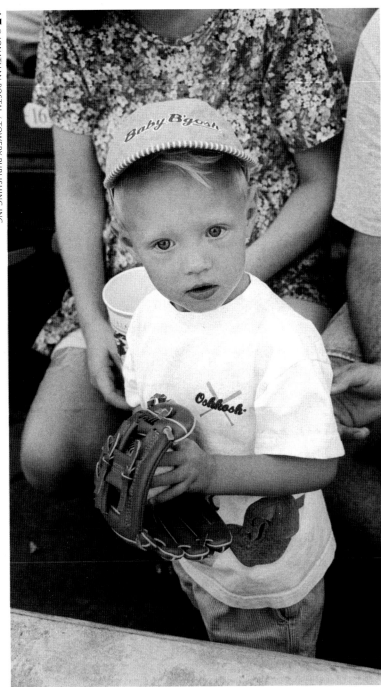

A T THE END OF THE 1999 season, *Baseball America* named the Indianapolis Indians the Triple-A Team of the Decade for the 1990s. The team's long-term success is destined to continue with the next generation of devoted fans.

WHETHER WITH A HAT OVER the heart or a steady salute, "The Star-Spangled Banner" evokes a patriotic response from Hoosiers.

THERE'S MORE THAN JUST clowning around involved for competitors in the Circle City Grand National Rodeo, an annual event held at Conseco Fieldhouse. Testing the prowess of cowboys from more than 30 states, the rodeo includes competition in five categories: bareback and saddle bronc riding, steer wrestling, calf roping, and bull riding.

Indianapolis

HOOSIERS SHOW THEIR TRUE colors in a variety of ways, from a high-stepping burger boy to dressing in traditional Mexican garb.

Indianapolis

ESTABLISHED IN 1905, SHAPIRO'S Deli is considered an Indianap- olis landmark. Family-owned for four generations, Shapiro's draws customers from miles away with its tempting Reuben and corned beef sandwiches.

T HE SILENT BUT REASSURING presence of the nation's armed forces is found throughout the Indianapolis area, including Lincoln Memory Gardens (TOP AND OPPOSITE) in Boone County and Union Station Crowne Plaza (BOTTOM).

Perhaps one of the most notorious Hoosiers of all time, John Herbert Dillinger Jr. (right) personifies the lawlessness of the gangster era. In the early 1930s, while fleeing the FBI, Dillinger and his gang conducted a cross-country crime spree. Dillinger was finally shot to death on July 22, 1934, and laid to rest in Crown Hill Cemetery in Indianapolis (opposite bottom). Most Hoosiers, however, respect the dedication of law officials and memorialize the sacrifices some have made (opposite top).

Indianapolis

© JONATHAN POSTAL / TOWERY PUBLISHING INC.

DEDICATED IN 1864 AND LISTED on the National Register of Historic Places, Crown Hill Cemetery offers a peaceful resting place for such political, commercial, and literary leaders as President Benjamin Harrison, Vice Presidents Charles Fairbanks and Thomas Marshall, Richard Gatling, Eli Lilly, and James Whitcomb Riley.

L e a d i n g   t h e   W a y

GOD

DISCIPLINE
COMPASSION

GREAT
EXPECTATIONS

© CHARLENE FARIS

THE BEAUTIFUL STAINED GLASS windows of area churches offer an affirmation of the inspiring faith of Indianapolis' residents.

L OCATED IN DOWNTOWN INDIANAP-
olis, the Scottish Rite Cathedral
is a massive Gothic-Tudor
structure containing a 54-bell
carillon and a 7,000-pipe organ.
Completed in 1929, the cathedral
was designed by George Schreiber,
an architect and member of the
Scottish Rite.

R ELIGIOUS IMAGERY DOESN'T necessarily have to be confined to a church. Whether in a storefront window or a neighbor's yard, heavenly visions abound in Indianapolis.

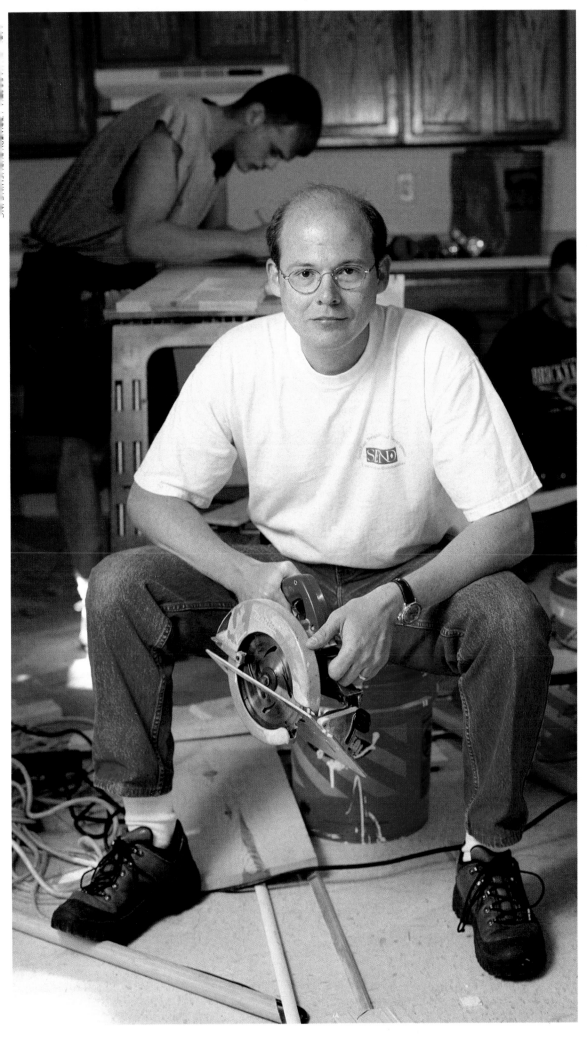

N AN EFFORT TO REVITALIZE THE southeast side of Indianapolis, residents and community leaders created SouthEast Neighborhood Development (SEND). Bill Taft (LEFT), executive director of SEND, leads the all-volunteer organization in its mission to restore beauty to neglected neighborhoods.

Oᴸᴰ ʜᴏᴍᴇs ᴀɴᴅ ʀᴇsɪᴅᴇɴᴄᴇs tell the history of Indianapolis and the surrounding areas. Lilly House (ᴘᴀɢᴇs 82 ᴀɴᴅ 83), the central feature of the 26-acre Oldfields estate, represents a stunning example of the American Country Place era, when wealthy businessmen escaped to their countryside retreats. Built in 1912, the house and gardens are located on the grounds of the Indianapolis Museum of Art. Poet James Whitcomb Riley spent the final 23 years of his life as a paying guest at 528 Lockerbie Street (ʙᴏᴛᴛᴏᴍ ʀɪɢʜᴛ). A National Historic Landmark, the Victorian building is now home to the James Whitcomb Riley Museum.

Indianapolis

THE PYRAMIDS, AN OFFICE complex and well-known landmark, creates a unique geometry in the Indianapolis skyline.

Indianapolis

THE INDIANAPOLIS BUSINESS
district mixes history and tradition with modern architecture.
Christ Church Cathedral (OPPOSITE),
the oldest religious building in
the city, was built in 1857 and
features stained glass windows
created by the Tiffany Studios in
New York.

WHETHER YOU ARE LOOKING in or looking out, the view is decidedly downtown at the Indianapolis Artsgarden. Opened in 1995, the facility features a glass-domed rotunda that serves as a performance, exhibition, and marketing space for the local arts community.

A N OASIS WITH LUSH LANDSCAPING, massive fountains, antique-style street lamps, walkways, and a pedestrian bridge, Central Canal provides a picturesque setting for residential and commercial complexes downtown.

▲ © JONATHAN POSTAL / TOWERY PUBLISHING INC.

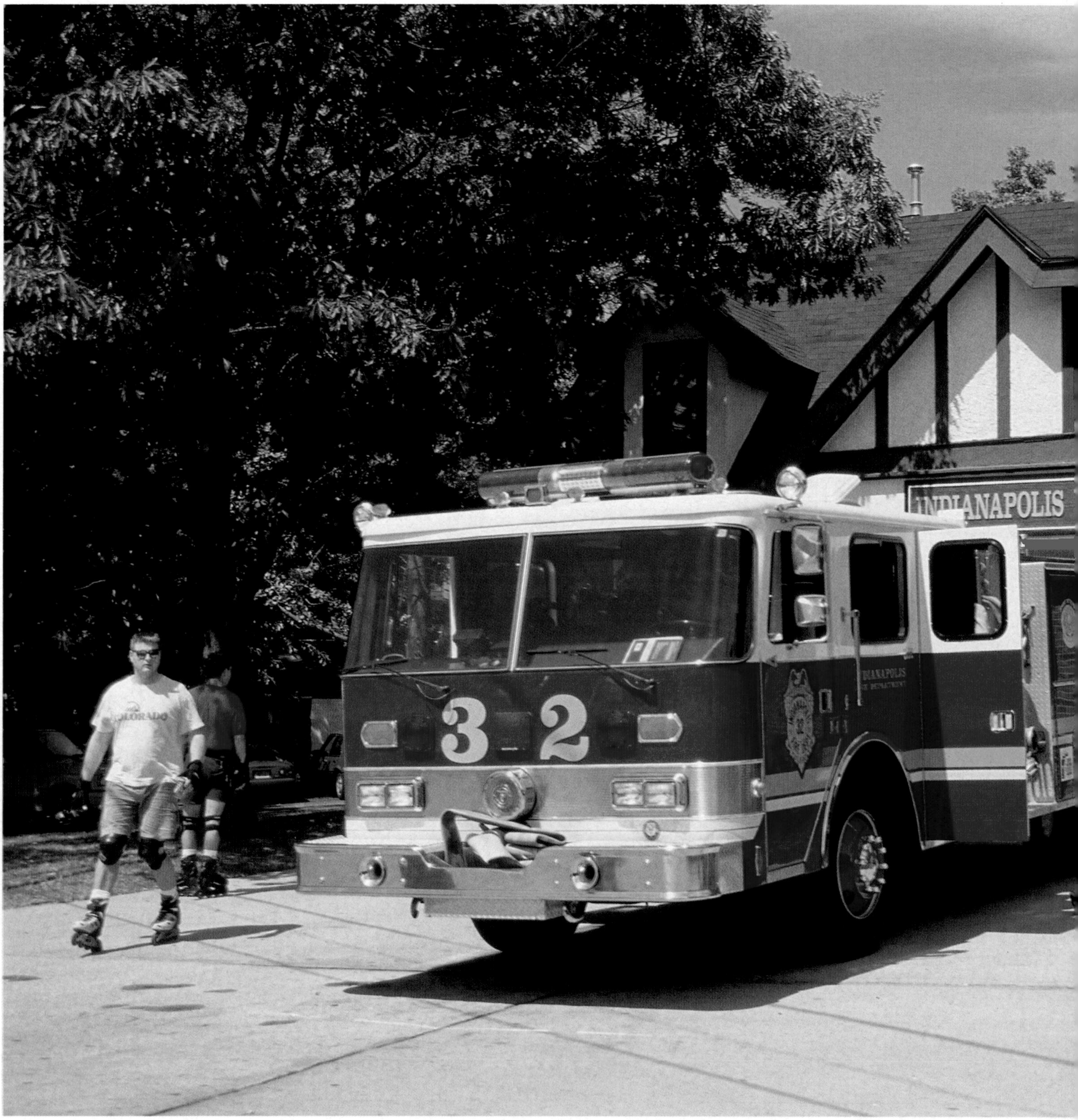

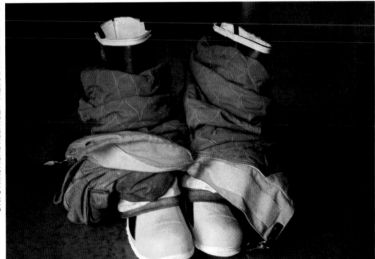

INDY KIDS WISHING TO GROW up and become firefighters will find that they have some very big shoes to fill. Each year, the city's fire department answers in excess of 95,000 fire alarms or rescue calls.

THOUGH FIRE FIGHTING IS A serious business, firefighters at Station Number 7 pause for some laughs served up with Jim Webb's award-winning chili.

Located in Mile Square since the 1800s, the station serves as the headquarters for the Indianapolis Fire Department.

INDIANAPOLIS' FINEST PROTECT the city with a lot of dedication—and a little bit of flare. When he's not on the job, Indianapolis policeman Dave Coffman (BOTTOM) can be found on the racetrack competing in Midget series races.

Indianapolis

NDIANAPOLIS YOUNGSTERS HOPING to follow in the footsteps of local heroes will find they have some mighty big shoes to fill. Congress-woman Julia Carson (ABOVE LEFT) made history in 1996 by becoming the first woman and first African-American elected to represent the metro area in Congress. Marion County Sheriff Jack Cottey (OPPO-SITE RIGHT) likewise has dedicated years to public service, working with the sheriff's department for much of his career.

I n d i a n a p o l i s

SOUTHERN LIGHTS / TOMPS PUBLISHING INC.

AN ANCIENT WORLD OF DINOSAURS and potentially scary creatures awaits visitors at the Children's Museum of Indianapolis. Founded in 1925, the facility is the fourth-oldest such museum in the world.

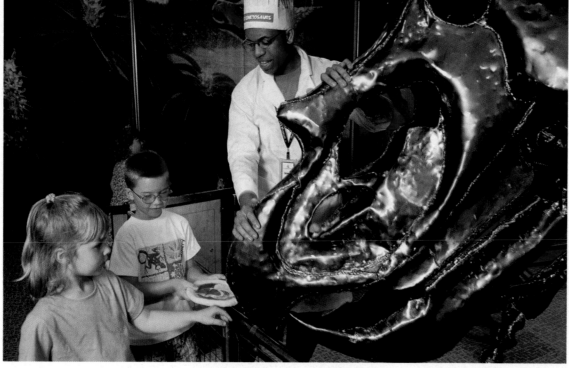

THE LARGEST FACILITY OF ITS KIND in the world, the Children's Museum of Indianapolis features five stories of interactive exhibits. The museum houses 10 galleries, a performing arts theater, SpaceQuest Planetarium, and CineDome, a large format movie theater with a 76-foot screen.

INDIANAPOLIS BOASTS SOME colorful personalities. Bob Kevoian and Tom Griswold (OPPOSITE, FROM LEFT) of *The Bob & Tom Show* received a 1999 National Association of Broad- casters Marconi Radio Award, one of the most prestigious honors in radio broadcasting. Known for their generosity, the team has generated millions of dollars for local charities.

LOCATED DOWNTOWN, THE ADOBE-style Eiteljorg Museum of American Indians and Western Art features paintings and bronzes by such artists as Charles Russell, Frederic Remington, Georgia O'Keeffe, and members of the original Taos, New Mexico, artists colony. Considered one of the finest of its kind in the country, the collection originated with Indianapolis businessman Harrison Eiteljorg.

L e a d i n g   t h e   W a y

NDIANAPOLIS AND THE SUR-
rounding area play host to a
plethora of wildlife. While some
are destined to become fodder for
local hunters, others are protected
by state and federal law.

FEW THINGS IN NATURE ARE
as beautiful as the sight of a
Midwest sunset, which lights
the sky in a wash of reds, oranges,
and pinks.

THE SITE OF THE 1994 WORLD Rowing Championships, Eagle Creek Park encompasses a nearly 4,000-acre forest and a 1,300-acre reservoir. One of the largest municipal parks in the nation, Eagle Creek is a favorite spot for Hoosiers to watch the changing hues of nature.

I T CAN NEVER BE SAID THAT Indianapolis doesn't have its share of flower power. Area roadways and greenways are brightened by the arrival of spring.

WHITE RIVER GARDENS, THE sister horticulture institution of the Indianapolis Zoo, includes a glass-enclosed conservatory that features special exhibits year-round, a water garden, a resource center, more than a mile of paths and walkways, and a dining facility with a view of the downtown skyline and riverfront.

Leading the Way

FEW THINGS GO TOGETHER LIKE a horse and carriage. Rides through local historical spots such as Crown Hill Cemetery (OPPOSITE), as well as the Indianapolis Zoo (LEFT), treat tourists and residents to a relaxing afternoon.

T HE ESSENTIALLY CAGELESS
environment of the 64-acre
Indianapolis Zoo creates an
uplifting atmosphere for both
woman and beast. Located in
downtown's White River State
Park, the zoo's thousands of
animals live in five biomes and a
totally enclosed, environmentally
controlled whale and dolphin
pavilion.

YIPES! STRIPES! IT'S A HERD of Grant's zebras from the Indianapolis Zoo. Known to express themselves through gestures, facial expressions, and sounds, this herd—whose ancestors originated in Africa—shows affection by grooming each other.

▲ © JONATHAN POSTAL / TOWERY PUBLISHING INC.

WHETHER YOU'RE MAN'S BEST friend or the cat's meow, Indianapolis can be a very eye-opening place to live.

Indianapolis

N INDIANAPOLIS, GOOD HEALTH IS not just for humans. Local veterinarians ensure that even man's best friend receives the absolute latest in health care.

THE POWER OF PUPPY DOG—
or cow—eyes can convince
even the most hard-hearted
of Hoosiers to break a few rules.

ATTRACTING MORE THAN 700,000 people to the Indiana State Fairgrounds in Indianapolis every August, the Indiana State Fair offers a variety of sights, sounds, and smells. While many people attend for the thrill of the midway or fair food delicacies, other Hoosiers roll up their sleeves to participate in the agriculture and livestock competitions.

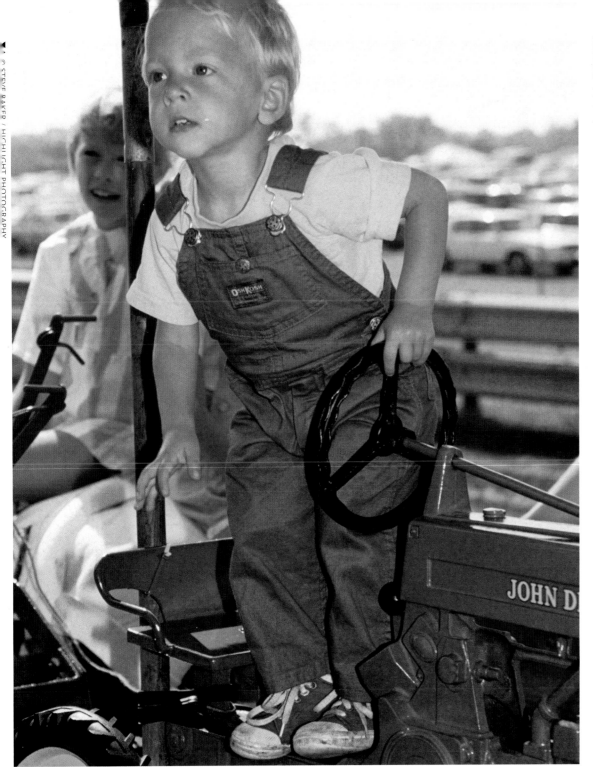

NDY KIDS KNOW THE TRUE meaning of poultry in motion. Whether by horsepower, Deere power, or other less conventional methods of moving on, these youngsters are true speed demons.

MOOOOOOOOOOOOOVE. THOUGH well-known for their lunar leaping abilities, cows have also been known to stop dead in their tracks for the tiniest of obstacles.

ACH YEAR, SOME 23,000 entrants begin in downtown and end up near Military Park for the Indianapolis Life 500 Festival Mini-Marathon. For those runners accustomed to shorter mileage, the event also includes the AmerUs Group 5K.

THE ANNUAL SUMMER CELE-bration (ABOVE), sponsored by the nonprofit cultural organization Indiana Black Expo, attracts thousands to its events, which include a rodeo, music performances, and a business expo. Artists come from around the country to exhibit at the Talbot Street Art Fair (OPPOSITE), which is considered one of the top such gatherings in the country.

EVERY OCTOBER, THE COCA-COLA Circle City Classic features a week of festivities leading to a match-up between two of the country's top, predominantly African-American, college football teams. Since 1984, when a college wide receiver named Jerry Rice led his Mississippi Valley State team to victory, the event has become, well, a classic for the city.

C ONNER PRAIRIE, AN OPEN-AIR living history museum located in Fishers, serves as a center for research and education about the life and times of early-19th-century settlers in the Old Northwest Territory. The 210-acre museum features three historic areas: the 1836 village of Prairietown, the 1823 William and Elizabeth Conner Home, and the Pioneer Adventure Area (PAGES 148 AND 149).

PONSORED ANNUALLY SINCE 1968 by the Tippecanoe County Historical Association, the Feast of the Hunters' Moon re-creates the rendezvous of French traders with the Miami people of Ouiatenon along the Wabash River. Held on the grounds of Fort Ouiatenon, the feast includes the celebrated arrival of costumed traders in 40 replica birchbark canoes. More than 8,000 people reenact the event, which lasts for two days and includes music, games, demonstrations, and exhibits.

Home to quaint shops, art galleries, and Indiana's largest state park, Brown County offers visitors a glimpse of sea-soned artisans practicing crafts and forms of music that have been around for centuries.

NDIANAPOLIS AREA RESIDENTS don't seem to have bees in their bonnets when it comes to reenacting local historical events.

▶ © CHARLENE FARIS

DOORS AND WALLS ARE THINGS of beauty in Indiana, where centuries of growth and development provide patterns and textures for those who stop to appreciate them.

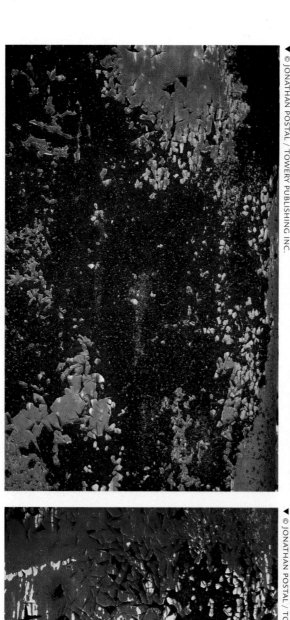

THE RUSTY PATINA OF TIME reflects an era when the simpler pleasures of life—like hanging out at the local country store—occupied a place of importance in our day-to-day existence (PAGES 162-163).

BEAN BLOSSOM BRIDGE
1880

WEIGHT
LIMIT
2
TONS

BEAUTIFUL IN ANY SEASON, the Bean Blossom Bridge has been covering travelers since 1880. Located in Brown County, the town of Bean Blossom brings to the 21st century some old-world charm and ambience.

© JEFFREY L. FORD

ELLENBERGER PARK IN INDIA-
napolis treats visitors to a
spectacle of ice, inside as well
as out: The park is the only one
in the city to house an indoor ice-
skating rink.

BEAUTIFUL FLOWERS AND natural foliage are just two of the sights awaiting visitors to Eagle Creek Park. The park is also home to one of two U. S. rowing courses sanctioned for international competition by the International Federation of Rowing Association.

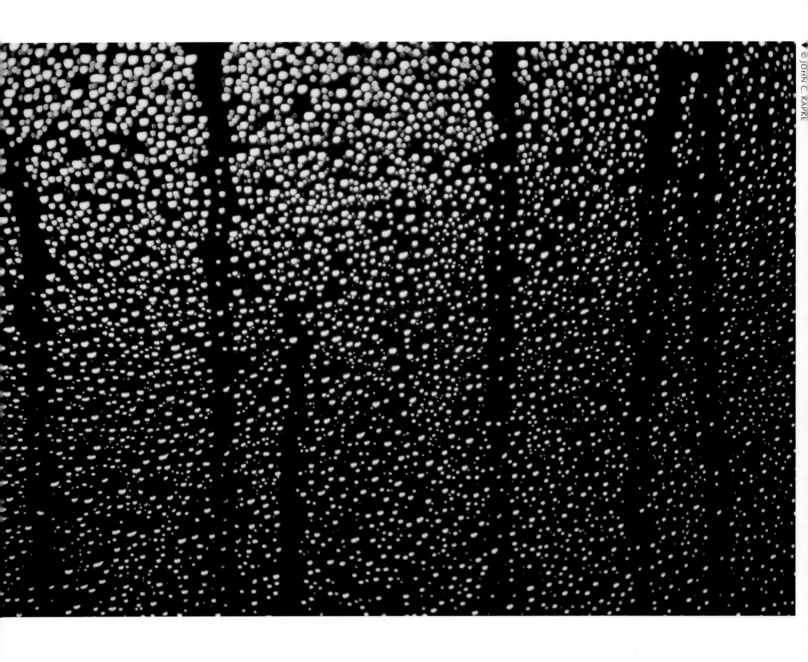

DELICATE BEADS OF WATER can turn any object into a be-jeweled wonder. But water never sparkles more invitingly than on lazy summer days, when an inner tube is the most relaxing place on Earth (PAGES 172 AND 173).

Indianapolis

EVERY CHILD HAS A FANTASY island of some sort, whether it's a figment of the mind or one composed of the fairy-tale sites around Indianapolis.

WHEN YOU'RE A KID, GOING in circles on the back of a vibrantly painted steed constitutes a rite of passage. For Indianapolis youths—and their parents, too—the smiles tell it all.

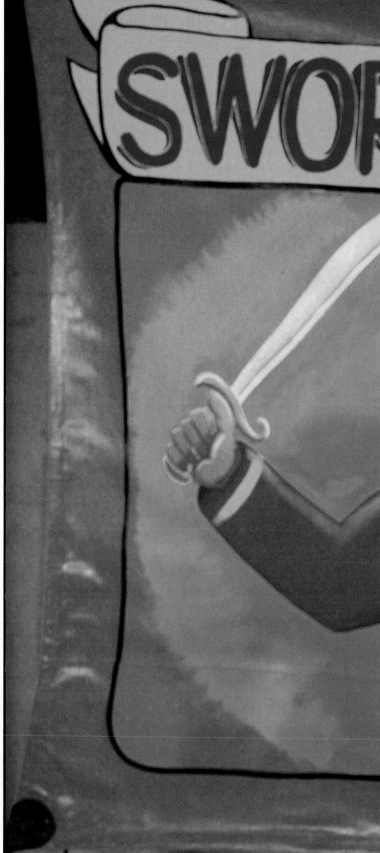

INDIANAPOLIS' **B**LUE **M**ONKEY Sideshow regularly stuns audiences with its old-fashioned circus acts, including the sword-swallowing Alex Kensington.

PUT ON A HAPPY FACE: FROM the traditional white faces of Japanese geisha to the festive markings of clowns and the rosy cheeks of the FAO Schwartz sign in Circle Centre Mall, a little makeup can bring out a whole new personality.

Indianapolis

When Christmas is a-coming, Indianapolis residents deck the halls with style—or a larger-than-life Styrofoam Santa.

Indianapolis

TALK ABOUT PUTTIN' ON THE dog. Decorated canines join their human friends—and one human/groundhog hybrid—to celebrate various holidays and events in the Indianapolis area.

L e a d i n g t h e W a y

I T'S STARS AND STRIPES FOREVER in Indianapolis, where patriotism abounds. Local residents who aren't waving the U.S. flag can be found wearing Old Glory instead— or at least a reasonable facsimile of her.

I n d i a n a p o l i s

MMACULATE GARDENING AROUND businesses and memorials in downtown Indianapolis makes the city a sight to behold, especially in the springtime. Obelisk Fountain (LEFT), a 100-foot, four-sided shaft of black granite at the center of the Veterans' Memorial Plaza, represents the powers of law, science, religion, and education.

© JONATHAN POSTAL / TOWERY PUBLISHING INC.

CULPTED DETAILS FOUND throughout Indianapolis and the surrounding area provide visual accents to the city's already luscious landscape.

THE INDIANA STATE FAIR-
grounds come to life every
August, offering a splendid
array of midway games, prizes,
and yummy treats.

Indianapolis

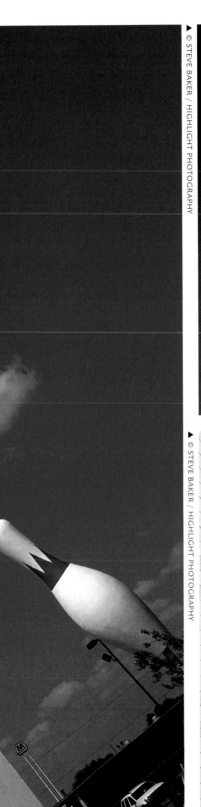

BOWLING, DONUTS, AND STEAMING hot coffee: Icons of Americana live on in Indianapolis today. Long a staple in cities everywhere, tenpin has enjoyed a resurgence in popularity of late, none too soon for Linton and Fern Calvert (BOTTOM RIGHT), who market a version of the game known as duckpin bowling. Using shorter pins and smaller balls, the high-energy variation has generated enough business for the Calverts to open three alleys.

mmy Sharpe Presents...
LIS B. DYER
the HAMMOND

J UMPIN', JIVIN', AN' WAILIN': Hepcats and kittens from Indianapolis hop on down to the Fountain Diner to jitterbug. Located in Fountain Square, the venue is part of an ensemble of shops and restaurants featuring 1950s-era memorabilia.

Indianapolis

S WINGIN' TO A FAMILIAR, NOSTAL-
gic beat, local artists such
as the Kelly Jay Orchestra
(OPPOSITE) and drummer Dick

Dickenson (ABOVE) bring the
sweet sounds of music to audiences
in Indianapolis.

Indianapolis

FOR DECADES SOME OF THE nation's best jazz musicians have called Indianapolis home, including such notables as Cliff White of the band Dog Talk (OPPO-SITE, TOP LEFT); Mingo Jones, former bassist for the late jazz guitarist Wes Montgomery (OPPOSITE, TOP RIGHT); veteran musician Jimmy Coe (OPPOSITE, BOTTOM RIGHT); and percussionist Lawrence Clark III (LEFT). Their music finds a home and an audience in numerous local venues, including David Allee's Jazz Kitchen (OPPOSITE, BOTTOM LEFT).

WHILE A REMOTE DISTANCE from the brilliance of Las Vegas, Indianapolis holds its own in the neon lights department. From local restaurants and hotels to the renowned Slippery Noodle Inn (BOTTOM LEFT)—the oldest bar in town, and recognized by *Rolling Stone* as one of the best blues venues around—the city's nightlife is anything but sleepy.

He may not be the King, but Danny Thompson (above) aspires to be Bigger than Elvis, the name under which he performs in Indianapolis' musical venues. Electric violinist Cathy Morris (opposite left) works tirelessly across the city as well, infusing audiences with her eclectic sounds that range from classical to jazz to Latin styles. One of the oldest nightspots in town, the Slippery Noodle Inn features performances by musicians such as Greg Deer (opposite right).

S ERVING UP 1950S NOSTALGIA in the form of burgers and shakes, the Fountain Diner (OPPOSITE, TOP LEFT AND BOTTOM) caters to a happenin' crowd. Whether you're the leader of the pack or a teen angel, the best grease in town is not in the hair, but sizzlin' on the grill.

I N Broad Ripple Village, everything old is new again. Hosting an eclectic mix of restaurants and shops, including Broad Ripple Vintage (LEFT), the village is an island of unusual sights and buys.

© JONATHAN POSTAL / TOWERY PUBLISHING INC.

THE CONTENTS OF INDIANAPOLIS painter Becky Wilson's studio will curl your hair. Working primarily with found objects, Wilson (OPPOSITE RIGHT) has been known to incorporate all types of unexpected articles in her works, dolls and mannequins among the lot. While Wilson works with replicas of the human form, local tattoo artist Mike Prickett (OPPOSITE LEFT) creates his designs on living models.

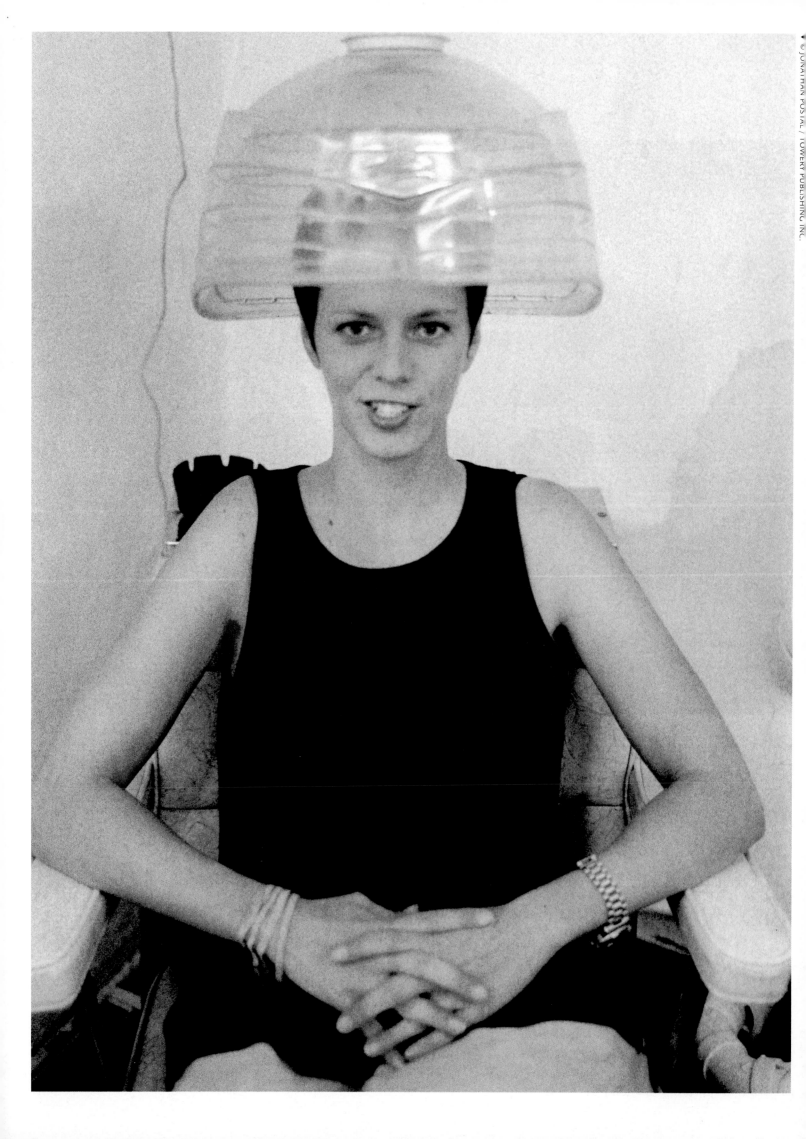

H OOSIERS ARE ALL ABOUT HAIR. From a nip and a tuck at a local barbershop to a professional 'do at a salon, residents find satisfaction in looking their best.

WELDED METAL AND VINYL provide a comfortable and steady perch in any establishment—but every alloy has its bending point.

Indianapolis

J AMES DEAN ARCHIVIST DAVID Loehr is quite at home among the hair tonics and barbershops of yesteryear (ABOVE). With the world's largest collection of Dean memorabilia, Loehr takes his devotion a step further, giving truth to the old adage that imitation is the sincerest form of flattery. But no matter what your style—or what the decor—a barbershop is a great place to take a load off and relax (OPPOSITE).

THE ORIGINAL REBEL, JAMES
Dean (OPPOSITE) was a Hoosier
born and bred. Buried in his
hometown of Fairmount, Indiana,
Dean lives on through tributes
such as the James Dean Memorial
Gallery, the seven-room private
collection of archivist and fan
David Loehr.

THROUGH THE DECADES, CE-
lebrities have flocked to the
Indianapolis Motor Speedway
to watch the incomparable Indianapolis 500. Shirley MacLaine
(ABOVE) and funnymen Jerry Lewis
and Dean Martin (OPPOSITE) paid
visits to the track in the 1950s,
bringing along their own unique
senses of humor.

I n d i a n a p o l i s

THOUGH A TALENTED ARTIST, Jan Martin (OPPOSITE RIGHT) didn't quit his day job. Vice president of Tarpenning-LaFollette, a custom sheet metal company, Martin spends his spare time creating bronze and steel works of whimsy. In Indianapolis, art imitates life (ABOVE)—but sometimes life has a way of imitating art (PAGES 240 AND 241).

NDIANAPOLIS' ARCHITECTURAL
elements possess a beauty all
their own. Bridges and buildings reflect similarities in form and
function.

I n d i a n a p o l i s

AREA MONUMENTS AND STATUARY represent a variety of tributes, and contribute a graceful beauty to Indianapolis.

T HE ARCHITECTURALLY STUN-
ning Indiana Historical Society
headquarters features hands-
on exhibits, films and lectures, and
the world's largest collection of
rare manuscripts, photographs,
documents, and artifacts devoted
exclusively to Indiana and the Old
Northwest.

A T NIGHT, INDIANAPOLIS glistens with the activities of thousands of residents who burn the midnight oil, whether working hard or playing hard.

T'S EASY TO CATCH AN EYEFUL in Indianapolis, where outdoor advertising, high technology, and local art create a panoply of optical illusions.

ACERS POINT GUARD TRAVIS
Best (OPPOSITE) gives Indiana
basketball two thumbs up. The
NBA Pacers combine the skill of
players like Best with the know-
how of legend, native, and coach
Larry Bird (LEFT). Bird retired
from his coaching job at the end
of the 1999-2000 season, which
saw the Pacers go all the way to
the NBA finals.

Designed to reflect the history
and tradition of basketball in the
state of Indiana, the Conseco
Fieldhouse (PAGE 256 AND 257) is
home to the Indianapolis Pacers.

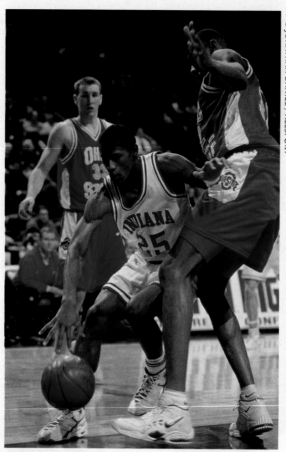

N A STATE WHERE BASKETBALL is not a pastime, but a passion, players and coaches are considered demigods. At the top of the list of the revered is Damon Bailey (LEFT), who led the Indiana University Hoosiers to greatness in the early 1990s, and has since passed the torch on to fellow players Dane Fife (OPPOSITE, TOP LEFT) and A.J. Guyton (OPPOSITE, TOP RIGHT).

Indianapolis

NO MATTER WHAT THE FORM of competition, a congratulatory hug or a good talking-to helps keep things moving in the right direction.

HOMETOWN NFL HEROES THE Indianapolis Colts have been led by an all-star group of players since the team arrived in 1984, including current quarterback Peyton Manning (TOP LEFT) and former players Aaron Bailey (TOP RIGHT), Tim Hauk (BOTTOM), and Elijah Alexander (OPPOSITE).

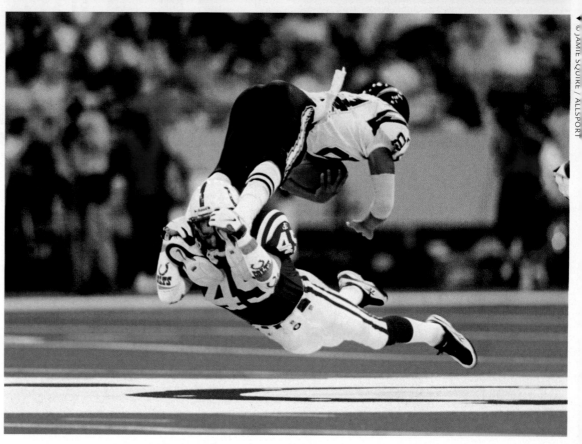

I n d i a n a p o l i s

Indianapolis

SPECTATOR SPORTS DEVELOP loyal followings in Indianapolis. Fans flock to the city's many excellent venues, including the RCA Dome (TOP LEFT AND RIGHT) for Indianapolis Colts' action, and the Velodrome (BOTTOM LEFT AND RIGHT) for national cycling events. The RCA Championhips are also a big draw for Hoosiers, and regularly feature tennis favorites like Pete Sampras (OPPOSITE).

IME TO ENJOY A REFRESHING drink? Perhaps. Or maybe it's time for a shopping spree at Parisian in the Circle Centre Mall (LEFT), where a landmark 5-ton electric clock greets visitors.

THE ARCHITECTURAL OPULENCE OF downtown landmarks suggests that no detail is overlooked in Indianapolis. The Circle Tower (OPPOSITE), located on Monument Circle, reflects the influence of art deco on 1930s architecture and design. The Central Library (ABOVE) has housed the city's literature for almost a century, but remains contemporary with up-to-the-minute technology.

I n d i a n a p o l i s

REFLECTING THE MAJESTY OF a modern-day metropolis, Indianapolis continues to lead the way to prosperity.

Profiles in Excellence

A LOOK AT THE CORPORATIONS, BUSINESSES, PROFESSIONAL GROUPS, AND COMMUNITY SERVICE ORGANIZATIONS THAT HAVE MADE THIS BOOK POSSIBLE. THEIR STORIES — OFFERING AN INFORMAL CHRONICLE OF THE LOCAL BUSINESS COMMUNITY — ARE ARRANGED ACCORDING TO THE DATE THEY WERE ESTABLISHED IN INDIANAPOLIS

ALLISON PAYMENT SYSTEMS, LLC ■ ALLTRISTA CORPORATION ■ AMERICAN AIRLINES, INC. ■ AMERICAN ART CLAY CO., INC. ■ ANTHEM, INC. ■ ASSOCIATED BUILDERS AND CONTRACTORS OF INDIANA ■ BANK ONE CORPORATION ■ BARTH ELECTRIC CO., INC. ■ BILL ESTES AUTOMOTIVE ■ BINDLEY WESTERN INDUSTRIES, INC. ■ BMG ENTERTAINMENT ■ BOVIS LEND LEASE, INC. ■ BRENWICK DEVELOPMENT COMPANY ■ BSA DESIGN ■ BUSINESS FURNITURE CORPORATION ■ BUTLER UNIVERSITY ■ CANTERBURY HOTEL ■ CARR METAL PRODUCTS, INC. ■ CARRIER CORPORATION ■ CATHEDRAL HIGH SCHOOL ■ CENTILLION DATA SYSTEMS/ E.NOVA, LLC ■ CITIZENS GAS & COKE UTILITY ■ CLARIAN HEALTH PARTNERS, INC. ■ COLLIERS TURLEY MARTIN TUCKER ■ COMCAST CABLEVISION ■ COMMUNITY CANCER CARE INC. ■ CONSECO, INC. ■ COVANCE ■ CROSSMAN COMMUNITIES, INC. ■ D.B. MANN DEVELOPMENT ■ DAIMLERCHRYSLER INDIANAPOLIS FOUNDRY ■ DEFENSE FINANCE AND ACCOUNTING SERVICE - INDIANAPOLIS CENTER (DFAS) ■ DELTA FAUCET COMPANY ■ DIVERSIFIED SYSTEMS INC. ■ EDS ■ ELI LILLY AND COMPANY ■ EMMIS COMMUNICATIONS CORPORATION ■ ERIS SURVEY SYSTEMS INC. ■ ESCIENT TECHNOLOGIES, LLC ■ FEDEX ■ FOX WXIN 59/ TRIBUNE BROADCASTING ■ G.M. CONSTRUCTION, INC. ■ GENERAL MOTORS (ALLISON

Transmission & Indianapolis Metal Center) ■ Globe Corporate Stay International ■ Goelzer Investment Banking ■ Goelzer Investment Management ■ GSC Industries ■ Guidant Corporation ■ Heritage Environmental Services ■ IBM Corporation ■ ImagineX Radiology Alliance, L.L.C. ■ The Indiana Hand Center ■ Indiana Health Industry Forum ■ Indianapolis Chamber of Commerce ■ Indianapolis Colts ■ Indianapolis Economic Development Corporation ■ Indianapolis Museum of Art/Indianapolis Symphony Orchestra ■ Indianapolis Private Industry Council ■ Ivy Tech State College - Central Indiana ■ Keane, Inc. ■ Keihin Indiana Precision Technology Inc. ■ Lauth Property Group ■ Lockwood Greene ■ Macmillan USA ■ Manpower Professional ■ Manufacturing Technology Center at Indianapolis (MTC-I) ■ Marsh Supermarkets, Inc. ■ Martin University ■ Mays Chemical Company ■ Monarch Beverage Company Inc. ■ Moorfeed Corporation ■ ONEX, Inc. ■ Pacers Sports & Entertainment Corporation ■ Park Tudor School ■ Paul Harris Stores, Inc. ■ The Permanent Magnet Co., Inc. ■ Pratt Corporation ■ Praxair Surface Technologies, Inc. ■ Protection Plus Inc. ■ Resort Condominiums International ■ Roche Diagnostics Corporation ■ SAFECO ■ St. Elmo Steak House ■ St. Francis Hospital & Health Centers ■ St. Vincent Hospitals and Health Services ■ Santarossa Mosaic & Tile Co., Inc. ■ Shiel Sexton Company Inc. ■ Simon Property Group ■ Smock Fansler Construction Corporation ■ Sprint Corporation ■ Standard Management Corporation ■ Star Environmental Inc. ■ Sterling Fluid Systems (USA) Inc. ■ Stuart's Moving and Storage, Inc. ■ The Sullivan Corporation ■ Telstreet.com ■ Tobias Insurance Group, Inc. ■ Top Notch ■ Trinity Homes ■ Union Planters Bank ■ United Signature Foods, LLC ■ Weiss Communications Inc. ■ WISH TV8 ■ Wishard Health Services ■ Woodard, Emhardt, Naughton, Moriarty & McNett

1834 BANK ONE CORPORATION

1834 UNION PLANTERS BANK

1851 CITIZENS GAS & COKE UTILITY

1855 BUTLER UNIVERSITY

1859 WISHARD HEALTH SERVICES

1876 ELI LILLY AND COMPANY

1879 WOODARD, EMHARDT, NAUGHTON,
MORIARTY & McNETT

1881 ST. VINCENT HOSPITALS AND HEALTH SERVICES

1883 INDIANAPOLIS MUSEUM OF ART/
INDIANAPOLIS SYMPHONY ORCHESTRA

1888 ALLISON PAYMENT SYSTEMS, LLC

1890 DAIMLERCHRYSLER INDIANAPOLIS FOUNDRY

1890 INDIANAPOLIS CHAMBER OF COMMERCE

1902 PARK TUDOR SCHOOL

1902 ST. ELMO STEAK HOUSE

1914 ST. FRANCIS HOSPITAL & HEALTH CENTERS

1915 GENERAL MOTORS (ALLISON TRANSMISSION
& INDIANAPOLIS METAL CENTER)

1917 PRAXAIR SURFACE TECHNOLOGIES, INC.

1918 CATHEDRAL HIGH SCHOOL

1918 COLLIERS TURLEY MARTIN TUCKER

Union Planters Bank

UNION PLANTERS BANK STRIVES TO BUILD A LOCAL REPUTATION for its community focus in every market it serves. Founded in Memphis in 1869, it is one of the 30 largest banks nationwide. With assets in excess of $30 billion and holdings in 12 states, Union Planters has been recognized by the Small Business Administration (SBA) as one of the

nation's top small-business-friendly lenders. The bank serves more than 1 million customers in Indiana, Alabama, Arkansas, Florida, Illinois, Iowa, Kentucky, Louisiana, Mississippi, Missouri, Tennessee, and Texas, maintaining more than 875 offices and 1,100 automated teller machines.

In 1998, Union Planters purchased Indianapolis assets from another bank to satisfy antitrust concerns, giving it access to a Hoosier legacy of community-focused banking dating back to the State Bank of Indiana, established by the Indiana General Assembly in 1851. Union Planters is keeping this legacy alive in spirit and practice; each bank franchise in the Union Planters network operates independently with local management and local decision making.

Calling Indiana Home

Union Planters did more than purchase 51 Indiana branches, $1.8 billion in deposits, $200 million in consumer loans, and $625 million in commercial loans from First Chicago NBD. The

bank provided meaningful employment for more than 500 former NBD employees—bankers with an average of 15 years' experience in the financial services industry—who were uniquely positioned to provide one-on-one customer solutions to Indianapolis-area customers.

Union Planters' franchise banks nationwide retain local boards of directors as well. In Indianapolis, where the firm

has 29 branches and is the fourth-largest bank, a 10-member board of local business leaders provides the management team with strategic and community investment direction.

"This board reflects a new way of doing business that's back to the community," says Steven J. Schenck, president and chief executive officer of the Central Indiana region. "It reflects an outreach to new customers and markets, and a commitment to neighborhoods and families."

Union Planters has also joined the Indiana Community Business Credit Corp., a group of 39 Indiana banks that provide pooled-risk financing to Indiana businesses in early stages of development. The bank leases much of the same office space its predecessors used, including the 36-story downtown tower, where it has options to expand operations.

Union Planters has continued the long-standing Fourth of July fireworks tradition from atop the downtown tower as an annual gift to the city of India-

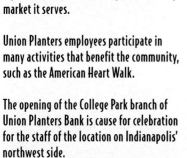

Clockwise from top:
Union Planters Bank strives to build a local reputation for its community focus in every market it serves.

Union Planters employees participate in many activities that benefit the community, such as the American Heart Walk.

The opening of the College Park branch of Union Planters Bank is cause for celebration for the staff of the location on Indianapolis' northwest side.

Union Planters CEO Steven J. Schenck (left) and then Mayor Stephen Goldsmith celebrate a bright economic outlook for downtown Indianapolis.

napolis. This pyrotechnic display, choreographed to music simulcast on WFBQ radio, is enjoyed by 250,000 viewers who gather to watch from surrounding buildings and the street 507 feet below.

Full-Service Offerings

Whether handling a $10 million business loan or a young couple's first mortgage loan, Union Planters seeks to find the right financial solutions to meet customers' needs. In addition to a full array of traditional deposit services and loan products, the bank offers individuals and businesses a variety of other financial options, including cash management, investment services, merchant card services, residential mortgages, leasing, trust services, private banking, international services, and on-line computer and telephone banking. The bank is one of only a handful of SBA-certified lenders in the state.

Union Planters is on the leading edge of electronic services. In fall 1999, the bank installed its first production model Internet ATM at a Tennessee administrative center to allow customers access to Internet

banking services through an ATM. Eventually, bank customers will be able to pay bills at any Internet ATM—similiar to the access they now have from their personal computers, utilizing UPOnline, Union Planters' secure Internet banking service.

Community Counts

Union Planters takes pride in its role as an active member of the Indianapolis community, lending support—both monetary and volunteer—to community organizations such as United Way, Junior Achievement, 500 Festival of Art, Indianapolis Women's Fund, and American Heart Association.

Employees serve on a variety of community boards, including the Indianapolis Zoological Society, Fairbanks Hospital, Indiana Small Business Development Corp., St. Vincent's Hospital Foundation, Gleaners Food Bank, WFYI, Girls, Inc., and the Indiana Repertory Theatre. The bank encourages employees to volunteer by publishing opportunities in its newsletter. Many employees sign up to take part in activities such as United Way Day of

Caring, Meals on Wheels, Black Expo, and health-related walks and races.

"We're committed to being a community bank in our one-on-one service to customers, while providing world-class financial solutions from our vast resources," adds Schenck. "From top to bottom, Union Planters Bank of Central Indiana is operated by Hoosiers for Hoosiers, bringing local decision making back to the Indianapolis banking community."

Union Planters employees in Indianapolis visit with the residents of A Caring Place as part of the United Way Day of Caring.

Bank One Corporation

BANK ONE CORPORATION CONTINUES TO LIVE UP TO ITS NAME and tradition of firsts in central Indiana. Not only is the company the leading financial institution in Indiana, the Bank One Tower is the state's tallest building, reflecting the status of its first-class address—111 Monument Circle. ■ With Indianapolis origins in one of the state's

Not only is Bank One Corporation the leading financial institution in Indiana, the Bank One Tower is the state's tallest building (top).

Bank One remains committed to the communities it serves. In central Indiana, that commitment extends from being the official bank of the Indiana Pacers and the new Conseco Fieldhouse to supporting United Way and human services agencies (bottom left).

Bank One floats to victory during the opening festivities for the Indiana Historical Society (bottom right).

oldest financial institutions, Bank One has become Indiana's top bank in terms of assets, locations, and offerings. As a result of its 1998 combination with First Chicago NBD, Bank One is now the leading commercial bank in the Midwest and the top credit-card issuer nationwide.

Other rankings place Bank One among the top 10 financial services providers in the world. Bank One is the number two cash-management bank, the number three provider of corporate banking services nationally, the number four agent/co-agent in the U.S. loan syndication market, and the number five U. S. banking corporation with assets of $240 billion.

From Wall Street to Main Street

Bank One's history in Indiana began in 1986, when it acquired American Fletcher National Bank, established in 1839. In 1992, a Chicago-based bank—First Chicago NBD—acquired the Indianapolis-based Indiana National Bank (INB), which had been a mainstay of the community since 1834.

Those combinations set the stage for the megamerger in 1998 of Bank One and First Chicago NBD. Today's Bank One boasts more than 90,000 employees, who serve more than 10 million households in 14 states and 11 countries.

Although headquartered in Chicago, Bank One maintains operations in Indianapolis for several subsidiaries and corporate functions. More than 5,000 Hoosiers work for Bank One Financial Services, Bank One Mortgage Corp., the consumer-lending call center, the Midwest processing center, education financing, Answer One, national accounts payable, and neighborhood banking centers.

"Our fusion of banking know-how with superior technology helps us compete strongly from Wall Street to Main Street," explains Joseph D. Barnette Jr., Bank One Indiana chairman. "The expansive portfolio of services we've created lets customers choose how they want to do business—at a banking center, at an ATM, or on-line."

Pioneer in Personalized Service

Bank One has always been a leader—from pioneering national credit cards in 1966 to introducing the first automated teller machines in 1970. In early 1999, the bank also began marketing credit cards through America Online Inc. and Excite Inc., and added a feature to its Internet banking site to approve home equity loans in less than a minute.

More than 400,000 customers have signed up to bank on-line since the service debuted in 1996, and Bank One hopes to triple that by the end of 2000. But the bank has no plans to curb any of its other choices. Worldwide, 2,200 offices and 6,000 ATMs ensure customer choice and convenience. Central Indiana's share includes more than 55 branches and 145 ATMs.

Bank One remains committed to the communities it serves. In central Indiana, that commitment extends from being the official bank of the Indiana Pacers and the new Conseco Fieldhouse to supporting United Way and human services agencies. Bank One officers are represented on virtually every not-for-profit and for-profit board in the central Indiana community, and the bank's work-life initiatives have been recognized by *Working Woman* magazine and the *Indianapolis Business Journal*.

"We've never hesitated to roll up our sleeves and get the job done in the communities we serve," Barnette adds. "After all, we have a number one name to live up to."

WOODARD, EMHARDT, NAUGHTON, MORIARTY & McNETT has maintained a commitment to the exclusive practice of intellectual property law since the firm's founding in 1879. Today, it is the state's largest legal firm devoted exclusively to the highly specialized areas of U.S. and international patent, trademark, copyright, trade secret, and unfair competition law.

Members of the firm work directly with a client or through the client's general practice attorney. All members of the firm are registered to practice before the U.S. Patent and Trademark Office in patent cases, and may represent clients in litigation in state and federal courts.

Founding Focus

The firm's founder, Charles P. Jacobs, Esquire, was a native of New York State who came to Indiana to practice law in the early 1860s. He served as chief deputy to the clerk of the Indiana Supreme Court, as private secretary to Indiana Governor Oliver Morton, and as secretary of the Republican State Central Committee before settling into a general law practice.

Jacobs' law practice gradually became more focused on intellectual property issues, which reflected his own interests in the fields of astronomy, music, literature, and religion. Jacobs was an astronomer as well, and had an observatory built into the roof of his home so he could entertain friends by pointing out features in the night sky.

Jacobs' role as a founder and instructor at several early law schools in the state— forerunners of the present Indiana University (IU) School of Law-Indianapolis—is a tradition that members of the firm have continued. Harold R. Woodard, the firm's current senior partner, taught intellectual property law at IU for 32 years and funds a scholarship in his name in that specialty.

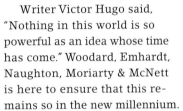

Depth of Technical Expertise

Today, Woodard, Emhardt, Naughton, Moriarty & McNett's 24 partners possess a wide diversity of technical and legal expertise. All 45 members of the firm hold engineering or science degrees, and many have technical work experience in science and industry. The firm represents major clients in the fields of electrical engineering, biotechnology, chemical engineering, mechanical engineering, computer software, and many others. The technical backgrounds of the firm's members more thoroughly equip them to provide counsel regarding the complex interrelationship of technical and legal issues that often exists in intellectual property law.

The firm has more than quadrupled in size since its centennial celebration in 1979, which reflects not only the growth in intellectual property law, but also the firm's clientele. Its client list includes many of the state's foremost technology-oriented organizations, including Eli Lilly and Company, Dow Agro-Sciences, Thomson Consumer Electronics, Allison, Cummins Engine, Great Lakes Chemical Corporation, Purdue University, and Indiana University.

Writer Victor Hugo said, "Nothing in this world is so powerful as an idea whose time has come." Woodard, Emhardt, Naughton, Moriarty & McNett is here to ensure that this remains so in the new millennium.

Growth in high-tech fields has fueled Woodard, Emhardt, Naughton, Moriarty & McNett's rapid growth as the largest intellectual property law firm in the state.

The firm has shown remarkable growth throughout the years, from its start in a home with a sky observatory to its present location as a multifloor tenant in the state's tallest building, located across from the Federal Courthouse.

Citizens Gas & Coke Utility

T CITIZENS GAS & COKE UTILITY, EVERYTHING GOES BACK to a long-standing tradition of trust—from the company's legal operating structure to how it relates to its more than 255,000 customers. ■ More than a century ago, the city's forefathers came up with the idea of operating a gas company as a trust, solely for the benefit of the residents of Marion County. City visionaries, including Colonel Eli Lilly, founded the company under the belief that a public charitable trust would remain viable in its mission to deliver low-cost, high-value, and excellent-quality energy services.

Citizens Gas still operates as a trust and is the only trust-directed utility in the country. As such, it remains dedicated to supplying its customers' energy needs and maintaining their trust with clean, low-cost, dependable natural gas service.

Trust Works

While the City of Indianapolis is the utility's trustee, tax money has never been used in maintaining Citizens Gas. Revenues pay operating costs and maintain the plant and property. Any remaining monetary benefits are passed along to customers in the form of lower energy costs. In fact, $21.3 million earned in other operations has been distributed to customers since 1995 in the form of lower rates on monthly gas bills.

Citizens' customers enjoy natural gas rates that are among the lowest in the nation—nearly 10 percent below the national average for snowbelt cities— and outstanding customer service. The utility maintains more than 7,000 miles of natural gas pipeline within Marion County, and recently invested about $15 million in modernizing underground mains and services systems.

Although Citizens' structure prevents it from achieving recognition in the Malcolm Baldrige quality assessment, the utility nevertheless goes through the rigorous process every year as a way to benchmark its services. Since it was first assessed in 1986, the company has experienced a more than 60 percent overall improvement in its ratings.

Citizens' manufacturing division, known as Indianapolis Coke, is one of the premier foundry and blast-furnace coke producers in the country. Of the five merchant foundry coke producers operating nationally,

Clockwise from top:
Citizens Gas & Coke Utility's corporate headquarters and customer service center are conveniently located on North Meridian Street in Indianapolis.

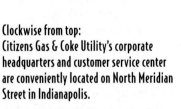

The company's Indianapolis Coke division is extremely proactive in meeting environmental standards. To date, it has met and exceeded all of the 1990 Clean Air Act amendments.

One of two Citizens Gas facilities that store natural gas in a liquid form, this liquified natural gas plant lights up the northern Marion County skies. Citizens Gas has enough stored natural gas to heat Marion County for several days.

Indianapolis Coke supplies about 25 percent of the nation's needs. For fiscal year 1998, this equated to sales of about 375,000 tons of foundry coke, 193,000 tons of blast-furnace coke, and 79,000 tons of industrial coke.

During 1998, Indianapolis Coke also demonstrated its commitment to the foundry and steel industry by being the nation's first coke producer to receive QS 9000 certification. The certification is required by auto manufacturers, who use coke to produce many of their products.

Beyond the Trust

Citizens Gas & Coke Utility's designation as a trust by the Indiana General Assembly allows it to have ownership in a stock corporation acquired as an asset. That stock corporation is Citizens By-Products Coal Company, established in 1935 as a wholly owned subsidiary operating in an unregulated environment. Citizens By-Products, in turn, has ownership in other subsidiaries and alliances, including Citizens Resource Development Corporation (CRDC), established in 1977; and Citizens Mechanical Services (CMS), LLC, established in 1996. CRDC buys, sells, invests in, and explores for oil and gas for the benefit of Citizens' customers and trust beneficiaries, and CMS provides residential and commercial customers with cost-effective solutions to their water heater, heating, and plumbing needs.

Citizens Investment Collaboration on Neighborhoods Inc. (Citizens ICON), a nonprofit corporation established in 1995, focuses on community revitalization initiatives. This group has successfully developed the River's Edge community on the site of the old Riverside Amusement Park—the largest market-rate housing development in Center Township in more than three decades.

Other Citizens By-Products ventures involve partnerships, three of which are with IGC Energy Inc. Established in 1996,

ProLiance Energy maximizes gas acquisition and supply resources currently available to both Citizens Gas and Indiana Gas Company (ICG), and administers the gas-supply portfolios of both companies, including all supply, transportation, and storage contracts, in addition to marketing fuels to other utilities and customers. ProLiance has been active in marketing its WeatherProof Bill, which guarantees customer costs regardless of weather. It also was approved as one of five gas marketers to participate in an Ohio natural gas customer-choice pilot program.

Energy Systems Group, LLC, established in 1997 with IGC and Southern Indiana Gas & Electric Company, provides performance contracting—a package of products, services, and skills to help consumers achieve enhanced energy and operational performance at a lower cost. Recent projects have involved Good Samaritan Hospital in Vincennes, Indiana; Mead Johnson's Evansville, Indiana, facility; the *Chicago-Sun Times*; and Rieck Mechanical in Dayton.

CIGMA, LLC provides warehousing and distribution of construction and maintenance materials used by Citizens, Indiana Gas, and third parties. An additional subsidiary, Remittance Processing Services

(RPS), LLC, involves an alliance with Indianapolis Power & Light (IPL) to provide high-volume, state-of-the-art payment processing services. In addition to processing for the partners, RPS also provides services to Indiana Gas.

"We view these collaborations as opportunities to bring an expanded array of services to our customers, reduce energy costs to our customers, and maintain a competitive position in an industry that is in the formative stages of deregulation," says President and CEO David N. Griffiths. "That's the trust and the vision of Citizens Gas & Coke Utility that is still at work today."

The River's Edge housing community represents the cornerstone of Citizens Gas & Coke Utility's community revitalization efforts. Ground breaking for the initial phase of 67 new homes was held in fall 1997.

Citizens Gas servicemen provide prompt, courteous service to more than 255,000 customers in Marion County.

Butler University

IN THE 1989 FILM *FIELD OF DREAMS*, AN IOWA FARMER FACES foreclosure because he heeds a whispered voice that says, "If you build it, they will come," and plows under his corn to build a baseball diamond. Knowing that good students will always follow the best faculty and programs, Butler University has heeded its own inner voice more than once since its founding in 1855.

Close attention to that inner voice has guided the university through a name change and three different campus locations. Alumni who haven't recently visited the current, 290-acre site five miles north of Indianapolis' center might not recognize their alma mater. But on closer inspection, they'll find the same traditions of excellence they experienced as students driving Butler's growth and physical change.

Enduring Traditions

Butler was founded in 1855 as North Western Christian University by Ovid Butler, a prominent Indianapolis attorney and abolitionist; its original mission was to prepare students to meet the challenges of the future. Through 1877, when the name was changed to Butler University, and each year since, a new class of students has encountered a challenging learning environment and a wide range of academic programs steeped in the liberal arts.

Butler has made headlines from the start. It was the first coeducational institution of higher learning established in Indiana and the second in the nation. It has admitted students of all races and religious persuasions since its founding, and was the first institution in Indiana to allow students to choose subjects under an elective system. Butler was the second university in the nation to employ a woman as a full professor and the first to endow a chair specifically for a female instructor. Its student newspaper, the *Collegian*, has published regularly since 1886. And its Hinkle Fieldhouse, the largest basketball arena in the nation when it was built in 1928, remains the heart and soul of Indiana basketball.

Butler was founded in 1855 as North Western Christian University by Ovid Butler, a prominent Indianapolis attorney and abolitionist; its original mission was to prepare students to meet the challenges of the future.

Butler's reputation for providing a quality education has survived the years as well. It is one of few midwestern universities included in the rankings of *U.S. News and World Report*, *Peterson's Competitive Colleges*, *Barron's Best Buys*, *Rugg's Recommendations on the Colleges*, and *The 100 Best Colleges for African-American Students*. Butler was one of only three Indiana colleges mentioned in a national survey of high school guidance counselors, who gave it the highest ratings for overall quality of education.

Today's students choose Butler for many of the same reasons national guides recommend it: academic excellence, personal attention from faculty, range of academic programs, quality facilities, emphasis on the liberal arts and sciences, and preparation for graduate school and careers. All students benefit from Butler's 13 to 1 student-faculty ratio, and a broad-based honors program provides additional opportunity for one-on-one mentoring from faculty. Qualifying freshmen can choose honors courses drawn from more than 60 fields of study in five colleges.

Changes Outside and In

Recent and planned site expansions, as well as innovative curriculum, also reflect the university's commitment to the best possible learning experience for its more than 4,000 graduate and undergraduate students. Renovations have included the Colleges of Business Administration, Education, and Pharmacy and Health Sciences.

Construction began in fall 1999 on the new communications complex, Fairbanks Center for Communication and Technology, to serve those pursuing careers in telecommunication arts, speech, journalism, and other communication studies. Planning is also under way for a Center for Arts and Culture, which will join Lilly and Clowes Memorial halls and provide additional recital facilities.

A bookstore expansion, completed in fall 1999, includes a Starbucks café. The university also recently enhanced the campus' park appeal by closing a dividing street and converting the space to a landscaped pedestrian mall.

Butler students are encouraged to study in international settings, and about 150 every year take advantage of semester, yearlong, or vacation opportunities. The Institute for Study Abroad, headquartered at Butler, is one of the largest such programs in the United States, placing students from American colleges and universities in academic programs in Argentina, Australia, Chile, Costa Rica, England, Ireland, New Zealand, and Scotland.

Reaching Out

Through the Butler Center for Citizenship and Community, students can round out their education by experiencing the link between scholarship and service. Working with practitioners in the public and private sectors, the center develops interdisciplinary and intercollege service-learning courses and experiences. A research laboratory also gathers and interprets data on community-generated research issues as a way to help identify and solve problems.

"We really have gone out and built the ballpark hoping 'they would come,'" says Dr. Geoffrey Bannister, who recently celebrated his 10th anniversary as university president. "And we haven't been disappointed. We've grown from 2,459 full-time undergraduates in the fall of 1989 to nearly 3,500. Consistently, 40 percent of our entering freshmen graduated in the top 10 percent of their high school class. Clearly, good students do follow the best faculty and programs."

Today's students choose Butler for many of the same reasons national guides recommend it: academic excellence, personal attention from faculty, range of academic programs, quality facilities, emphasis on the liberal arts and sciences, and preparation for graduate school and careers.

Wishard Health Services

Wishard Health Services has been serving the citizens of Marion County since 1859.

Wishard's primary care network includes six community health centers, including the Grassy Creek Health Center on Indianapolis' far east side.

THE 19TH-CENTURY FACADE OF WISHARD HEALTH SERVICES reminds passersby on West 10th Street of the building's historical significance as Indianapolis' first hospital. However, observers who look beyond the twin wings and stately pillars will discover one of the top hospitals in the nation, committed to the science of health and healing.

Wishard's history dates back to 1859, when a smallpox epidemic prompted Indianapolis to build a hospital. In 1975, the hospital was named in memory of William Niles Wishard, a superintendent who oversaw an expansion and many improvements in the quality of care.

Today, the older buildings, erected in the 1920s, house administrative functions and a nursing museum. But behind them is an ever evolving, modern, and diverse health care service delivery organization of 3,200 employees providing a full range of care to more than 200,000 Marion County residents every year.

Top-Rated Services

Wishard contributes to the next generation of medical practitioners as a teaching hospital staffed by Indiana University (IU) School of Medicine physicians. It's the only hospital in Indiana to be named one of the top 100 hospitals nationwide for three consecutive years by Health Care Industry Association (HCIA)/ Mercer Inc., an international management consulting firm.

The Wishard name is synonymous with exemplary emergency care. The Indiana University/ Wishard Trauma Center became the first Level I trauma center in the state in 1992 and remains one of only two citywide. Wishard's state-of-the-art Regional Adult Burn Center, which serves the entire state, is the only burn treatment facility in Indiana

verified by the American College of Surgeons and the American Burn Association.

Additionally, Wishard houses one of 12 National Centers of Excellence in Women's Health in the United States. This distinction is awarded through a granting process by the U.S. Department of Health and Human Services. Operated by the IU School of Medicine, the center assesses women's health needs and current medical procedures, then works to develop a coordinated national resource center to provide comprehensive care. The center also develops educational programs to raise awareness and conducts research into women's health issues, in addition to providing clinical care for Wishard Health Services.

Expanding Its Reach

Recently, Wishard has undergone a $100 million expansion and renovation that has vastly improved its ability to provide quality health care. In addition to the hospital, Wishard Health Services encompasses a new primary care center, six new

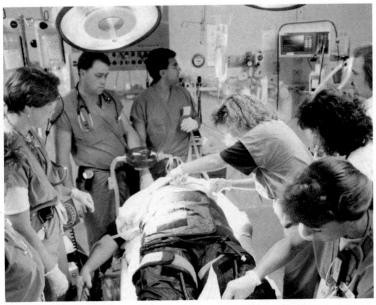

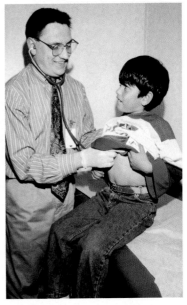

community health centers throughout the city, and Locke-field Village Nursing Home—all open since 1995.

Waiting, reception, and entrance areas to Wishard's Emergency Room and Urgent Visit Center (UVC) have been upgraded and expanded to enhance patient flow, family privacy, and staff efficiency. Nonemergency visits are now directed to a separate area, and Center of Hope sexual assault treatment and counseling facilities have been relocated in the UVC.

A new intensive care unit expanded Wishard's Close Observation Unit from 19 to 29 beds, while consolidating the unit into one location adjacent to existing intensive care units. The new, $3.8 million unit increased hospital flexibility in managing patients according to their medical needs.

Other major renovations have expanded treatment facilities and made new services available as well. A new cardiac catheterization lab expands the level of service provided from diagnostic-only to intervention. The new lab can now perform percutaneous transluminal coronary angioplasty and place intracoronary stents. The Center for Senior Health and the Acute Care for Elders (ACE) unit are both new additions at Wishard. The Center for Senior Health

provides consultative care on an outpatient basis, while the ACE unit provides acutely ill patients age 70 years or older with special services.

The Women's Visit Center also grew in 1998—from four examination and treatment rooms to 10, and from four labor/delivery/recovery/post-partum (LDRP) rooms to 11. Additionally, Wishard introduced a new care coordination program of home visits made to at-risk women, beginning in pregnancy and continuing through the child's first year of life. A team of social workers, nurses, and nutritionists works together to assess a mother's needs, educate her about the contribution a healthy lifestyle makes to birth outcome and infant health, and link her to community services that can help.

Building on the shift to outpatient-oriented health care, Wishard built the Westside Health Center to replace the Tibbs Health Center. The 22,000-square-foot facility, which opened in 1998, serves residents in the neighborhoods of Haughville, Stringtown, and Hawthorne with 18 examination rooms, a laboratory, a pharmacy, and women's, infants', and children's services.

Midtown Community Mental Health Center, another Wishard agency, offers services on-site

as well, and a large community room provides a meeting place for local civic and community organizations. Like all six Wishard Health Centers, Westside has an advisory council made up of neighborhood residents to provide feedback on services.

"As Wishard approaches 150 years of service, we remain dedicated to constantly improving and updating the scope and quality of our many patient services," says Director Randall Braddom, M.D. "The pace of change in medical care is accelerating, and Wishard is changing rapidly to meet the challenges it will face in the new millennium. We're truly proud of the evolution we've experienced thus far, and look forward to many more years of service to Marion County's citizens."

Clockwise from top left:
Wishard's Level I Trauma Center serves more than 90,000 patients each year.

Wishard's Hispanic Health Project provides translation, information, and counseling services to the area's growing Hispanic population.

Among the recent renovations at Wishard are 11 new labor/delivery/recovery/postpartum (LDRP) rooms at the Family Beginnings department.

Eli Lilly and Company

ELI LILLY AND COMPANY PLANS TO MAKE ITS MARK IN THE 21ST century by meeting unmet medical needs at a pace unrivaled in its nearly 125-year history. Headquartered in Indianapolis, this pharmaceutical giant has long been driven by innovation and science. ■ But Sidney Taurel, chairman, president, and chief executive officer, believes the next level of accomplish-

ment will demand relentless acquisition and development of innovative medicines, and a strategy that derives the greatest benefit from each.

Always at the Forefront

Since its beginning in 1876, Lilly has been at the forefront of many significant breakthroughs in modern medicine. Founder Colonel Eli Lilly, a pharmaceutical chemist, recognized the importance of research and development, and hired the company's first full-time scientist in 1886, laying the foundation for the commitment to scientific innovation for which the firm continues to be known today.

In the 1920s, Lilly scientists working with University of Toronto researchers introduced the first insulin product, which revolutionized the treatment of diabetes. During the 1950s, the company developed long-acting, orally administered penicillin products, as well as erythromycin, the first compound in a major class of antibiotics called macrolides. Lilly research teams expanded on discoveries by European scientists in the early 1960s to develop the first agents in another class of antibiotics, the cephalosporins, which today include Lilly's Ceclor®, one of the world's most widely used antibacterial products.

For the treatment of diabetes in the early 1980s, the company introduced Humulin®, human insulin, the world's first human health care product created using genetic engineering technology. The late 1980s brought the launch of Prozac®, the first product in a new class of antidepressants and Lilly's most successful product to date.

Other Lilly products include Zyprexa®, for treatment of schizo-

phrenia; Gemzar®, for pancreatic and lung cancers; Axid®, an antiulcer agent; ReoPro®, used in angioplasty procedures; Humatrope®, a therapy for growth hormone deficiency in children; Evista®, to prevent osteoporosis; and Vancocin®, an injectable antibiotic.

In addition to its major Indiana facilities in Indianapolis, Clinton, Greenfield, and Lafayette, which together employ about

12,000 individuals, the company has manufacturing plants and research and development facilities around the globe, bringing its total employment to more than 30,000 individuals worldwide. Lilly also conducts clinical research trials in approximately 50 countries and markets its pharmaceuticals in more than 160 nations.

Fueling Growth

In 1999, Lilly invested nearly $2 billion in research and development (R&D). R&D as a percentage of sales is the highest in the pharmaceutical industry and double the investment level of most high-technology companies. The firm also unveiled long-term growth plans that included a planned $1 billion expansion of operations and the creation of up to 7,500 new jobs during the next decade.

Expansion plans include development and infrastructure improvements at two of Lilly's

More than the miracle of breakthrough drugs, says Sidney Taurel, chairman, president, and chief executive officer of Eli Lilly and Company, "the real miracle is the people who labor to create them."

Founder Colonel Eli Lilly, a pharmaceutical chemist, recognized the importance of research and development, and hired the company's first full-time scientist in 1886, laying the foundation for the commitment to scientific innovation for which the firm continues to be known today.

main Indianapolis campuses— Lilly Corporate Center and Lilly Technology Center. The expansion encompasses nearly 20 new construction projects, ranging from a $100 million project to increase the company's recombinant DNA human-insulin production facilities to a $6 million project that will create high-tech research laboratories.

The expansion will create new jobs mainly in Indianapolis, including scientists, physicians, technicians, and production operators. City officials liken the effect of the investment to a Fortune 500 company relocating to Indianapolis every two years for the next decade.

Meeting Unmet Needs

Lilly directs all of its efforts toward patients' unmet medical needs. The firm's strategy in meeting those needs emphasizes discovering innovative medicines first, and then helping patients maximize benefits from them. By improving the research and development process, investing in new research technologies, and expanding its research team, the firm will strengthen its ability to identify high-potential drug candidates.

A significant part of the company's efforts to speed the discovery and development of innovative pharmaceuticals has been to enter into research alliances with leading scientific companies and universities. Today, Lilly is engaged in more than 100 ongoing collaborations that are focused on new product discovery and development, product delivery approaches, and technology platforms that can be used across all areas of discovery research. This strategy enables Lilly to share ideas and learn from some of the world's distinguished researchers.

Many of Lilly's current products, including ReoPro, were developed as a result of a partnership. Lilly markets the drug, which was developed by Malvern, Pennsylvania-based Centocor, Inc., to help prevent acute cardiac complications in patients undergoing balloon angioplasty. ReoPro is also the subject of a broader trial for unstable angina, as well as trials for treatment of heart attack and heart-related stroke.

The Human Element

Increased competition for qualified employees makes Lilly's time-honored principle of putting people first more important than ever. A reputation for investing

Headquartered in Indianapolis, Eli Lilly and Company has been driven by innovation and science throughout its 125-year history.

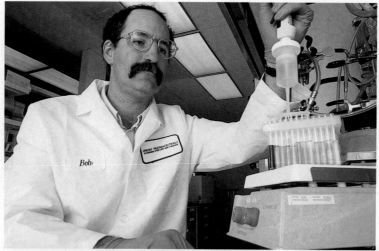

Lilly's policy of putting employees first grew out of its origins as a family business.

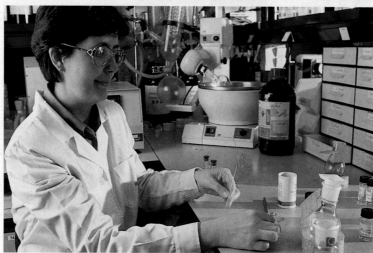

In 1999, Lilly invested nearly $2 billion in research and development. R&D as a percentage of sales is the highest in the pharmaceutical industry.

in the development of its people drives recruitment of partners as well as employees, especially as many of the top scientists migrate toward start-up biomedical firms.

What draws both camps to connect with Lilly is its sterling reputation. Putting its employees first grew out of the company's origins as a family business. Increasingly, Lilly recruits top talent on a global basis, so fostering a culture of inclusion where diversity is valued is a key goal. The company works hard to develop employees with a global perspective by sending them on global assignments, as well as by bringing non-U.S. employees to Indianapolis.

Half of Lilly's current senior management team were born outside the United States—including Taurel, a U.S. citizen who was born in Morocco and has represented Lilly in Brazil, Austria, France, and the United Kingdom. The company has been recognized in lists like

Fortune magazine's 50 best companies for Asians, African-Americans, and Hispanics, and *Working Mother* magazine's 10 best companies.

In addition, the company fosters employee development by encouraging community involvement. Indianapolis employees participate in a variety of programs designed to impact the city's young people and neighborhoods. For example, the Science Education Coordination Committee works with teachers and students to increase awareness of and interest in careers in sciences for Indianapolis youth. Scientists in the Schools sponsors visits by Lilly employees, and laboratory tours and Summer Education Experience for the Disadvantaged (SEED) bring young people into Lilly facilities. Partnerships to refurbish used but usable computers place much-needed equipment in Indiana schools, and participation in Junior Achievement and Partnership

in Education further extend the Lilly reach.

The Lilly Hammers group of employees helps with home rehabilitation projects in low-income neighborhoods as well. Since 1992, employees have built 20 homes in conjunction with Habitat for Humanity.

Lilly sponsors an employee recognition grant program, which makes it possible for employees who volunteer a minimum of 50 hours per year to one organization to have a $250 grant awarded to that organization in their names. Since 1995, this program has donated more than $65,000 to employee-supported efforts.

The Point of Convergence

But the point at which customers, communities, and employees converge perhaps provides the best insight into Lilly's success and certainly is, as Taurel explains, "the reason we come to work every day.

"A breakthrough drug is often hailed in the media as a miracle, but the real miracle is the extraordinary perseverance, the commitment, and the caring of all the people who labor to create it," Taurel says. "A new drug is one huge success built out of 100,000 small failures. People invest years, sometimes decades, overcoming each failure, fearing that each new one might prove insurmountable.

"At a certain point along this chain of invention, when the new compounds reach real patients, if the results are favorable, we begin to hear reports from clinics and physicians, sometimes from patients or their families. And that moment is when those who have worked so hard get the best reward possible—another human being says thank-you for healing his pain, healing his child, or saving his life

"There's nothing to compare to that feeling of meeting the unmet need. This is the bonus that goes far beyond any quantitative or economic measure. Call it a dividend that continually accrues."

As Indianapolis' only independent, college preparatory school for children in prekindergarten through grade 12, Park Tudor School has been upholding a tradition of educational excellence for nearly a century. Its more than 3,500 alumni have included local philanthropists J.K. Lilly III, Ruth Lilly, and Allen Clowes, along with business lead-

ers Russ Pulliam, Myrta Pulliam, and Tom Binford.

"Park Tudor helps children prepare for an increasingly complex and diverse world by providing a high-quality, well-rounded college preparatory education in an atmosphere responsive to the needs of both children and parents," says Headmaster Bruce W. Galbraith. Many of our graduates are inextricably linked to both the history and the future of the city."

A Long-Standing Tradition of Excellence

Park Tudor School was established in 1970 by a merger of Tudor Hall School for girls and Park School for boys. Tudor Hall's history dates to 1902, while Park School's history dates to 1914, when it was first formed as the Brooks Preparatory School for boys. The two schools originally were neighbors, first downtown near 16th Street, then later at sites on Cold Spring Road. Park School moved to the current 55-acre Park Tudor campus in 1967, when the land was donated to the school by the Lilly estate. The school recently completed a $22.5 million capital campaign that included construction of the Hilbert Early Education Center and expansions of two of the campus' seven buildings.

Park Tudor students regularly earn among the highest SAT scores of any four-year public or private school in the state, with 100 percent of students accepted to attend college. The school has graduated several Presidential Scholars, the first female student on the U.S. Math Olympiad team, and a first-prize winner in the national Westinghouse Science Honors

Institute for high school seniors—a contest won by five Nobel Prize recipients.

A Challenging Curriculum Makes Well-Rounded Students

Park Tudor's challenging academic program includes more than 20 advanced placement courses and boasts a low student-teacher ratio of nine to one. More than two-thirds of faculty members hold advanced degrees—including several with doctorate degrees—and they have a reputation for providing a safe and caring environment.

The school's 900 students have many opportunities to balance their education with fine arts programs, athletics, and a host of volunteer clubs. The "no-cut" athletic program enables all students to participate in any activities in which they hold an interest. More than $1.4 million in financial assistance is awarded annually, with about 20 percent of the school's students receiving some form of financial aid.

At Park Tudor, students learn to use technology as an essential tool in research. Technology offerings include a full-campus fiber-optic network, more than 400 personal computers, and Internet access. Computer learn-

ing is fully integrated into the curriculum with each classroom having at least one computer workstation.

In addition, foreign-language instruction is part of the curriculum starting in preschool. Up until fifth grade, all children learn Spanish. Thereafter, students can also choose from courses in French, German, Japanese, Latin, and Greek.

"We take pride in fostering a child's sense of esteem and accomplishment," Galbraith adds, "teaching high standards of behavior, responsibility, ethics, and citizenship."

From top:
With a low student-teacher ratio and numerous faculty with master's degrees or higher, Park Tudor School takes pride in fostering a child's sense of esteem and accomplishment.

The school's 900 students have many opportunities to balance their education with fine arts programs, athletics, and a host of volunteer clubs.

As Indianapolis' only independent, college preparatory school for children in prekindergarten through grade 12, Park Tudor School has been upholding a tradition of educational excellence for nearly a century.

St. Vincent Hospitals and Health Services

ADVANCES IN MEDICAL SCIENCE AND TECHNOLOGY ARE reshaping how doctors understand and treat diseases, while expanding their vision of what is humanly possible. But at St. Vincent Hospitals and Health Services, the staff realizes that the human experience is more than the physical body—there is a mind and a spirit to be treated as well. Health and healing of the whole person is the mission. And since the beginning, the hospital has reached out to the community in hundreds of places and programs, with special concern for the poor and vulnerable.

When four Daughters of Charity arrived in Indianapolis in 1881, their efforts to help the poor were supported by a budget of $34.77. Their hope and faith, however, were limitless, and their strength was drawn from devotion to God and from the traditions of St. Vincent de Paul, St. Louise de Marillac, and St. Elizabeth Ann Seton.

Serving the Indianapolis area and nearby Carmel from two hospital campuses—a 691-bed facility on West 86th Street and a 54-bed facility in Carmel—its ministry extends into central Indiana with hospitals in Elwood, North Vernon, Williamsport, and in 2000, Randolph County. Throughout the country, the Daughters of Charity serve as part of Ascension Health, a national health ministry cosponsored by the Daughters of Charity National Health System and the Sisters of St. Joseph Health System.

Specialty Centers and Service Lines

St. Vincent's health ministries are organized as specialty centers and individual service lines, giving each the autonomy to develop medical, surgical, educational, and community service-related programs.

Excellence in children's medicine is a priority. The pediatrics program has newborn intensive care and pediatric transport technologies that are among the most advanced in the nation. An eight-bed Pediatric Intensive Care Unit opened in 1998 to serve children with critical-care needs. St. Vincent's Children's Specialty Hospital, a separate facility, embodies the hospital's pledge of family-oriented care, where acute comprehensive rehabilitation, ventilatory management, and transitional care are provided in a comfortable setting.

A commitment to women's health is evident both inside and outside St. Vincent's walls. The Family Life Center delivers more babies than any single hospital in Indiana. At the Lazarus department store in Castleton Square, women can receive a high-quality mammogram screening and bone density testing for osteoporosis.

St. Vincent is a leader in the treatment of cardiovascular disease through the Indiana Heart Institute, which pioneers new strategies and techniques in prevention, diagnosis, and treatment. Investigation of more than 15,000 procedures is performed annually, with leading-edge work done in the advancement of surgical alternatives, including less invasive procedures and drug therapies.

Comprehensive joint replacement services are a growing specialty. Technical innovation and multidisciplinary medical expertise focus to help afflicted patients return to pain-free mobility. Extensive presurgery education and conditioning, along with involved postsurgery follow-up, supplement knee, hip, and shoulder replacements.

St. Vincent's Neuroscience Service Line offers a wide range of services to aid in the prevention of and recovery from strokes, the leading cause of disability and the third leading cause of death. A stroke risk assessment guide helps identify risk factors and direct potential stroke sufferers toward healthier choices.

St. Vincent Sports Medicine has been expanded to meet the needs of athletes of all ages, and features education and wellness activities to help improve the health of the entire community.

St. Vincent and Westview Hospital joined to create Healthplex, the first and only dedicated wellness center in the state. Med- ical, wellness,

St. Vincent Hospitals and Health Services' mission is guided by the teachings of St. Vincent de Paul. Its commitment to charity, care of the poor, and community benefit is supported by an annual investment of more than $32 million.

and therapeutic resources combine to offer a holistic approach lacking at traditional fitness facilities.

Alternative approaches to ease pain are an emerging component of St. Vincent's holistic health services. The John S. Marten & Family Center for Complementary Medicine and Pain Management incorporates both traditional and alternative treatment models to help patients with chronic pain.

St. Vincent Stress Centers offer specialized programs in mental health and chemical dependency. In addition, St. Vincent New Hope provides services for adults with congenital or acquired disabilities.

In Hamilton County, St. Vincent Carmel is expanding its services, including orthopedics, imaging, surgery, bariatric weight-loss treatments, and pulmonary rehabilitation to meet the needs of the growing northside community.

In 1998 and 1999, St. Vincent received several local and national honors. It placed on the annual 100 Top Hospitals list developed by HCIA Inc. and

William M. Mercer Inc., recognizing hospitals that deliver the most cost-efficient and highest-quality medical care. In both years, *U.S. News & World Report* recognized St. Vincent's cardiac program as one of the best in the nation, and in 1998, the magazine recognized the ear, nose, and throat program. In addition, the National Research Corp. reported that central Indiana health consumers made St. Vincent the number one consumer choice in the market for the fourth straight year.

Spirit of Caring

In 1999 alone, St. Vincent contributed more than $32 million in charity care and community benefits. At the center of its advocacy is the Building Healthier Communities program, which places St. Vincent as a catalyst for improved community and individual health. It incorporates dialogue with community leaders to identify community-specific issues and create partnerships that share a vision of holistic health.

At the Unity Development Center, St. Vincent serves as a multidimensional resource for

a low-income neighborhood. Children age six to 12 can participate in programs and activities that include sports, dance, computer training, and tutoring.

By calling a single number, 388-CARE, the people of Indianapolis and surrounding communities can connect with St. Vincent services to find answers to health care questions. More important, they will find someone who cares. Again and again, St. Vincent's mission is strengthened and renewed: to minister to the minds, bodies, and spirits of those in need.

From a growing campus on Indianapolis' northwest side, St. Vincent plays a major role in the city's good economic health, as well as its physical, emotional, and spiritual well-being. Some 5,800 people are employed at this facility and at St. Vincent Carmel (top).

St. Vincent's continuum of care includes a full range of services for elderly and geriatric patients, with a special emphasis on those unable to pay (bottom).

Allison Payment Systems, LLC

ALLISON PAYMENT SYSTEMS, LLC (APS) WAS ON THE cutting edge when it was founded in 1888 as the first coupon book company in the nation, and takes pride in the fact that it still is on the cutting edge as a pioneer in on-line electronic payment. Today, as a specialty commercial printer providing a broad range of computer-printed products and services to financial businesses, APS is one of the largest mailers of first-class materials in Indianapolis, posting more than 85 million pieces of mail in a year.

An Idea That Took

In a city where the Allison surname is synonymous with innovation, APS President and Chief Executive Officer Joseph H. Thomas likes to describe APS as the first Allison success story. Long before James A. Allison was associated with either the Indianapolis Motor Speedway or General Motors Corporation, he worked for his father, Noah, at Allison Coupon Company.

In the late 1800s, the practice of buying on credit was gaining acceptance as America's consumer economy became more complex. Yet, many debtors either could not or would not repay the debts they incurred on a timely basis. Noah Allison came up with the idea of the coupon book as a profitable way to help both debtors and creditors. He negotiated with local merchants so people could purchase many necessary commodities with scrip instead of cash, then sold the coupon books to workers on payday. Coupons were good only for particular items, such as groceries, and valid only when detached by the grocery store clerk.

Coupon books helped consumers because store owners sold them at a small discount and people could buy more with them than if they used cash. The books helped merchants by giving them their money up front. The idea worked and spread so quickly that Allison Coupon could barely get the books printed up fast enough.

Allison Payment Systems, LLC (APS) provides "timely products" with "timeless quality" (top).

Noah Allison founded APS in 1888 as the first coupon book company in the nation. Today, it is one of the largest mailers of first-class materials in Indianapolis (bottom).

Workmen building the Panama Canal from 1904 to 1914 were paid in part using Allison coupon books, as were soldiers at army posts nationwide. The country's first installment loans in 1919 were repaid using Allison loan coupon books, and appropriately, General Motors Acceptance Corporation (GMAC) began using Allison payment books in 1922.

A New Family Dynasty

Allison Coupon was eventually sold to Cummins Chicago, a manufacturer of document perforators, and the name was changed to Cummins-Allison. Thomas became its president in 1988 and bought the company in 1995. Today, the company is a family business once again, with Thomas' four sons and a daughter-in-law among the approximately 165 employees working out of 100,000 square feet of space at two westside locations.

Sales have more than doubled, approaching $35 million, since the ownership change. Coupon books, which constituted 85 percent of the business in 1995, today account for less than 50 percent. Focus has instead shifted to multifaceted payment systems, including an on-line payment option.

APS offers a complete line of billing statements and invoices, from a basic black-and-white statement to a full-color marketing and billing campaign, with an emphasis on reliability and speed. Client data files, once submitted to APS, are converted into customized, individual statements and mailed either the same day or the next day with no more than three errors per 6 million transactions—which is an average monthly workload.

"We take accuracy very seriously," Thomas explains. "To illustrate the difference we can make, a major St. Louis-based mortgage company had as many as 6,000 customer service calls per month when they came to us. Within a month of APS mailing their statements, that number had dropped to 2,000."

Clients opting for instant job tracking can access APS computer systems through the Internet to check progress on their jobs and spot-check statements sent to customers. APS can selectively insert secondary marketing and information materials into the outgoing envelope before presorting takes place at its in-house postal facility. All told, APS uses more than 160 million envelopes a year for its coupon book and statement business.

Other Leading-Edge Options

For clients who want to do their own processing of financial information, APS offers Electronic Document Generation (EDGE), a proprietary desktop laser-printing software that generates checks and other printed documents from blank paper. EDGE works with customer accounts payable, payroll, or other PC-based systems to format payment documents with signatures, logos, and bank codes for machine readability,

eliminating the need for pre-printed check stock, signing machines, and other equipment. American United Life, Indianapolis Life, and the Eli Lilly Foundation all use the APS EDGE system.

PaySense, the latest APS offering, gives clients still another advantage—electronic bill presentment and payment via the Internet. The proprietary on-line system is the result of a partnership between APS and a Minneapolis-based software development firm. The software includes data security and two-way processing so that bills can be sent out over the Internet and paid the same way.

Consumers receive an E-bill that replicates the traditional paper bill, and they can pay it immediately or delay payment. Payments are then processed through an electronic post office that forwards transactions to the biller's bank using an automated clearinghouse network. Billers receive duplicate notices when transactions go through and can

choose to process them daily or twice weekly by clicking on the PaySense button on the APS Web site.

"Our growth is tied to staying on top of developments in technology," says Thomas. "We plan to continue investments in newer and more modern equipment and systems to stay on the leading edge of our clients' needs."

Clockwise from top:
Computer operations area where clients' data files are converted for production processing of billing statements and payment coupon books.

Company partners Joseph H. Thomas, president and CEO (seated); John M. Mentzer, vice-president administration (right); and Richard A. Lippitz, vice president sales and marketing (left).

APS offers a complete line of billing statements and invoices, from a basic black-and-white statement to a full-color marketing and billing campaign, with an emphasis on reliability and speed (bottom).

DaimlerChrysler Indianapolis Foundry

THE DAIMLERCHRYSLER INDIANAPOLIS FOUNDRY PRODUCES cast-iron engine blocks for most DaimlerChrysler car, minivan, and truck engines manufactured in North America at a rate of 800 per hour, or 2 million per year. ■ Engine block demand has increased year after year, necessitating parallel increases in productivity, quality, facility size, and capability. To meet demand, the foundry runs two shifts, six days a week. A four-year, $300 million modernization and expansion will increase that production capacity by 20 percent and assure the plant's viability well into the 21st century.

Quality, however, is the crucial measure at DaimlerChrysler, since the foundry's performance affects work at all engine plants. The foundry is ISO 9002 certified and has won a state award for quality improvement in 1997.

Spanning the Centuries

The present foundry grew out of a small specialty operation in the 1890s called the American

Foundry. American began making engine castings for the emerging automobile industry in 1901. In the mid-1920s, acquisition of an existing customer directed more Chrysler work to the foundry until shortly after World War II, when Chrysler bought the foundry and began operating it as a wholly owned subsidiary.

Construction on the current plant occurred between 1946 and 1949, and Chrysler made the foundry an official part of Chrysler Corporation in 1959. In 1998, Chrysler announced its latest investment in the foundry: a $100 million expansion project. In November of that year, Chrysler merged with Daimler-Benz, makers of Mercedes-Benz, to form DaimlerChrysler.

The number of foundries in the United States today is significantly lower than it was just a few years ago. Indianapolis Foundry is one of the major foundries in the country, which is reversing the trend by continuing to expand. The 748,000-square-foot facility is situated on 48 acres on the west side of Indianapolis.

Indianapolis Foundry is the only DaimlerChrysler-owned North American foundry, and it employs more than 1,100 workers. The foundry melts and pours 200,000 tons of iron every year at temperatures reaching 2,600 to 2,800 degrees Fahrenheit. Another 200,000 tons of sand are used in the casting process to make cores and molds for the castings.

Protecting the Environment

As one of the largest and most effective recyclers in Indiana, the foundry uses scrap metal from shredded automobiles, engine blocks, and discarded

The DaimlerChrysler Indianapolis Foundry produces cast-iron engine blocks at a rate of 800 per hour, or 2 million per year (top).

Indianapolis Foundry is the only Daimler-Chrysler-owned, North American foundry, and it employs more than 1,100 workers (bottom).

and dismantled equipment.

Many automotive manufacturers are getting out of the foundry business, or even sourcing abroad, because environmental regulations make it difficult to bring new plants on line. In response to the Clean Air Act Amendments of 1990, much of the recent modernization and expansion at the Indianapolis site employs state-of-the-art methods to minimize the foundry's environmental impact.

A new cupola installation uses a revolutionary afterburner system that eliminates 99 percent of all carbon monoxide (CO) and organic compounds. The heat from igniting CO is then reused in a recuperator. This process reduces the requirement for natural gas to produce the 1,100-degree, preheated air needed for melting iron.

Transporting new sand to the site costs more than the sand itself, so a sand reclamation system helps reuse sand many times over. The reclamation system consists of a first-stage mechanical sand screening, followed by a thermal treatment of 1,200 degrees to burn off chemicals used as binders during molding. The reclaimed sand, which is no longer waste, is used instead of new sand. In 1998, the plant recycled 132,000 tons of sand that would normally be disposed of in a landfill.

Building the DaimlerChrysler Community

Plant employees take their community roles seriously as well. Every year since 1984, employees have banded together to make the holidays brighter for several hundred Indianapolis families through its Clothe-A-Child program at Christmas. DaimlerChrysler employees take disadvantaged children shopping for clothes, shoes, and coats. The day includes lunch, snacks, and pictures with Santa.

DaimlerChrysler further contributes to the quality of its local community and state through vigorous support of many organizations devoted to education, health and human services, the environment, the arts, and the community at large.

Plant Manager Tony Watt, a seasoned company executive, grew up right around the corner from the plant. "This plant provides a great opportunity for the future of DaimlerChrysler and for Indianapolis," Watt says. "The current expansion gives us a world-class process. But it's the spirit of our employees, and their commitment to quality and to community, that makes us a world-class operation."

Plant Manager Tony Watt says, "It's the spirit of our employees, and their commitment to quality and to community, that makes us a world-class operation. (top)"

As one of the largest and most effective recyclers in Indiana, the foundry uses scrap metal from shredded automobiles, engine blocks, and discarded and dismantled equipment (bottom left and right).

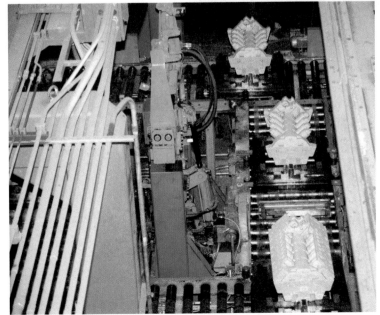

Indianapolis Chamber of Commerce

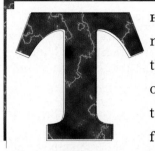

THE INDIANAPOLIS CHAMBER OF COMMERCE'S LEGACY OF BUSIness and community advocacy spans more than a century of the city's growth and development. Formed in 1890 by a group of business leaders interested in infrastructure improvements, today's chamber continues that tradition by paving the way for more than 3,000 businesses and corporations.

On an average day, the chamber fields more than 300 telephone calls, processes nearly 60 requests for information, and serves about 20 newcomers and potential new residents. While its mission centers on advocacy for and promotion of business rather than tourism, the Indianapolis Chamber of Commerce plays an integral role in promoting the benefits of living and working in the Circle City to potential businesses and residents.

Helping to Manage Growth

The environment that spawned the chamber's forerunner, the Commercial Club, had a great deal in common with Indianapolis' current national status. In 1890, Indianapolis was a relatively new city of the American West, which in fewer than 70 years had grown to be one of the 25 largest in a young nation.

At that time, infrastructure was not able to keep pace with growth, creating a less-than-appealing environment in which to live and work. Perhaps most distressing were piles of dirt left along the streets by two competing companies digging

and installing natural gas lines along the city's unpaved thoroughfares. Out of these conditions emerged a group of 27 business leaders, led by Colonel Eli Lilly, with the initial mission: "to promote prosperity and work for the general welfare of Indianapolis." Lilly was elected the first president of the Commercial Club, whose name was changed to the Indianapolis Chamber of Commerce in 1912.

In its first week of operation, the club sponsored the Street Exposition of Indianapolis, which resulted in paving major downtown thoroughfares. Other early accomplishments included creating a city park system, supporting the first city hospital, facilitating a major cleanup of downtown property, securing a location for the airport, and revising the city charter to establish the mayor/city council system.

The organization continued to respond to the needs of businesses well into the 20th century,

Indianapolis Chamber of Commerce founder Colonel Eli Lilly served as the chamber's first president from 1890 to 1894 (left).

Today's vibrant downtown reflects the commitment and involvement of the Indianapolis business community (right).

protecting manufacturing interests during the war years and assisting veterans with job placement in the 1950s and 1960s. In more recent years, the chamber has acted as an advocate for interstate highways, education, metropolitan planning, the environment, construction of the Hoosier (now RCA) Dome, and Unigov, the system of government that united the City of Indianapolis and Marion County in 1970.

In 1991, in commemoration of more than 100 years of service to the city, the chamber issued its Getting Indianapolis Fit for Tomorrow (GIFT) report, which renewed the organization's focus on the city's infrastructure. GIFT recommended a dramatic increase in infrastructure spending—$1.1 billion—much more than the planned expenditures on streets, sanitary and storm sewers, parks, and public buildings. Stephen Goldsmith, who was elected mayor in November of that year, incorporated many aspects of the chamber's GIFT report into his Building Better Neighborhoods program.

A Collective Voice

Advocacy for issues that impact business has set the Indianapolis Chamber of Commerce apart throughout its history. The organization remains a voice for progress and improvement, and is still focused on serving mem-

bers, whether through legislative influence on issues that affect business, networking opportunities and member discounts, discounted health insurance, or exclusive demographic surveys and database information.

"The Indianapolis Chamber is known as a convener," says Ronald K. Pearson, 1999-2000 board chair. "We have a reputation for creating private sector solutions to community problems. Whether it is an innovative plan for infrastructure investment or tough recommendations for education, we get things done."

A relatively new chamber effort involves creating neighborhood business alliances to focus on the special concerns of a specific business district and to help manage its growth more effectively. So far, alliances have been formed in the Castleton and Lafayette Square areas, and more are planned for the future.

In addition, the chamber has won accolades for a video it produced to help employers convince prospective employees to relocate to the Indianapolis area. "Invitation to Indianapolis" features interviews with many new residents, who discuss all the city has to offer, including easy commutes, friendly neighbors, low housing costs, and a rich offering of cultural and leisure activities. The video won

two national awards following its release in spring 1998—a Telly Award from the video/ film industry and an Award of Excellence from the American Chamber of Commerce Executives (ACCE).

"Invitation to Indianapolis" has been supplemented with the introIndianapolis.com Web site, for people and businesses relocating to Indianapolis. The site provides access to area businesses and service providers, in addition to comprehensive relocation information, news, calendars, maps, and on-line forums. It also links to the chamber's membership site, which includes detailed demographic information about the city and on-line registration for the chamber's numerous monthly networking opportunities.

"Indianapolis has always been blessed with business leaders and companies who see the big picture, who have a vision of where the community ought to be headed, and who are willing to fulfill that vision," says John S. Myrland, chamber president. "Our members will continue to be at the forefront in pursuit of that vision, and the Indianapolis Chamber of Commerce will continue to lead those efforts."

Carrying on the legacy of Lilly's strong leadership are (from left) Ronald K. Pearson, chamber board chairman; Yvonne H. Shaheen, vice chairman; and John S. Myrland, chamber president.

Traffic congestion was just one of the problems the Indianapolis Chamber of Commerce tackled in its early days.

St. Elmo Steak House

INDIANAPOLIS IS THE LARGEST CITY IN THE NATION WITHOUT A navigable port, yet strangely, the restaurant with the longest history in the city at a single location is named for the patron saint of sailors. ■ There's nothing ironic, though, about the success of St. Elmo Steak House. The restaurant, which is located on South Illinois Street, opened in 1902 as Joe Stahr's Tavern.

Shortly after opening, Stahr added a buffet that gained a local following and changed the name to reflect his nautical interests. With a dedication to quality and unfaltering customer service, the restaurant has been an Indianapolis mainstay ever since.

A perennial favorite among Indianapolis residents and visitors alike, the eatery has played host to a long list of celebrities, whose photos and autographs grace the walls of the establishment. Lyle Lovett has ducked in for a private meal before sound check, borrowed an employee's motorcycle to unwind, and said thank you with front-row concert tickets and backstage passes. The rock band Aerosmith has even made an appearance at St. Elmo. "It really burst my bubble of what rock stars are supposed to be like," recalls current owner Stephen M. Huse. "They were all drinking non-alcoholic beer and killing time before catching a movie at Circle Centre."

Doing What It Does Best

Huse purchased the restaurant in 1986 from longtime owners Harry Roth and Isadore Rosen, and is now the restaurant's sole owner. "We offer a limited menu—only 14 entrée selections—but what we do, we do really well," Huse says. The wet-aged steaks, shrimp cocktails, and wine selections are the favorite items on the restaurant's menu. On a weekly basis, the establishment serves up 1,300 filets, 600 16-ounce strip steaks, 100 porterhouses, and 100 24-ounce strip steaks. More than eight tons of shrimp per year go into its famous shrimp cocktails, and the staff

grinds the horseradish used in the homemade cocktail sauce fresh every day. Tours are available of the 25,000-bottle wine cellar, where the temperature is always 60 degrees and each bottle is stored at the optimal 15-degree angle.

Huse has expanded the restaurant during his years of ownership. Most recently, a $2 million expansion and renovation added private dining rooms for larger upscale private events. One private dining room, the Board of Directors' Room, overlooks the wine cellar. The newest addition is the Hulman Room, which incorporates many artifacts related to the career of the late Tony Hulman, former owner of the Indianapolis Motor

Speedway. For groups using these new rooms, the staff can prepare custom, preprinted menus; provide private bar setups; and oversee audiovisual needs for business meetings.

But the most unique features of St. Elmo, the ones that solidify its reputation as an Indianapolis tradition, are the staff and the service they provide. "The man who cooks the shrimp and grinds the horseradish every day has been with us 30 years," Huse says. "Many more have been here 10 and 20 years. Our servers stay because they develop a clientele. The more the rest of the world changes, the more things at St. Elmo stay the same."

Clockwise from top:
St. Elmo Steak House has remained one of the most popular eateries in downtown Indianapolis for almost 100 years.

"The members of our staff are professionals," says owner Stephen Huse. "Guest service is our number one priority."

Steaks are carefully aged to prime tenderness and cooked at a high temperature to seal in flavorful juices.

CATHEDRAL HIGH SCHOOL PROVIDES A HOLISTIC EDUCATION ENcompassing spiritual, intellectual, and social growth, building on the same mission that established the Fighting Irish tradition more than 80 years ago. ■ Today, its 39-acre wooded campus houses 48 classrooms, administrative offices, and special services for a student body of 1,050, which is approximately 80 percent Catholic, as well as 52 percent male and 48 percent female. At least 40 percent of each freshman class is chosen based on diversity of faith, race, geography, academic level, and economic circumstances. About one-fourth of the school's students receive some form of financial aid.

Bishop Joseph Chartrand founded Cathedral High School in 1918 as an all-boys Catholic high school, naming it after its original location across the street from the Cathedral of Saints Peter and Paul at Meridian and 14th streets. When the Archdiocese of Indianapolis closed the downtown location in 1973, the administration of a private Cathedral High School shifted to a 24-member lay board of trustees. Three years later, when Ladywood-St. Agnes girls school closed, Cathedral purchased the northeast-side campus on the former Stoughton-Fletcher estate and opened the new school year as a Catholic, private, co-educational, preparatory high school.

A Tradition of Success

Students of all academic levels attend Cathedral High School, and 98 percent go on to college. Its honors program includes eight advanced placement courses, along with a language support program to help college-bound learning-impaired students. The graduating classes of 1998 and 1999 earned $9.6 million in college scholarships, with graduates going on to such prestigious institutions as the University of Notre Dame, Boston College, Northwestern University, Wabash College, and Yale University, among others. Graduates include two Olympians, five professional football players, the inventor of the artificial kidney, a Nobel Peace Prize winner, a Pulitzer Prize winner, and a host of others who went on to become leaders in the Indianapolis community and abroad.

Cathedral maintains interactive distance-learning equipment and more than 300 personal computers for student use—a ratio of about one for every three students—and offers basic and advanced computer courses. Computer skills are integrated into the general curriculum as well, with all classrooms containing at least one computer wired for network and Internet access.

A Tradition of Heart

The Fighting Irish tradition extends beyond the classroom to athletics and community service. Students can choose from 12 interscholastic sports teams for boys and 10 for girls, as well as a wide variety of social and service clubs. Seventy-five percent of all freshmen at Cathedral participate in at least one of these extracurricular activities. The school has won state championships in football, boys basketball, girls volleyball, and girls tennis, and has had numerous individual state champs in wrestling, swimming, and tennis.

"While our immediate objective is to prepare students for college admission, our ultimate goal is to guide them toward being competent, concerned, responsible, and ethical members of society," says Father Patrick J. Kelly, principal. "Our students and our graduates are the best proof of our success."

The stone crucifix overlooks the outdoor altar on the Cathedral High School campus, where each year the graduating class celebrates the Baccalaureate Mass (top).

Cathedral High School is a Catholic, private, co-educational, preparatory high school dedicated to the holistic development of its students (bottom).

CHRIS C. KAUFMAN

CHRIS C. KAUFMAN

CATHEDRAL

5225

St. Francis Hospital & Health Centers

EVERY TIME A BABY IS BORN AT ST. FRANCIS HOSPITAL, A lullaby rings over the public address system. This modest gesture serves as a simple but powerful reminder that each new life is precious. The understanding that each individual has a contribution to make, that life should be cherished—these are the distinguishing characteristics of St. Francis Hospital & Health Centers.

True to Its Roots

Since 1914, St. Francis Hospital has been a center of physical and spiritual healing, combining sophisticated treatments with an overriding concern for the patient as a whole person. The hospital was founded by the Catholic Sisters of St. Francis of Perpetual Adoration. The Sisters are actively involved at St. Francis Hospital to ensure its mission of continuing Christ's healing ministry is carried out in the many Indiana communities St. Francis touches.

In the more than 85 years of service to the central Indiana area, St. Francis' original campus in Beech Grove has grown from a 75-bed community hospital to a full-service medical facility offering a wide range of medical specialties. Today, St. Francis serves more than 670,000 outpatients and 17,000 inpatients yearly. It is one of the largest tertiary-care hospitals in Indiana, and has 4,000 employees and 650 physicians at three locations.

In 1995, St. Francis opened its Indianapolis facility—the only new hospital opened by an Indianapolis-based health care system in more than a decade. The expansion facility cost more than $80 million, and includes ambulatory surgery, a cardiac care center, outpatient diagnostics, a 24-hour emergency department, an outpatient cancer center, obstetrics and pediatric services, and medical offices for primary and specialty physicians.

In early 2000, Kendrick Memorial Hospital in Mooresville, Indiana, joined the St. Francis team. The newly named St. Francis Hospital-Mooresville offers proven expertise in several specialty areas, including orthopedics, colon and rectal surgery, sports medicine, and women's services.

Pioneer in Patient Care

From open-heart surgery to cancer-fighting linear accelerators, St. Francis' technology is superb. Nowhere is that more visible than on the doors of patient rooms. Computer units mounted on all patient doors allow paperless record keeping, immediate access to patient records, and access by more than one health care provider simultaneously.

St. Francis was also one of the first locations in the state to have digital imaging between two sites, including doctors' offices. In the coming years, this service will grow as fiber optics are added throughout the city.

Centers of Excellence

St. Francis offers several Centers of Excellence—superior medical practice areas with exceptional physicians, staff, and technology. These practice areas include cardiology, emergency medicine, oncology and bone marrow transplant, orthopedics, diagnostic imaging, women's and children's health services, and occupational medicine.

The St. Francis Hospital & Health Centers' Beech Grove facility was opened in 1914 and, along with the Indianapolis and Mooresville sites, provides compassionate, high-quality care to patients in south-central Indiana.

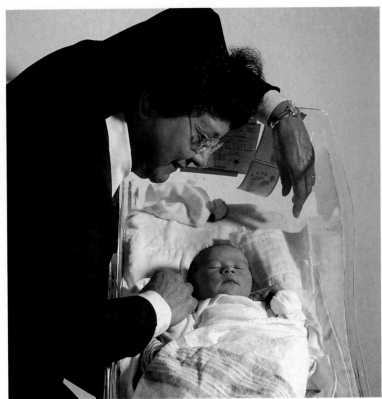

The St. Francis Regional Heart Center, for example, is a nationally recognized cardiac center offering a multidisciplinary team of specialists who focus on all aspects of heart health, including research, education, prevention, diagnosis, treatment, and rehabilitation. The team performs more than 600 heart surgeries every year, ranking in the top 25 percent of all U.S. hospitals based on heart surgery volume.

St. Francis' cardiothoracic surgeons perform open-heart surgery, transmyocardial revascularization (TMR), and minimally invasive bypass surgery. These specialists were the first in Indiana to use the Heartport system, and the hospital serves as a national training site for this procedure. Instead of reaching the heart through the more traditional chest incision, Heartport enters through small access sites between a patient's ribs. This less invasive method can be used to perform a wide range of heart operations, including multivessel bypass and valve surgery. Because it is minimally invasive, Heartport reduces trauma, complications, and pain associated with traditional bypass surgery.

In the area of emergency medicine, board-certified emergency physicians and nurses at both Beech Grove and Indianapolis provide around-the-clock emergency services to more than 74,000 patients a year.

At Indianapolis, the Cancer Care Center offers the latest cancer-fighting procedures and treatments. Moreover, the Beech Grove campus houses the Indiana Blood and Marrow Transplantation program— one of only 14 accredited bone marrow transplant programs in the United States.

In the field of orthopedics, St. Francis is the fourth-leading joint replacement center in the United States, with more than 1,500 joint replacements performed each year.

St. Francis performs nearly 200,000 diagnostic imaging tests annually. Technology includes both open-sided and traditional magnetic resonance imaging (MRI).

St. Francis offers a comprehensive array of services for both women and children. In addition to modern labor/delivery/ recovery/postpartum rooms, St. Francis has an exceptional neonatal intensive care unit (NICU) and skilled neonatolo-

gists and nurses for high-risk newborns. St. Francis delivers more than 2,700 babies yearly.

In addition, St. Francis physicians and staff have the most specialized training in occupational medicine in the Indianapolis area.

Community Concern

St. Francis is deeply committed to its aggressive community-giving program, reinvesting 10 percent of its operating margin—more than $1.5 million annually— into the Indianapolis-area community for health and wellness initiatives. Part of that budget supports the hospital's Senior Promise program, which provides insurance assistance and services for the elderly. Other philanthropic initiatives support Catholic education and one of the largest recreational soccer complexes and programs in the state.

These funds also help underwrite the St. Francis Neighborhood Clinic on Indianapolis' near southeast side, further extending the hospital's mission to reach underserved, low-income families.

Although technological and governmental changes continue to impact health care, St. Francis Hospital & Health Centers' mission remains unchanged. This mission of healing successfully guides the organization to provide high-quality, compassionate care to Indianapolis and south central Indiana communities.

St. Francis Hospital & Health Centers embraces Christ's healing ministry in its mission of improving the physical, emotional, and spiritual health of children and adults (top).

St. Francis focuses on technology to best serve its patients. The cardiac catheterization labs are continually upgraded with the latest technology and equipment (bottom).

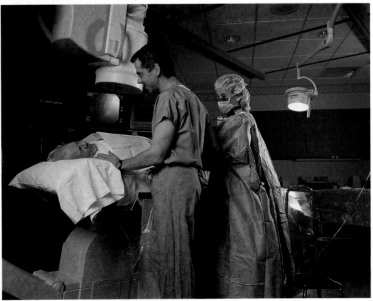

Indianapolis Museum of Art

THE INDIANAPOLIS MUSEUM OF ART (IMA) IS ONE OF the nation's largest general art museums where visitors can "Discover Art—Inside & Out." Founded in 1883, the IMA offers a varied collection of world-renowned art in a spectacular setting. It is a leading cultural and creative resource, serving central Indiana and the Midwest.

The IMA features outstanding collections of African, American, Asian, and European art, including paintings, sculpture, prints, drawings and photographs, decorative arts, textiles, and costumes. Considered a "collection of collections," the IMA holds the largest collection of watercolors and prints by J.M.W. Turner outside of Great Britain, as well as a magnificent African art collection with more than 1,400 objects, and the Clowes Collection of Old Master works with more than 100 paintings, drawings, and sculptures. Other highlights of the museum's permanent collection include Chinese vases, West Asian rugs, neo-impressionist paintings, works from *Gauguin and the*

School of Pont-Aven, contemporary studio glass, and works by Indiana artists. The IMA also offers temporary special exhibitions throughout the year drawn from collections and museums around the world, as well as from the permanent collection.

The IMA is located on a 52-acre, parklike campus offering beautifully landscaped grounds with formal and informal gardens. Most of the gardens are part of Oldfields, a historic,1930s estate complete with a greenhouse and mansion overlooking the White River Valley. The Oldfields estate is the former residence of J.K. Lilly Jr. and was donated to the museum by his children Josiah K. Lilly III and Ruth Lilly. The estate is a rare midwestern example of the design of the American Country Place movement (1890-1945), a time when a tranquil retreat from the stresses of city life was the desire of the wealthy and middle class alike. The Oldfields estate features the informal Ravine Garden, the Formal Garden, and an apple orchard.

Throughout the year, the IMA presents lectures and offers classes and workshops for all ages. Lectures feature nation-

ally known artists, critics, and historians. Studio workshops explore watercolors, charcoal, painting, and drawing. The IMA libraries offer resources for visitors to research or learn how to properly care for artwork. Program offerings include films, concerts, poetry, storytelling, puppet shows, and tours.

Each year, the IMA presents an extensive list of special programs and events. Host to Sunday afternoon recitals, upbeat Friday evening receptions, gourmet dinners, and relaxing outdoor festivals of film, music, and art, the IMA offers variety and entertainment.

Visitors enjoy shopping and dining at the IMA's shops and restaurants. The Alliance Museum Shop features souvenirs from the special exhibitions and permanent collection along with books, handcrafted jewelry, and museum reproductions. Original artwork is available for sale or rent at the Alliance Rental Gallery. The museum's Madeline F. Elder Greenhouse includes a wide assortment of plants, garden accessories, and gifts for the garden lover. Treasures are also found at the Better Than New Shop, which sells new and used items.

Clockwise from top:
The Indianapolis Museum of Art (IMA) is one of the nation's largest general art museums, where visitors can enjoy world-class art and 152 acres of beautifully landscaped gardens.

Emile Bernard's *Breton Women at a Wall* is one of the highlights of the museum's permanent collection.

Visitors enjoy the IMA's contemporary art collection.

Indianapolis Symphony Orchestra

INDIANAPOLIS IS KNOWN FOR ITS SUCCESSFUL MAJOR-LEAGUE TEAMS that feature world-class professionals who perform at the highest level of skill and proficiency. The NBA's Pacers and the NFL's Colts readily come to mind, but a third major team—the Indianapolis Symphony Orchestra(ISO)—fields the largest number of players with 87 full-time musicians from around the world, attracts more

than 500,000 people to its events each year, and owns and operates its performance facility, the Hilbert Circle Theatre.

Founded in 1930, the orchestra's accomplishments include acclaimed national and international tours (including three trips to the musical capitals of Europe since 1987), a 50-year broadcasting and recording history, and a stellar artistic reputation. The ISO is heard on its own nationally syndicated radio series, *Eli Lilly Presents Indianapolis On-the-Air*, which is carried in more than 220 U.S. markets in 41 states and Puerto Rico, and has recorded compact discs with Decca, Koss Classics, and New World.

One of only 18 full-time American orchestras, the ISO performs more than 200 concerts each year to serve a wide variety of musical tastes in classical, pops, family, holiday, patriotic, and educational outreach programming at the Hilbert Circle Theatre, as well as in cities and towns across Indiana and in neighborhoods throughout the Indianapolis metropolitan area.

The orchestra is recognized for its innovative and attractive programming to reach new audiences, including the Studio Series, which features insightful analyses and performances of classical masterworks; preconcert Words on Music discussions; the Young People's Discovery Concerts for elementary school children; thematic Midwinter and Spring festivals; and outdoor Marsh Symphony on the Prairie concerts.

The ISO has pioneered two projects that have set a new standard for the industry: the creative holiday presentations of Ameritech's Yuletide Celebration and the Symphonic Pops

Consortium. Yuletide Celebration is the first and largest orchestra-produced holiday production of its kind in America, and incorporates orchestral music, dance, musical theater, and larger-than-life puppetry and imagery. The ISO now offers a packaged version of this colorful program, complete with costuming and artistic direction, for other orchestras to present to their audiences.

The new Symphonic Pops Consortium was spearheaded by the ISO to create high-quality programs that orchestras otherwise could not afford to produce separately. Joining the ISO in this one-of-a-kind partnership are the Detroit, St. Louis, Seattle, Milwaukee, and National (Washington, D.C.) symphony orchestras. The first of these newly created programs was launched by the ISO in the spring of 2000.

The artistic leadership of the ISO is provided by its music director since 1987, Raymond Leppard, an internationally renowned conductor, performer, composer of film scores, author, music scholar, Cambridge don, and recording artist who has earned five Grammy Awards

and other prestigious international prizes for his artistry. After 14 years of dynamic leadership, Leppard will end his tenure as music director at the conclusion of the 2000-2001 season to assume the post of conductor laureate, the first ever to be honored in the ISO's history.

Administrative leadership is provided by President and CEO Richard R. Hoffert, who will guide the Indianapolis Symphony Orchestra into its next decade of financial and artistic growth and commitment to an even higher level of excellence.

Sponsored by Ameritech, the Indianapolis Symphony Orchestra's (ISO) Yuletide Celebration is the first and largest orchestra-produced holiday production of its kind in America, and incorporates orchestral music, dance, musical theater, and larger-than-life puppetry and imagery (top).

One of only 18 full-time American orchestras, the ISO performs more than 200 concerts each year to serve a wide variety of musical tastes in classical, pops, family, holiday, patriotic, and educational outreach programming at the Hilbert Circle Theatre (bottom).

General Motors
(Allison Transmission
& Indianapolis
Metal Center)

ENERAL MOTORS (GM) AIMS TO BE THE WORLD LEADER IN transportation products and related services with a mission to "earn customer enthusiasm through continuous improvement driven by the integrity, teamwork, and innovation of GM people." Representing GM in Indianapolis for more than 70 years, the Allison Transmission and Metal

Fabricating divisions are striving toward the same goal. The Allison Transmission Division of General Motors leads the world in the design, manufacture, and sales of medium- and heavy-duty automatic transmissions for trucks, buses, off-road vehicles, and military equipment. This ability is part of what makes Allison Transmission a world leader. The division employs 4,000 people, 2,800 of which are represented by United Auto Workers Local 933.

Indianapolis Metal Center (IMC), part of GM's Metal Fabricating Division, evolved from a simple factory that manufactured horse-drawn carriages to the highest-tonnage sheet metal producer for the world's number one automaker. The facility specializes in the metal forming and fabrication of truck parts for world-class vehicles under GM badges such as Chevrolet, GMC, Oldsmobile, and Cadillac.

A History of Strength and Durability

In 1915, James Ashbury Allison, one of the cofounders of the Indianapolis Motor Speedway and the Indianapolis 500, founded the Indianapolis Speedway Team Company to make race car parts. Eventually becoming Allison Engineering Co., the company ultimately played an integral role in the aircraft industry dur-

ing World War I. Because of its technological advancements, Allison sparked the interest of GM, which purchased the company in April 1929. Throughout the years, GM has invested significantly in Allison, showing confidence in its innovation capabilities and growth potential.

Allison Transmission literally invented heavy-duty automatic transmissions in 1946. Since

In North America, nearly every bus, fire truck, refuse vehicle, transit coach, and motor home is equipped with an Allison Automatic transmission (top).

The Allison Transmission Division of General Motors (GM), located in Indianapolis, leads the world in the design, manufacture, and sale of medium- and heavy-duty automatic transmissions.

then, it has expanded its product line and served as a supplier to more than 250 original equipment manufacturers, such as International, Spartan Motors, Freightliner, and GMC. In North America, nearly every school bus, fire truck, refuse vehicle, transit coach, and motor home is equipped with an Allison Automatic.

Having gone through various name changes and statuses within GM, the company earned divisional status in 1987, becoming the Allison Transmission Division. Today, the company continues to thrive as an important division within GM. Its worldwide growth continues with its six plant facilities and parts distribution center covering more than 4 million square feet and occupying 225 acres of land in Indianapolis and Speedway. In addition to the Indianapolis operations, Allison Transmission has facilities in Baltimore, Brazil, and Europe.

Industry-Leading Technology

Development and implementation of business practices designed to improve transmission technology are parts of what Allison Transmission contributes to GM's mission to remain a world leader. This productive stance allows the company to pursue new technologies and to investigate innovative peripherals.

Allison Transmission has a rich tradition of product and manufacturing innovation. Considered one of the most prolific patent organizations within GM, the company has nearly 600 registered patents. Its technological leadership in Indianapolis prepares the way for significant company growth into the next century. The headquarters and Indianapolis operations remain within walking distance of the Indianapolis Motor Speedway, but the company's markets continue to expand to include new global customer groups.

Allison Transmission's long heritage of innovation is evident

in its new 1000/2000 Series™ transmissions. These commercial transmissions, which the company began producing in 1999, are bringing the Allison standard of reliability and performance to commercial vehicles such as heavy-duty pickup trucks and delivery vans—markets that, until now, the company had not directly served. These products bring an entirely new area of business opportunity to Allison Transmission and the Indianapolis community. The new product line is expected to nearly double the company's manufacturing capability in the Indianapolis area. GM's Chevrolet and GMC Truck Group divisions recently announced that the 2001 model Silverado and Sierra pickups will offer the strength and durability of an Allison Automatic.

Allison Transmission continues to expand its technology focus to include the development of hybrid propulsion systems. In 1999, the company's hybrid electric drive system was placed in revenue service in New York City in one of the city coaches.

The company's reputation for superior quality products

is proven by the fact that it is ten times the size of its closest competitor, and boasts more than an 80 percent market share of all commercial-duty automatic transmissions produced and sold worldwide.

Employee involvement is key to the company's continued growth. Allison Transmission recognizes that creating an environment where all employees can contribute will allow continued strong business performance, ensure ongoing growth, and place the company in a solid strategic position to meet and exceed customer expectations.

GM's Chevrolet and GMC Truck Group divisions recently announced that 2001 model Silverado and Sierra pickups will offer the strength and durability of an Allison Automatic (top).

The 1000 Series™ transmissions are bringing the Allison standard of reliability and performance to commercial vehicles such as heavy-duty pickup trucks and delivery vans (bottom).

Horse-Drawn to Horseless Carriages

The rich history and diversity of IMC and its expansion and progress mirror that of the entire General Motors Corporation. The continuous and sustaining effort of the plant as a member of the GM family plays a critical role in the design, engineering, and manufacture of GM trucks. IMC is dedicated to helping GM deliver the highest-quality products on the market to ensure customer enthusiasm and to maximize shareholder value.

GM is the world's largest purchaser of rolled steel, and the Metal Fabricating Division is the group responsible for transforming those sheets of metal into parts for world-class vehicles. As one of the division's seven large-scale metal-stamping plants, IMC has evolved into the highest-tonnage producer of sheet metal in the GM family.

Overlooking the downtown Indianapolis skyline from the banks of the White River, IMC once was known as Martin-Parry Carriage Works. Chevrolet Motor Division purchased the factory in 1930, and additional facilities were constructed to increase production and efficiency. Upon completion of the renovated facility in 1936, Chevrolet-Indianapolis began production of its famous, all-steel truck tops and bodies. From 1930 to 1941, Chevrolet became the largest producer of trucks in the industry, and this plant gained recognition as the largest exclusive truck body plant in the world.

IMC led the industry in the 1980s as it invested millions of dollars in transfer press technology, a continuing focus that has contributed to its reputation as a premier metal center. In 1982, the plant became part of GM's Truck and Bus Group. It later joined the Metal Fabricating Division in a strategic corporate move to consolidate all of GM's metal-stamping activities. Ongoing improvements in equipment systems and organizational development, coupled with a committed Hoosier workforce, have helped IMC sustain a leadership role in the industry.

Technology and Automation

Through the dedication of more than 2,800 employees,

GM has invested heavily in high-speed automation equipment (at right) to expedite the production of parts, such as truck door panels. This line marries an inner and an outer panel to create a finished door.

GM's Indianapolis Metal Center (IMC) specializes in producing large metal stampings for GM trucks such as the GMC Yukon sport utility vehicle. The Yukon is a sister sport utility of the Chevrolet Suburban, the longest-running nameplate in automotive history, and the Chevrolet Tahoe.

IMC continues to play a critical role in manufacturing GM's trucks. As part of the Metal Fabricating Division, IMC is responsible for the metal forming and fabrication of truck parts. These parts include major sheet metal panels and assemblies, such as doors, roofs, dash panels, and most pickup box metal for GM's popular line of pickups and sport utility vehicles.

The parts made at IMC are highly visible in the Hoosier community. IMC produces parts for vehicles such as Chevrolet S-10 and GMC Sonoma pickups and sport utility models— Chevrolet Blazer, GMC Jimmy and Envoy, and Oldsmobile Bravada; Chevrolet Silverado and GMC Sierra full-size pickups; Chevrolet and GMC Suburban, Tahoe, Denali, and Yukon sport utilities; Cadillac Escalade; and the GMC medium-duty trucks.

IMC employees are committed to providing quality to their customers. Through teamwork and continuous improvement, the people of IMC work to put quality in everything they do. United Auto Workers Local 23 and the International Association of Machinists Lodge 2819 represent much of IMC's proud workforce.

Community Outreach

Impressive in both Allison Transmission and IMC is the dedication that extends beyond the workplace to the community. GM and Allison Transmission recently have introduced a volunteer program that encourages employees to take an even more active role in their communities. Both companies are strong contributors to the economic well-being of Indianapolis and its surrounding communities.

In addition to financial support offered by GM, Allison Transmission and IMC employees participate in fund-raising and charity collections to benefit those in need. Such organizations include Junior Achievement, United Way of Central Indiana, and the Children's Museum.

In fact, Allison Transmission has become a model of local corporate giving. In 1998, the company was ranked number one in giving per employee and number two in total giving. United Way granted its prestigious A Company That Cares award to Allison Transmission for its successful campaigns and employee generosity. In 1999, the company received the coveted Mayor's Eagle Award in the category of Innovative Methods/Research & Development, along with an honorable mention for community/charitable involvement.

As two unified groups with strong visions and the support of well-prepared employees, Allison Transmission and IMC are helping General Motors manufacture the world's best products.

IMC stamps out metal sheet parts for GM's medium-sized sport utilities such as the Oldsmobile Bravada, the GMC Jimmy and Envoy, and the Chevrolet Blazer (top).

GM employees review data on a truck door stamping placed on a special fixture that measures the part's dimensions. This analysis takes place in one of three quality labs at the plant dedicated to achieving customer enthusiasm with high-quality products.

Praxair Surface Technologies, Inc.

THE TOWN OF SPEEDWAY SITS SEVEN MILES NORTHWEST OF THE center of Indianapolis and boasts many sites that played historical roles in central Indiana's development. Praxair Surface Technologies, Inc. carries the legacy of one of those sites. ■ Today one of the world's leading suppliers of surface coatings for a variety of industries, Praxair Surface Technolo-gies grew out of a business started by two of the founders of the Indianapolis Motor Speedway, Carl G. Fisher and James A. Allison. And in a town such as Speedway, with historic sites in no short supply, Praxair is historic for more than "surface" reasons.

Historic Beginnings and Growth

Speedway's founders envisioned it as a city without horses, built around industries supporting the manufacture of the horseless carriage: the automobile. In 1912, Fisher and Allison founded Prest-O-Lite Company—a manufacturer of acetylene cylinders for automobile headlights—one block south of the motor speedway.

Fisher and Allison sold their firm to Union Carbide in 1917. In the ensuing years, Union Carbide established itself as an industry leader, developing and introducing an extraordinary range of practical gas uses crucial to the growth of many industries, from steel to food to electronics to medicine. The business as it exists today developed in the 1940s, with the invention of thermal spray technology at the Speedway site.

The company began making wear-resistant coatings and powders in the early 1950s, as jet-engine manufacturers looked for ways to improve engine performance and reliability. The solution, pioneered in Speedway, was a variety of super-hard ceramic and metallic coatings and powders that, when applied to surfaces, resisted wear, prevented corrosion, and offered temperature protection. These products have since become crucial to superior engine performance and durability, multiplying the life span of some parts by 10 to 20 times. In addition to coating jet engine components, Praxair Surface Technologies refurbishes and repairs such components.

Union Carbide spun off its industrial gases and surface technology businesses as a separate company in 1992, creating Praxair, Inc.; the name was derived from a combination of praxis, the Greek word for practical application, and air, Praxair's primary raw material. Today, the Speedway complex, where more than 900 patents originated, houses Praxair Surface Technologies' world headquarters and employs 500 people. The complex is one of

The Speedway laboratory and world headquarters of Praxair Surface Technologies, Inc. occupies the site of the former Prest-O-Lite Company, founded by Carl G. Fisher and James A. Allison. In 1998, ASM International designated the Speedway facility a historical landmark in the development of engineered materials, calling it an "idea factory" where more than 900 patented inventions were created and a new industry was born. Today, the company provides products and services to industries ranging from aviation to semiconductors.

semiconductors. The ceramic powders and sputtering targets this specialty products group develops are used to make medical devices, superconducting components, and transducers, as well as semiconductors and components for memory storage and inkjet applications.

Single-Source Solutions

Praxair Surface Technologies prides itself on providing customers with single-source solutions. In addition to manufacturing and applying coatings for customers, Praxair designs, builds, installs, and services coating systems for use at the customers' sites. The company offers a full line of spray booths, air-filtration units, parts handling, and other peripheral equipment for designing and installing facilities to meet individual thermal spray needs.

A staff of industry-trained application engineers and technicians can recommend the most economical equipment and materials to meet a customer's surface modification requirements, and industry-trained engineers can install the system and perform complete testing and training. They can offer solutions—available on a global basis—from one of the broadest portfolios of thermal spray products and services in the industry.

Not only did Praxair invent equipment and processes such as the detonation gun and plasma spray, the firm has kept the technology flowing through later refinements such as the shrouded plasma torch and Super D-Gun system. Today, Praxair offers the broadest range of products and services of any surface technology manufacturer.

Praxair's investment of more than $30 million in the company's Speedway site during 1998 and 1999—including renovation of existing facilities, doubling of powders manufacturing capacity, and construction of an additional building—are all geared toward assuring a continued place in Indianapolis history for many years to come.

Praxair Surface Technologies' Detonation Gun (D-Gun®) facilities use industrial robots to help control coating application, ensuring consistent results in all of its plants worldwide (top).

The shock wave generated by the detonation of this D-Gun as it fires is largely responsible for driving the coating powder onto the surface of the part to be coated—creating a superior mechanical bond (middle).

Praxair protective coatings are applied to a wide variety of components used in many industries (bottom).

more than 40 Praxair Surface Technologies manufacturing plants and service sites employing more than 3,500 people worldwide.

Reducing Wear and Tear

The people of Praxair Surface Technologies have been creating solutions for more than 40 years by helping people in production, maintenance, and engineering solve problems caused by abrasion, erosion, and corrosion. Technologically advanced coatings extend the life and improve the performance of critical components, keeping equipment running longer and more reliably.

In addition to the aircraft industry, Praxair Surface Tech-

nologies customers include the printing, textile, chemical, primary metals, semiconductor, and optical industries. Applying wear-, temperature-, and corrosion-resistant coatings to enhance performance of parts is the company's main business, but the expansion of related businesses has broadened the company's horizons to encompass other areas of surface enhancement technologies.

A specialty products group develops and manufactures polishing products, specialty ceramics, and sputtering targets. Praxair polishing products are advanced materials used for high-precision polishing applications such as plastic eyeglass lenses, computer hard disks, and

Colliers Turley Martin Tucker

LOCAL AND NATIONAL BUSINESSES OF ALL SIZES HAVE relied on the expertise of Colliers Turley Martin Tucker (CTMT), formerly a division of F.C. Tucker, for their commercial real estate needs. The company, which was founded in 1918, now ranks as Indiana's largest comprehensive commercial real estate firm. ◼ Fred

Tucker Jr. oversaw the development of the commercial division of F.C. Tucker in the mid-1950s. Over the years, the Tucker name has been associated with downtown revitalization, including pioneering projects such as the downtown Hilton Hotel, the Indiana National Bank Tower (INB) Tower, and Market Square Arena. More recently, CTMT associates have been instrumental in the development of outlying areas such as the Plainfield, Indiana, industrial market.

In 1998, the division was spun off and merged with Colliers Turley Martin, headquartered in St. Louis, to form Colliers Turley Martin Tucker. Today, in addition to its Indianapolis office, CTMT operates in Cincinnati; Dayton; Kansas City, Missouri; Nashville; and St. Louis.

The blended firm's mission is to focus on customers' long-term needs as a partner. Added ownership in Colliers International Property Consultants gives clients one-stop shopping by providing access to the global knowledge of 4,440 professionals from more than 225 offices in 47 countries—experts at affiliated firms who are intimately familiar with their local markets.

It is a blueprint for success, and the numbers prove it. CTMT is one of the dominant commercial real estate firms in the central United States, with more than $1 billion in transactions, more than 27 million square feet under its management, and nearly 500 professionals representing more than 20 specialties.

The Indianapolis office currently has 34 brokers, 100 employees, and more than 6 million square feet of space under management. The company maintains its local office in the American United Life (AUL) Tower, which it currently leases and manages.

Broad Service Offerings

The growing array of CTMT services ranges from site selection and construction management, to database design and ongoing administration of a client's entire real estate portfolio. Known for its continuous investment in research, information systems, and technology, CTMT is the recognized source in each of the cities it serves for the most up-to-date information and resources.

Corporate services clients can opt for facilities management, transaction management, and portfolio administration, changing services as their business goals evolve. In addition to allowing clients to manage their core businesses better and capitalize on new opportunities, these services save money and improve productivity.

The development and construction services divisions can help companies improve productivity and efficiency with tailored

Colliers Turley Martin Tucker (CTMT) associates have been instrumental in the growth of the Plainfield, Indiana, industrial market by representing developers and users. In 1999, Saint-Gobain signed a 10-year lease of this 400,000-square-foot facility owned by Opus North Corporation. The two parties were represented by two different CTMT teams.

solutions that include consolidating multiple locations into a single facility or replacing the physical structure of an old facility. CTMT can manage a project from beginning to end, starting with strategic planning and conceptual programming, through design development, construction management, move in, and operations. As the client's representative, CTMT assembles the full team of professionals, including architects, space planners, engineers, consultants, and contractors to deliver each project, large or small, on time and on budget.

The firm's alliance with the Economic Development Group (EDGe) lends additional expertise to client projects. The division possesses an in-depth knowledge of the public sector and has experience in working with public officials to secure economic incentive packages that result in the largest possible financial return. Among the incentives for which companies could qualify are real and personal property tax abatement, training grants, tax credits, and other programs.

Keeping pace with technology, CTMT is also using the Internet to market its properties. Its Web site contains all of its current listings, including site plans, floor plans, direct contact information, maps, demographics, and even virtual tours.

Top-Notch Professional Staff

Colliers Turley Martin Tucker recognizes the importance of providing its clients with highly educated and knowledgeable professionals with expertise in areas that complement client objectives. As such, the firm encourages active participation in local, regional, and national professional associations. CTMT professionals are well represented in the Society of Industrial and Office Realtors, an international network covering 450 cities worldwide; the

Commercial Investment Real Estate Institute, which awards the certified commercial investment member designation; and the Counselors of Real Estate, an organization of professionals recognized for exceptional competence in real estate practice.

Employees are also active in two professional associations devoted to increased sophistication in the fields of building management and leasing—the Building Owners and Managers Association and the Institute of

Real Estate Management. CTMT's team of professionals includes certified property managers, certified public accountants, civil and mechanical engineers, constructions managers, interior designers, and real estate brokers.

The focus on integrity, professionalism, and development of the individual entrepreneur is an Indianapolis Tucker tradition that is being further developed under the name Colliers Turley Martin Tucker.

CTMT leases and manages the 692,000-square-foot, Class A office tower owned by American United Life Insurance Company (AUL). The tower serves as AUL's corporate headquarters and is located in downtown Indianapolis.

Indianapolis

1919	AMERICAN ART CLAY CO., INC.
1921	SMOCK FANSLER CONSTRUCTION CORPORATION
1922	BUSINESS FURNITURE CORPORATION
1924	SANTAROSSA MOSAIC & TILE CO., INC.
1931	AMERICAN AIRLINES, INC.
1931	MARSH SUPERMARKETS, INC.
1936	BMG ENTERTAINMENT
1936	STUART'S MOVING AND STORAGE, INC.
1944	ANTHEM, INC.
1945	BARTH ELECTRIC CO., INC.
1946	THE PERMANENT MAGNET CO., INC.
1946	PRATT CORPORATION
1946	STERLING FLUID SYSTEMS (USA) INC.
1947	MONARCH BEVERAGE COMPANY INC.
1949	MOORFEED CORPORATION
1950	CARRIER CORPORATION
1952	PAUL HARRIS STORES, INC.
1953	DEFENSE FINANCE AND ACCOUNTING SERVICE - INDIANAPOLIS CENTER (DFAS)

American Art Clay Co., Inc.

A VISIT TO MOST ART AND CRAFT SUPPLY STORES THROUGH-out the United States will turn up dozens of American Art Clay Co., Inc.'s (AMACO®) more than 4,800 products. For more than 80 years, the company has helped shape the creativity of millions of artists and children worldwide. ■ In addition to producing modeling clay

Clockwise from top:
American Art Clay Co., Inc. (AMACO®) stores dry clays and other raw materials in eight silos, each 40 to 50 feet high.

Representing more than 70 years of experience at AMACO are (from left) Roger Halpin, executive vice president, chief financial officer, and treasurer; William Berry, president and chief operating officer; and Edward J. Walsh, senior vice president, sales and marketing.

Valri P. Sandoe, owner, and her husband, L. Bond Sandoe Jr., chairman and chief executive officer, now lead the company founded by her father, Ted O. Philpott.

products and paints from its Indianapolis-based facilities, AMACO continues a tradition of service to art educators, students, professional and amateur ceramists, hobbyists, and craftsmen with the manufacture of kilns, glazes, and the Brent® line of fine potter's wheels. Not satisfied with being the nation's leading supplier of ceramic materials and equipment, the company is launching a new artist's paint brand that could make other artist paints obsolete.

From the Pharmacy to the Final Product

Ted O. Philpott, a Purdue University-educated pharmacist, founded American Art Clay in 1919 in partnership with a friend who wanted to develop ceramic plaques using photographic images and needed the help of Philpott's background in chemistry. Their joint venture

was unsuccessful, but the modeling clay created in the process evolved into American Art Clay's initial product. Permoplast® clay became the first nonhardening children's modeling clay in the United States, and remains familiar to generations of young people who reformed its colorful, square-extruded logs into animals, bowls, and gifts for mom.

AMACO's first facilities were located next door to Philpott's pharmacy. Eventually, Philpott sold the pharmacy to give his full attention to Permoplast production. The firm moved to its current Speedway location in 1931, and Philpott expanded the product line in 1934, manufacturing the first kilns designed specifically for school and studio use.

Not one to be unprepared, Philpott maintained his pharmacist's license all his life, so he would always have a backup profession. AMACO became a

growing concern whose focus has changed somewhat through the years. Philpott died in 1966 at age 78. His daughter, Valri Sandoe, now owns the company, and her husband, L. Bond Sandoe Jr., serves as chairman and CEO. When Bond Sandoe joined the company in 1954, children's art supplies made up 90 percent of sales and ceramics constituted 10 percent. Those percentages reversed by the early 1970s, so the firm stopped producing items such as chalk and crayons, and focused primarily on ceramics.

Today, the firm has few national competitors, thanks to its unique product blend. The Speedway facility has grown to 165,000 square feet and employs approximately 150 people. Its eight cavernous silos, each 40 to 50 feet high, have a storage capacity of 2 million pounds. The silos hold clay and other raw materials

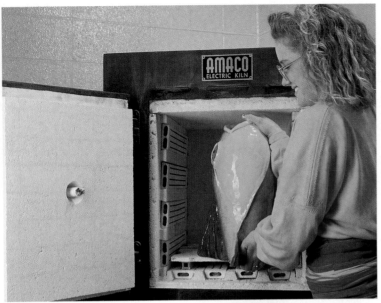

until needed by the firm's advanced clay handling and processing system. The system electronically controls batching, blending, extruding, and packaging of dry and de-aired moist clays to produce a consistent product.

On the Forefront of Education

To ensure a market for its products and their proper use, AMACO has led an extensive effort since the 1950s to train art teachers and occupational therapists in teaching ceramics. The firm even teamed with instructors from Indianapolis' Herron School of Art to hold a summer workshop series for teachers. AMACO was an industry leader in removing lead from glazes, and continues to promote the safe use of its products through catalogs, labeling, and special product encyclopedias and safety manuals.

The firm works with a variety of demonstrators to promote its products through trade shows, workshops, demonstrations, and television shows such as HGTV's *Carol Duvall Show*. Its catalogs also feature the work of artists who use its products. AMACO collaborates with many of those artists to improve and develop products, and works with start-up firms interested in selling a product to AMACO that the firm can in turn manufacture and market.

That's how AMACO acquired its new Genesis Artist Colors™ line of paint, which Bond Sandoe believes has the potential to double company sales. The proprietary paint incorporates a heat-fixing agent that prevents drying until heat is applied. This makes Genesis paints easier to use than oil paints, which dry very slowly, or acrylics and watercolors, which dry very quickly. The paint's nondrying nature simplifies preparation, correction of mistakes, cleanup, and storage. Most important, Genesis Artist Colors are certified nontoxic and odor-free, which is unique among artist oil colors.

Advocate for Children

AMACO catalogs regularly include pictures of employees as they are now, alongside pictures of them as children. "We

have long-standing relationships with many of our customers, and this helps them put faces with names," Bond Sandoe says. "And since many of our products are created for the school art supply field, it helps us keep the focus on children."

Another way the company maintains that focus is through support of the Children First, an advocacy group dedicated to the cause of abused and disadvantaged children. AMACO supports the group's benefit ball and cycling team, and has made fund-raising appeals through its catalogs.

"We believe all children should have the right to explore the magic of their imagination free from abuse or neglect," Bond Sandoe says. "It is one more way American Art Clay helps shape creativity in the world."

Clockwise from top left:
AMACO kilns are well-insulated for minimum heat radiation, making them completely safe for school use.

Recently developed by AMACO, Genesis Artist Colors™ is a revolutionary new painting medium that offers artists unlimited spontaneity, flexibility, and freedom.

Art teachers incorporate quality art, craft, and ceramic products from AMACO into their lesson plans by allowing students to create an object relating to the topic being studied.

Brent® potter's wheels have a solid reputation among ceramic artists worldwide for reliability and long-lasting performance.

Smock Fansler Construction Corporation

IN ITS NEARLY 80-YEAR HISTORY, SMOCK FANSLER CONSTRUCTION Corporation (SFC) has grown from a small trucking company to a full-service general contractor that specializes in heavy construction and architectural site work. The company initiates approximately 400 projects per year, including building construction, site amenities, earth work, underground utilities, and concrete work. The company's growing client list includes institutions, public school systems, and Fortune 500 companies such as DaimlerChrysler, Navistar, Target, Rolls-Royce Allison, Ford, and the U.S. Postal Service.

Providing Construction Solutions

The firm started out in 1921 as Kenneth Smock Associates, a trucking company with a single dump truck, hauling fly ash for Indianapolis Power & Light Company. In the 1930s, the firm expanded from trucking into excavation, establishing its reputation for providing quality construction from the ground up.

Founder Kenneth Smock retired in 1965 and sold the company to its current owner, Tom Fansler Jr., who continues as chairman and chief executive officer. His son Tom Fansler III joined the business in 1982 and serves as president and chief operating officer. Two other sons are also part of the management team.

Over the years, Fansler Jr. has expanded the business into general contracting, and today, SFC has annual sales in excess of $26 million. Highway contractors aside, SFC is the third-largest contractor in the city in terms of concrete construction, operating from a 12-acre site on the city's southwest side.

Known for providing construction solutions to heavy industry, Smock Fansler's 180 employees perform well on extremely difficult jobs. The firm is comfortable coming in on an emergency basis or during a plant shutdown to finish a project under tight time constraints. Doing much of its work with employees rather than subcontractors, and drawing from its own fleet of more than 75 vehicles and heavy machines, the firm maintains control over quality and adheres strictly to schedule.

"When it comes to satisfying a customer, there are 24 hours in our day," Fansler Jr. says. "We like finding solutions when other contractors say it can't be done. Our goal is to be the first company called in when there's a construction problem or when a business needs help envisioning the growth of its facilities."

Signature Aesthetic Solutions

SFC has also made a name for itself and won a number of awards for its skill in architectural site work, such as parks, greenways, recreational facilities, trails, gardens, and fountains. "Years ago," says Fansler Jr., "a fountain was part of a project we were bidding. We liked doing it so much that now we look for that kind of work and are often sought out because of our experience. We often help clients make simple changes in their plans that add appeal and enhance quality of life for employees."

High-end, unique water features—complete with lights, choreographed water, and overflow basins—are a SFC signature.

Clockwise from top:
Smock Fansler Construction Corporation (SFC) has grown from a small trucking company to a full-service general contractor.

SFC has also made a name for itself and won a number of awards for its skill in architectural site work at parks like the Indy Parks skateboard facility.

The pyramid-shaped, cascading fountain on the campus of Indiana University-Purdue University at Indianapolis is a good example of Smock Fansler's expertise in finding construction solutions.

The pyramid-shaped, cascading fountain on the campus of Indiana University-Purdue University at Indianapolis is a good example of Smock Fansler's expertise in finding construction solutions. The project originally had a long lead time and a higher price tag because of the South African granite the designer had specified, but SFC was able to save time and money by finding a comparable Canadian product.

SFC recently finished its largest project, the Indianapolis Zoo and South Park segments of the White River Riverfront Development. In fall 1999, the firm completed the construction at White River State Park. Smock Fansler built a new courtyard entry to the zoo, a shelter house, a parking area, a promenade, and pedestrian barriers, in addition to improving the levee.

Renovation and redevelopment at Marian College included drainage work, road construction, landscaping, and fountain work, as well as building parking lots and an amphitheater. Across the street from the college, at the Major Taylor Velodrome, SFC built the Indy Parks skateboard facility.

SFC also built the cable-stayed SerVaas Bridge across Fall Creek, near the Veterans Hospital. In 1998, it constructed the World War II Memorial in downtown Indianapolis.

Maintaining a Family Orientation

Smock Fansler Construction takes pride in its record of employee retention. More than half of its employees have been with the firm eight years or longer. Some retired and current workers span three generations of a single family. Clarian Health's Buchanan Counseling Center recognized SFC in 1998 with the Family Life Enhancement Award for its family-centered employment policies.

SFC's family orientation extends into the community as well. Fansler III serves on the Keep Indianapolis Beautiful board, and the firm is active in Habitat for Humanity, helping to create the first-ever planned greenspace in a Habitat community near Beech Grove. In 1998, the firm was the largest United Way donor, both in dollars and in participation, among general contractors.

"The Smock Fansler family takes its reputation very seriously," Fansler Jr. says. "Because we are personally involved in every project, there isn't a client in our family of clients who would not have us back."

Clockwise from top left:
SFC also built the cable-stayed SerVaas Bridge across Fall Creek, near the Veterans Hospital.

This second-story addition to a telephone switching facility typifies the difficult work SFC is accustomed to performing.

The historical interior restoration of the Hamilton County Courthouse reflects the company's attention to detail.

The historical restoration of the Pagoda was one of many projects completed at Garfield Park, such as the aquatic center, gym, Sunken Garden, and trails.

Business Furniture Corporation

INNOVATION, CREATIVITY, AND SURPRISE ARE NOT WHAT MANY MIGHT expect from Indianapolis' oldest and most respected office furniture dealership. But that's where the surprise comes in. ■ For more than 77 years, workplaces of all sizes have turned to Business Furniture Corporation for help in creating work environments and relationships that get results. Owned by Richard and Debra

Oakes, Business Furniture places high priority on understanding each customer's individual needs before any product knowledge is applied. It also realizes that office spaces today are at once more intuitive and more complex than ever before, and that it takes experience and talent to create outstanding results—along with the right product partners. Business Furniture is the exclusive Steelcase dealer in Indianapolis, and offers products from such top-quality manufacturers as Metro, Brayton, Vecta, Turnstone, OFS, and National Office Furniture.

Its progressive, needs-driven approach has made Business Furniture the area's largest office furniture dealer as well. Sales in excess of $50 million in 1999 testify to the firm's success, along with an extensive client list that includes Eli Lilly, Thomson Consumer Electronics, Dow Agro-Sciences, GTE, Roche Diagnostics, PSI Energy, and Bank One. Yet, while these companies are large and long established, Business Furniture works with a full spectrum of business types, giving personal attention to each project and organization, regardless of size.

The success the company has experienced has also meant physical growth. Moving from its downtown location in 1997, Business Furniture has expanded throughout the state. In addition to its state-of-the-art, 70,000-square-foot showroom and warehouse facility on Indianapolis' northwest side, the firm has a retail store on the city's northeast side, offices in Lafayette and Terre Haute,

and a subsidiary—Business Furnishings—in South Bend.

The Space Age

Since 40 percent of businesses in America will soon find themselves either moving to new space or renovating their existing offices, the need for a partner who understands the changing face of the work process is critical. Business Furniture offers a wide range of services to fit each client's needs. The company's experienced designers and workplace consultants can develop and coordinate complete office projects that effectively utilize valuable office space. Every client is assured efficient, accurate space planning with minimal downtime, error-free plans, and maximum project flexibility through the use of computer-aided design.

For companies that do not wish to purchase all new furnishings, Business Furniture offers a range of reconfiguration, rental, and repair services. The reconfiguration service involves taking inventory of and analyzing existing office furnishing and systems, evaluating how the components coordinate with the changing needs of the client's environ-

One of Indianapolis' most respected office furniture dealers for more than 77 years, Business Furniture Corporation's corporate headquarters is on the city's northwest side, with additional locations throughout Indiana.

Business Furniture has expanded, adding a state-of-the-art, 70,000-square-foot showroom and warehouse. The company uses the climate-controlled, secured warehouse to provide inventory staging and asset management.

Clockwise from left:
Business Furniture offers installation, delivery, repair, and a range of services to companies throughout the state of Indiana.

Business Furniture consultants utilize extensive resources to provide customers with the best solutions and products to fit their needs.

Employees can increase productivity though informal communication on the "Street."

ment, and empowering employees to better understand new spaces and work methods.

Business Furniture helps clients manage their assets, as well, with a bar-coded scanning system for accurate, efficient inventory management. Customized service plans can cover regular, emergency, or as-needed maintenance and repair. Clients can store their surplus furniture at Business Furniture's warehouse at a fraction of standard real estate costs. The company considers these services part of exceeding client expectations through a true working partnership.

For the team at Business Furniture, it is a long-held truth that any company's physical space represents far more than just a cost center. Work space can and should be a strategic resource that not only supports business demands and fosters productivity, but also attracts good people and encourages them to stay.

Innovations at Work

Technology development and changing management philosophies are just two of the important trends driving modern workplace design. Large executive suites and private offices are giving way to more responsive, team-focused, shared work environments where knowledge can be most effectively leveraged. With many employees engaged in information services, companies are rethinking traditional design to provide a range of work settings that are flexible and mobile—settings based on the work done rather than job title or status.

Business Furniture's philosophy, Innovations at Work, recognizes the transition fueling today's office. According to a Steelcase study, knowledge workers spend 70 percent of their days engaged in activities that take them away from their individual desks. Solutions are derived from activity-based

planning focused on a balance of private and shared environments. In response, Business Furniture strives to create spaces where workers can occupy an individual, personalized work space, but also have immediate access to mutual areas containing files, conference tables, and group tools.

"Ultimately, workplace performance is the relationship between a work space and the technology, people, and processes that it connects and supports," says CEO Richard Oakes. "We work with customers to develop a plan for optimizing space and creating an environment designed around their most valuable asset—their employees and the intellectual capital they possess. We don't just sell furniture to our customers; we partner with them to produce business results."

Santarossa Mosaic & Tile Co., Inc.

A T SANTAROSSA MOSAIC & TILE CO., INC. THREE GENERATIONS of the Santarossa family have made many Indianapolis building projects special by providing the finest ceramic, terrazzo, marble, carpet, vinyl, and stone finishes imaginable for more than 75 years. The company has fulfilled the flooring needs for countless institutions, corporations, hospitals, retail malls, and education and government buildings throughout Indiana and the Midwest. Its handiwork is seen—and walked on—daily at locations as diverse as the Indiana Soldiers and Sailors Monument on Monument Circle, Thomson Consumer Electronics, Conseco Fieldhouse, and Circle Centre mall.

Three Generations of Craftsmen

The story of Domenic Santarossa, who founded Santarossa Mosaic & Tile, is not unlike the stories of many European immigrants who came to America through Ellis Island in the early 20th century. He had left his native Italy at the age of 13 to study the terrazzo and mosaic trade in Bremen, and in 1913, he arrived in the United States at the age of 20 to seek his fortune. In 1920, he settled in Indianapolis and, a year later, moved his business into the building the firm still occupies on the city's east side. His son Mario joined the business after completing training as an architect at Notre Dame in 1948, and today, a third generation of the Santarossa family is at the helm of the still-burgeoning business. Mario's son David serves as president, while his brothers John and Robert and sister Theresa Piggott all serve as company officers, and Lewis Carraro, Domenic's nephew, serves as the company's vice president. The company has seen its business double in volume every seven years since 1978, and today, it completes more than 300 projects a year.

Expanding Product Line

Terrazzo is a process of setting small chips of marble in cement and polishing them. The floor style fell out of favor in the 1950s, so Santarossa added ceramic work to its repertoire in 1968, followed by marble, granite, and stone in the early 1970s, and vinyl, carpet, and wood in the mid-1980s. Today, terrazzo is experiencing a rebirth. Like the many Italian-American craftsmen who used terrazzo to transfer love for their homeland to a new home, architects, designers, and builders are re-discovering the flooring's beauty, durability, and versatility for both commercial and upscale residential use. Santarossa goes to great lengths to provide customers with the best in finished products made from the finest-quality raw materials. The firm has access to virtually every major domestic and foreign supplier of ceramic, stone, and terrazzo in the world, and represents the most respected and established mills for its carpet and other resilient materials.

The Santarossa custom marble and granite workshop is unequaled in Indiana and offers a variety of marble and granite fabricating, refinishing, and custom design work. Santarossa artisans can fashion custom marble and granite fireplaces, tables, countertops, basins, and entire walls. Individual items can be made to exact specifications and shipped anywhere in the world.

"We're honored to continue the legacy of excellence established by our grandfather," says David Santarossa. "Just as he did, we truly care about the quality of our products, the superiority of our workmanship, and the integrity of our reputation."

Santarossa Mosaic & Tile Co., Inc. has made many Indianapolis building projects special by providing the finest ceramic, terrazzo, marble, carpet, vinyl, and stone finishes imaginable for more than 75 years.

The terrazzo floor, treads, and stone base at the fashion mall at Keystone at the Crossing were completed in 1988. The installation looks as good today as it did when the company installed this project.

MERICAN AIRLINES, INC. AND INDIANAPOLIS HAVE BEEN partners in aviation since the Indianapolis International Airport first opened in 1931. Today, the airline has 70 employees based in the city, providing support for 14 daily departures. ■ American traces its corporate history to just five years before its arrival in Indianapolis, when Charles A. Lindbergh—who was then chief pilot for Robertson Aircraft Corp. of Missouri—flew a single bag of mail from Chicago to St. Louis. By 1937, the airline had celebrated carrying its one-millionth passenger.

American opened its Dallas/Fort Worth headquarters in 1979. Today, along with regional partner American Eagle, it operates a fleet of more than 900 aircraft, employs more than 111,000 people, serves about 230 markets, and completes more than 3,800 flights daily. On an average day, American receives more than 338,000 reservation calls, handles nearly 300,000 pieces of luggage, serves more than 200,000 in-flight meals and snacks, and changes more than 70 airplane tires.

Industry Pioneer

American Airlines' history is packed with innovation. In 1933, American was the first to introduce flight attendants, and in 1934, it originated an air traffic control system. A mid-1930s collaboration with Douglas Aircraft Co. resulted in development of the DC-3, one of the most famous commercial airplanes ever built. In 1953, American flew the first nonstop transcontinental route from Los Angeles to New York, and in 1959, it introduced the first computerized reservations system.

In 1981, American debuted the AADVANTAGE travel awards program—the first and largest of the frequent flyer programs—which today boasts more than 35 million members worldwide and more U.S. flyers than any other airline awards program. In 1998 alone, American awarded more than 2 million trips to AADVANTAGE members.

American Airlines also hosts one of the Internet's busiest electronic commerce sites. American launched the Web site www.AA.com in 1995, added on-line booking in 1996, and incorporated personalized content in 1998. Since then, more than 2 million AADVANTAGE members have logged on, with the site receiving more than 300,000 visits on peak days and 25 million page views each month.

A Corporation with a Conscience

American's heritage also includes many examples of corporate citizenship. Environmental responsibility has been an integral part of corporate culture since the early 1930s, when American Airlines decided to fly its aircraft with polished, unpainted fuselages.

American flight attendants initiated an in-flight recycling program in 1989 that collects more than 10 million aluminum cans annually. Other recycling efforts involve tires, oil, plastics, glass, paper, and cardboard. To date, American's recycling program has saved more than 71,000 trees, 1.6 million gallons of oil, 29.4 million gallons of water, 17.2 million kilowatt-hours of electricity, and 13,860 cubic yards of landfill space.

The recycling program has also earned more than $390,000 for charity. In addition to designating recycling funds for the Nature Conservancy and the National Parks Association's Miles for Trails program, American supports a variety of community, arts and culture, education, and health- and welfare-related organizations in the communities it serves.

From the days of Lindbergh's mail route to today's increasingly global and technologically driven industry, American continues to prove that it's something special in the air and on the ground.

American Airlines christened this 1940s-era DC-3 *Flagship Indianapolis* to commemorate American's air service to Indianapolis (left).

American Airlines, Inc. and Indianapolis have been partners in aviation, from the opening of the Indianapolis International Airport in 1931 to the introduction of American's 777 (right), which represents a new era in air travel.

Marsh Supermarkets, Inc.

VALUE PLAYS AN ENDURING ROLE AT MARSH SUPERMARKETS, Inc.—from its We Value You slogan reflecting its customer-driven philosophy, to the lasting value it creates as an innovator in grocery merchandising, to the community values the company displays as a corporate citizen. ◼ Created as a family enterprise in 1931, Marsh began in

Value plays an enduring role at Marsh Supermarkets, Inc.—from its We Value You slogan reflecting its customer-driven philosophy, to the lasting value it creates as an innovator in grocery merchandising, to the community values the company displays as a corporate citizen.

"We will continually change by implementing programs focused on the ever changing needs of customers," says Chairman and CEO Don E. Marsh. "We're committed to identifying and implementing industry best practices."

Muncie, with one store. By 1953, when the company went public, the chain had 16 stores. Marsh's first Indianapolis store opened in 1957 at 53rd Street and Keystone Avenue. Now headquartered in Indianapolis, Marsh is one of the largest regional grocery chains in the United States, with 71 Marsh Supermarkets; 22 LoBill Foods; 178 Village Pantry convenience stores in Indiana and Ohio; and Savin' $, whose slogan bills it as "the little store that saves you more." In addition, Marsh Supermarkets manages the Convenience Store Distributing Company (CSDC), a distribution firm serving more than 1,300 nonaffiliated convenience stores in nine states, and Crystal Food Service, the largest food service operator in Indiana.

Marsh's 14,000 employees serve more than 2 million customers every week in stores throughout central Indiana and western Ohio—from West Lafayette in the north to Bloomington in the south. Marsh's market share is the highest in the state, with fiscal year 1999 income of $11.6 million on sales of $1.6 billion. In spite of the best year ever in sales and operating income, Chairman and CEO Don E. Marsh is quick to point out that "anything done in retail today is obsolete tomorrow. We will continually change by implementing programs focused on the ever changing needs of customers. We're committed to identifying and implementing industry best practices."

State-of-the-Art Innovations

Innovation is a long-standing value at Marsh Supermarkets as well. True to Don Marsh's promise, the supermarket giant isn't standing still. Its regional

presence makes implementing new technology relatively simple and cost effective, so the company is always looking for new innovations that simplify customers' lives. For instance, Marsh made history in 1974, when a 10-pack of Wrigley's Juicy Fruit Gum became the first retail item scanned using a UPC laser scanner, ushering in a whole new era in retail sales.

With the introduction of Marsh.net, customers can shop via the Internet, as well as over the phone or by fax, and they can have groceries delivered to their doors by Marsh Fresh Express. Because 40 percent of families are still looking for meal solutions at 4 p.m., customers who frequent Marsh's stores will find plenty of prepared foods and grab-and-go sections that cater to busy families and professionals looking for convenience.

In a late-1995 joint venture with National City Bank, Marsh issued the first co-branded credit card of its kind in Indiana: the Marsh Fresh Idea Visa, which combines Marsh's existing customer loyalty card with all the uses of a Visa card as well as a 1 percent rebate check for all

card purchases, regardless of vendor, redeemable for free groceries at Marsh. The Fresh Idea Rewards program also mails a customized shopping list to customers' homes every two weeks, along with special savings opportunities, based on purchase patterns.

A recent innovation, IQ Shopper will expand from its two initial test sites to additional stores in the future. This time-saving system allows customers to scan and sack their own groceries as they shop. A hand-held unit keeps a running total of exactly how much they have spent at any time during the shopping visit, and with the press of a button, totals the bill for payment at a special station.

A Variety of Options

Marsh's various store concepts provide customer choice and extra value as well. Its LoBill Foods, which grew to 22 stores in 1999, serves price-conscious customers with everyday low prices and weekly specials in smaller stores that provide a neighborhood shopping experience. LoBill has been well known in county seat towns

in Marsh's service area, and debuted in the metropolitan Indianapolis market in 1995. Savin' $, a new concept store that's part of the LoBill division, opened in Frankfort, Indiana, and operates as a stock-up store with an every-day-low-price format.

Village Pantry convenience stores began converting to a new-generation format in 1998 with a sandwich-made-to-order program, full-service and self-serve delis, drive-up windows, and bakeries featuring fresh bread, pizza, rotisserie chicken, fried chicken, and home meal replacement take-home items.

Crystal Food Services Inc., Marsh's catering division, now includes three divisions—cafeteria management, vending, and event catering. In 1999, Marsh also launched Coffee Etc., a coffee service available in offices and convenience stores, as well as in 27 area Baskin-Robbins ice-cream stores.

The Marsh name is also synonymous with another value—corporate citizenship. The company continues to support a broad spectrum of events, including the Indianapolis Symphony Orchestra's summer concert series, Symphony on the Prairie at Conner Prairie historic village in Fishers, north of Indianapolis. "We take seriously the importance of giving back to the community," says Marsh. "These efforts require not only our financial support, but the participation of employees who proudly represent the company and their communities. They repeatedly personify the Marsh vision of service."

Marsh Supermarkets offers its customers the freshest and finest foods from around the world.

BMG Entertainment

MUSIC HAS PLAYED A LARGE ROLE IN INDIANAPOLIS' RICH cultural heritage, and BMG Entertainment is proud to be a part of that tradition. As one of the world's premier entertainment companies, it is home to more than 200 record labels in 53 countries, the world's largest music club, the industry's most highly regarded distribution company, and the fastest-growing music publishing company today. BMG is a leader in marketing and selling artists' music over the Internet, as well as one of the world's largest compact disc and cassette manufacturing companies.

BMG-Indianapolis traces its local roots back to 1936, when RCA Records began pressing phonograph records at its near-east-side production facility located on North LaSalle Street. Records manufacturing continued at this address until 1979, when RCA consolidated all business activity at its East 30th Street complex.

Becoming part of the Bertelsmann Music Group (BMG) in 1986 when Bertelsmann AG acquired RCA Records, BMG-Indianapolis continues as the company's principal operations location. At its 600,000-square-foot facility, BMG provides a comprehensive membership service for the millions of members of BMG Music Service, as well as the members of BOOKSPAN. BMG-Indianapolis also is home to BMG Distribution's National Order Service,

Clockwise from top:
Since the mid-1960s, BMG Entertainment has been an anchor for the 30th Street/ Shadeland Avenue business corridor in Indianapolis.

High-speed mail-opening machines (bottom right) and advanced remittance-processing equipment (bottom left) are part of the leading-edge technology that services millions of BMG customers weekly.

BMG Indianapolis' mural of stars is a constant reminder of the artists who help make the company great.

National Inventory Management, and Financial Services organizations, in addition to being the North American base for Bertelsmann mediaSystems' (BmS) global information systems strategy.

Each day, BMG's 1,500 Indianapolis employees continue the tradition of innovation, creativity, efficiency, teamwork, and customer service excellence that has been the hallmark of the company's operations for more than 60 years. Nowhere are these characteristics more evident than in the services local BMG employees provide for the millions of customers of BMG Direct's Music Service Clubs.

America's Number One Music Direct Marketer

BMG Direct is a direct marketing company that interacts with consumers through the mail, by telephone, and through the Internet, offering a wide variety of music and additional products to its members. It's a business that requires processing huge volumes of information in many

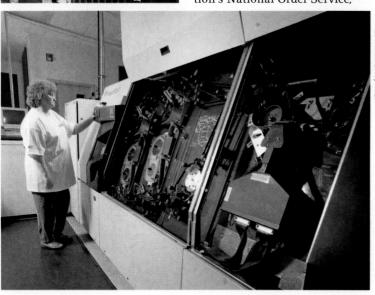

different formats, all passing through BMG's Indianapolis-based operations.

The marketing group divides its efforts into two categories: marketing to current members and soliciting new ones. Every time a current member receives one of the company's catalogs in the mail, BMG-Indianapolis has the opportunity to market the firm's entire music repertoire to that individual.

The largest club, BMG Music Service, customizes the catalogs to its members by listening preference, including Alternative, Country, Dance, Hard Rock, Light Sounds, Metal, R&B, Rap, Soft Rock, Classical, Jazz, Latin, and Sound & Spirit.

When a BMG club member receives a catalog, bill, or other correspondence, that's the result of the company's Indianapolis-based Mail Systems and Services team. A combination of teamwork and technology assembles millions of announcements each month using Selectronic inserting machines and high-speed bar code sorters to ensure postal discounts and improve delivery.

A Mountain of Mail Each Week

In Indianapolis, BMG Direct receives millions of pieces of mail every week. Its highly automated Inbound Mail operation sorts and opens approximately 30,000 pieces every hour and delivers the mail to the processing, enrollment, imaging, or data entry departments. Inbound Mail takes care of more than 85 percent of incoming mail the day it is received.

Orders are processed using

high-speed scanners and leading-edge character recognition capabilities. Enrollment information and order cards are scanned to create images and data, which can be edited if necessary or sent directly to the mainframe computer to create customer orders. In addition, the Remittance Processing department handles payments totaling millions of dollars each day, using the best equipment and technology developed for the banking industry.

Providing Superior Customer Service

BMG Direct offers customers a variety of options, and customers ask a lot of questions. Those questions and other service-related customer contacts are handled through the Customer Relations department. Customer contact comes to BMG through regular mail, E-mail, and telephone calls. Tens of thousands of calls and E-mail requests are received each week.

In fact, more and more of BMG Direct's customers are contacting the company through electronic mail and by telephone. To handle the rising activity, the company's call center stays up to date with the telecommunications and computer equipment needed to support the demands of today and tomorrow.

Best Systems Support in the Industry

Utilizing more than 2 million lines of computer code, the Information Systems department brings all of the company's systems together locally and

links the Indianapolis operation with other BMG Direct facilities, including the New York headquarters and the distribution facilities in South Carolina.

BMG is always looking for ways to improve customer service, and spends millions of dollars each year upgrading its leading-edge technology.

An Indianapolis Employer of Choice

BMG's business thrives on the creativity and enthusiasm of its employees, and strives to create a work environment that attracts and retains high-quality people. It emphasizes promoting from within and offers a generous benefits package. The flexible, smoke-free, casual work environment includes an on-site fitness center, employee discounts on club memberships, and access to a popular, on-site employee store. In addition, BMG keeps its team members updated with regular business reviews, roundtable discussions, and companywide meetings.

Ultimately, anytime a consumer receives one of BMG's mailers, sees one of its magazine ads, visits its Web site, places an order, makes a payment, asks a question, or receives an order, that individual's correspondence will be handled with the utmost care and efficiency by one or more of the people, processes, or technologies found at the Indianapolis home of BMG Direct.

Clockwise from top:
At its Indianapolis location, BMG has transformed warehouse space into a productive and pleasant office environment.

Millions of BMG customers receive announcements mailed from the Indianapolis facility every month.

The company's mission is to provide the best-possible customer service in the industry.

▲ MEDIAWRIGHT, INC.

▲ MEDIAWRIGHT, INC.

Stuart's Moving and Storage, Inc.

SINCE 1936, STUART'S MOVING AND STORAGE, INC. HAS PROVIDED first-class transportation and warehousing of commercial and household goods. A third-generation, family-owned business, it has built and maintained a steady reputation for meeting the changing needs of families and businesses, whether they are relocating across the street or across the continent.

Founded by Marion H. Stuart with only $74, one truck, and a single employee, Stuart's today operates a fleet of 200 trucks, employs 50 people, and has moved thousands of families and businesses millions of miles across 48 states.

While Marion Stuart is still involved in the business, the leadership role has been held by nephew Anthony "Tony" Stuart since 1965. Tony's son, Todd, has also worked for the firm since the age of 14. The trio oversees the day-to-day operations and brings continuity to the firm, which embraces service and dependability as mainstays of its success.

"We differentiate ourselves from the national competition through our commitment to customer service," Marion Stuart says. "Our drivers maintain a professional appearance, are neatly uniformed, arrive on time with clean equipment, and are always polite. They handle our customers' possessions as if they were their own. We view our customers' expectations in this as a trust, and we are committed to honoring that trust."

Valued Reputation

Stuart's customers confirm this trust in their long-term relationships with the moving and storage firm. Customers have included a long line of Indiana governors and their families; many prominent corporate clients, including Thomson Consumer Electronics, Eli Lilly and Company, Conseco, and Browning Investments; and a broad, steady base of residential accounts.

The company is also entrusted with ongoing relationships through the Indianapolis Museum of Art and the Indiana State Museum. "People who need to move or store fine antiques and works of art depend on us to customize our service to their specific needs," Marion Stuart explains. "Our custom-built vans have special safety features, air-ride suspension, and temperature controls to protect even the most delicate and sophisticated cargo, regardless of the weather or altitude during transport. And, we have housed many antique museum pieces in our custom humidity- and climate-controlled warehousing vaults."

A 1948 photo of its crew moving the renowned English Hotel and Opera House from its Monument Circle location attests to Stuart's established reputation in Indianapolis, as well as its competence in handling virtually any request.

The Personal Touch

Stuart's recognizes that for families and businesses alike, moving is a time of apprehension. Because that apprehension can translate into anxiety, or even a loss of job productivity, Stuart's handles all customers with special care and in a timely manner.

Premove consultations with families or corporate relocation coordinators start the process by identifying areas of concerns and allaying apprehensions. Specialized brochures provide helpful guidelines and checklists to customers. And a color-coding system ensures the placement of belongings in their proper locations.

Ongoing and responsive communication are critical components to the moving process, and continuity is assured because the same crew that packs a customer's belongings also unpacks them—a hallmark of Stuart's dependable and reliable service.

Tony Stuart believes that the sooner employees or families are settled into their new surroundings, the sooner they will be able to return to normalcy. "It's a big responsibility on our part, and we look upon it as such," he says. "We are honored that our customers choose us, and we are pleased to be able to do return business with repeat customers. People, more than just furniture, are at the heart of all our moves."

At Stuart's Moving and Storage, Inc., founded in 1936, tradition is an art. A 1948 photo of its crew moving the renowned English Hotel and Opera House from its Monument Circle location attests to Stuart's established reputation in Indianapolis, as well as its competence in handling virtually any request.

THE MISSION OF ANTHEM, INC. IS TO IMPROVE THE HEALTH OF THE people it serves. Its network of physicians and hospitals helps policyholders improve their current state of health, while reminders about regular checkups and screenings maintain health awareness. In addition, its disease management and prevention programs help policyholders avoid future problems.

An Indiana-based company established in 1944, Anthem helps ensure wellness far beyond Indiana's borders. Not only is it the Blue Cross and Blue Shield licensee for Indiana, Ohio, Kentucky, and Connecticut, but it has also extended its reach to Nevada, Colorado, New Hampshire, and, soon, Maine.

Nationwide, Anthem insures more than 6 million people and employs about 13,000. About 2,300 of its Indiana employees are located in a new operations center in the historic Fountain Square area of downtown Indianapolis. The new center consolidates more than a dozen locations into one and centralizes many of its administrative functions.

With a motto of "Healthy minds. Healthy bodies. Healthy communities," Anthem, Inc. strives toward its mission: "to improve the health of the people we serve."

Setting New Standards

Striving to be at the forefront of health care trends, Anthem is currently exploring health indexing, a process that helps define base levels of health for a given population, then ties the compensation of partner providers in that area to improving that population's health. The project is defining new standards for financing and health care access in the years to come.

Anthem Chairman L. Ben Lytle was part of a 34-member advisory commission on consumer protection and quality in health care appointed by President Bill Clinton in 1997. The group crafted a comprehensive Consumer Bill of Rights to protect health care consumers, and developed a strategy for improving the quality of care through increased access and lower costs. Anthem then became the first health plan in the country to endorse and begin voluntary implementation of the bill of rights.

Addressing Community Health

As part of its goal to help people live more productive lives, Anthem also impacts the health of the individual communities where its major operations are located. Anthem contributes to charitable, civic, and social causes to make these communities better places for families and individuals to live, learn, and grow.

In 1998, net income for the Anthem network was $172 million on revenues of $5.9 billion. Corporate giving was about .9 percent of before-tax net income, compared to the national industry average of .7 percent.

Anthem's community service efforts are health related, involving activities such as free blood pressure screenings, health fairs, and other education programs. But the company is also a strong supporter of music, theater, visual arts, sports, and community events, believing a well-rounded community is one where everyone has access to a rich cultural and civic life.

Targeted areas of giving are Healthy Minds, in support of education; Healthy Bodies, in support of health and fitness; and Healthy Communities, in support of arts, economic development, and social services. In making funding decisions, Anthem also takes into account the volunteer involvement of its employees.

"Healthy communities happen when we all work together," Lytle says. "Anthem is proud to share its resources with our communities and help shape a better future for us all."

Barth Electric Co., Inc.

BARTH ELECTRIC CO., INC.'S ATTENTION TO CUSTOMER satisfaction—bringing a job in on time and at or under budget—has contributed to the firm's phenomenal growth and signal reputation. ■ Barth's 76,000-square-foot office and warehouse near downtown Indianapolis serve as headquarters for more than 350 employees and 90 service and specialty vehicles. The company is a full-service electrical construction and maintenance provider, offering around-the-clock emergency service to its clients.

Postwar Success Story

In 1945, Mike Barth Sr. returned from active duty with the Seabees in World War II, looking for a way to put his construction knowledge to work. His first job was installing a frozen food locker in an Acton grocery. For his services, the store owner paid Barth with a truck and some cash. He used the cash to rent a storefront on Virginia Avenue and repainted the truck with the Barth name to give him the mobility to take on additional electrical jobs.

From the very beginning, it was a family business. Mrs. Barth sold appliances, did paperwork, and answered the telephone, while Mike Jr. did odd jobs. They were so successful that within 18 months, they had sold the Barth appliance business to specialize in electrical contract work and moved to larger facilities on South Meridian Street. Sales tripled every decade from 1950 through 1990, and steady growth since then has

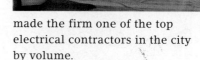

made the firm one of the top electrical contractors in the city by volume.

Top-Notch Service

Barth Electric still prides itself on delivering service, whether for one 120-volt receptacle or a million dollars' worth of wiring for a major project or a telephone and computer system. A list of longtime Barth customers and jobs reads like a who's who of Indianapolis business and industry.

Barth has served area grocers since the late 1940s, followed

by a host of other retail relationships. Longtime customers have included The Kroger Company since the 1950s, Carrier Corporation since the 1960s, and Duke Realty Corp. and Simon Property Group since the1970s. Barth's expertise also played a role in Circle Centre Mall, the Indiana Historical Society headquarters, and the Indianapolis Motor Speedway expansions, just to name a few.

More recently, the company installed electrical distribution and telephone wiring for the Formula One track at the Indianapolis Motor Speedway. The job capped a lifelong love affair with racing for the Barth family, which counts a former United States Auto Club (USAC) and a current Indy Racing League (IRL) official among its ranks.

The family is also known locally for its generosity to organizations such as Habitat for Humanity and United Way. Barth electricians have wired many of the Habitat homes in the area at the company's expense. "We attribute our success to treating the community, customers, and employees the same way we want to be treated," says Mike Barth Jr. With concern not only for its customers, but also for its constituency, Barth Electric Co., Inc. brings corporate citizenship to a new level in Indianapolis.

From its modest beginnings in 1945, Barth Electric Co., Inc. now claims a role in many major construction projects dotting the Indianapolis skyline, including (from top) the 9100 Building at Keystone at the Crossing Circle Center Mall, and the Indiana Historical Society headquarters.

WITHOUT MAGNETS, ORDINARY LIFE WOULDN'T BE SO ordinary. No one knows that better than Stan Malless, president of The Permanent Magnet Co., Inc. Magnets have certainly changed his life, and indeed, have more impact on everyday life than most people realize. ■ Magnets are found in everything from cell phones and thermostats to computers and sophisticated satellites. Whatever their use, there's a good chance they were made by Permanent Magnet, whose products have gone to the Moon and to Mars, been aboard every space shuttle flight, and played a key role in the operation of guided missiles.

A Ground Floor Opportunity

In 1946, after returning from active duty in World War II, Malless had an engineering degree from Purdue University and a job waiting for him at his prewar employer, General Motors. Instead of returning to his old job, he teamed up with two friends to explore a life-long fascination with the mysteries and theories surrounding magnets.

At the time, there were only six permanent magnet producers in the United States, and Malless saw the potential for growth in the industry. And he was right—the partners found themselves with purchase orders for 300,000 magnets before they had a building or equipment.

Their first manufacturing facility was a small Quonset hut they constructed themselves, installing grinders, a punch press, and a small, heat-treating furnace. The heat produced by the equipment often was not enough to keep them warm, and the men would have to wear heavy mittens for office and production work. However, they did not let those inconveniences get in the way of exploring new and better methods for manufacturing and grinding.

Jewelry Manufacturer

A permanent magnet provides two measurable qualities—

Stan Malless, president of The Permanent Magnet Co., Inc., founded the company in 1946 to explore a lifelong fascination with the mysteries and theories surrounding magnets.

strength of magnetic field and resistance to demagnetization. A reliable supplier must precisely control scores of variables to deliver the right product for the customer's specific application. The magnet alloy must be a mix of elements to an exact chemical formula.

Permanent Magnet makes cast magnets, as well as ones that are sintered or are compressed from powdered materials. Materials used include nickel, cobalt, aluminum, zirconium, copper, titanium, and silicon, and must be imported from such places around the globe as Canada, Zaire, South America, and China. At Permanent Magnet, metals are heated to temperatures as high as 3,000 degrees Fahrenheit, then cooled at set rates in the presence of a magnetic field. Rare earth magnets, which Permanent Magnet also produces, require magnetic alignment before tons of pressure are applied to form the final shape.

Permanent Magnet's expertise in bringing all the right variables together in the right way has created the need to expand its Lawrence Township facilities six times since its founding, to 46,000 square feet and 200 employees. Through the years, the firm's ability to set new standards in manufacturing and grinding precision has also earned it the nickname "jewelry manufacturer" within the industry. It's an appropriate moniker for a firm harnessing the power of nature every day.

Pratt Corporation

BEGINNING WITH A MINIMAL INITIAL INVESTMENT AND STATIONing headquarters in the family's basement in 1946, Ryland Pratt worked with his three sons—Ryland Jr., Daniel, and Richard—to print made-to-stock promotional signage, including generic posters and pennant strings for businesses such as retail stores, gas stations, and car lots.

Signage was printed with phrases like Sale, Grand Opening, or Open for Business, and was eventually marketed through catalogs and flyers. By the late 1990s, the company came to be known as Pratt Corporation, and through three generations of dedication and hard work—a fourth has just started—it has established itself as a successful designer and printer of retail graphic signage.

Steady Growth

While the current management team is a blended mixture of Pratts and non-Pratts, the ownership and board of directors is still a family affair.

"I like to say that the company is two years young and 52 years old," says Dan Pratt Jr. "It took us about 52 years to get to $15 million in sales, but only two years after that to reach $25 million."

Today, the company designs, produces, and distributes multi-

piece graphics kits and displays for nationwide chains, such as Lowe's Home Improvement warehouse stores, Napa Auto Parts, and McDonald's restaurants. A strategic plan acquisition prompted Pratt to acquire local companies; launch a new company, One Source Fulfillment; create four business divisions, Creative Services, Digital Services, Screen Printing Services, and Fulfillment Services; add two locations in Indianapolis; and increase the employee base from 150 to 180, all in the last two years.

As sales continuously increase, the Pratts hope to build their grandfather's legacy into a $100 million business in the near future.

Keeping Pace

In 1997 and 1998, Pratt Corp. invested more than $3 million in new technology. The company currently owns two of only a handful of large-format, multi-

color in-line screen printers in use in the United States.

Technology leadership for Pratt means specialized training to help employees keep pace. The company recently turned a section of its plant facilities into a learning center for teaching job skills and basic support skills. Pratt has enlisted the help of trained high school and college teachers, and employees with reading problems or learning disabilities receive individual tutoring. The company received a Literacy Guild award for its efforts.

Now, learning is a part of the corporate culture, and every employee is expected to learn a new skill every year. "The pressure to change and learn new ways of doing things is hard on some of our people," Dan Pratt says. "But it helps them as much as it helps the business. If something ever happened to Pratt Corp., we owe it to our employee family to make sure they have the skills to get a job somewhere else."

Improving the skills of current employees creates an invigorating work environment and attracts even more qualified employees to the company. With investments in the company's technological infrastructure and its employees, Pratt Corp. is laying the groundwork for a promising future.

Pratt Corporation has established itself as a successful designer and printer of retail graphic signage.

FOR MORE THAN A HALF CENTURY, STERLING FLUID SYSTEMS (USA) Inc. has manufactured its Peerless Pump brand of industrial fluid-handling solutions at its Indianapolis plant. The Peerless Pump name reflects the product's reputation, particularly in the vertical pump market, as a pump without equal for quality, performance, and reliability.

Sterling Fluid Systems (USA) Inc.

Sterling is a world leader in fluid handling, specializing in pumps, vacuum technology, engineering systems, water treatment technology, and valves. The company employs 4,000 people worldwide and maintains operations in more than 50 countries, making it one of the leading suppliers of pumps to the world.

Created in the Orange Groves

Peerless Pump Company was founded in 1923 near Los Angeles, first manufacturing well pumps to irrigate local orange groves. A decade later, the company became an integral part of the Food Machinery Corporation, which provided the resources Peerless needed to become the world's largest producer of deep well turbine pumps.

The Indianapolis manufacturing facility was established in 1946, as demand for Peerless products grew. Thyssen-Bornemisza Group (TBG) acquired Peerless in 1976, as part of its North American operations.

In 1993, Peerless manufacturing operations that had been previously headquartered in California were consolidated at the Indianapolis plant. The city's central location for distribution, talented personnel, and room for expansion made consolidation worthwhile. In 1997, TBG North America changed its name to Sterling Fluid Systems (USA), but continues to be known by the Peerless brand name in key sectors of the industrial pump market.

Known Worldwide

Today, the 300,000-square-foot Indianapolis facility employs nearly 300 people and is capable of testing all sizes of Sterling

pumps. It is one of three Peerless Pump plants in North America and one of more than 30 Sterling manufacturing and assembly facilities worldwide.

When combined, the Indianapolis manufacturing plant and its Sterling sister facility in the United Kingdom create the world's largest supplier of industry-listed fire-fighting pumps. Indianapolis is also a major supplier of pumps for the municipal water supply

industry, the chemical process industry, and other general industrial applications.

The company is known for producing state-of-the-art designs and has computer-controlled machine-tooling capabilities. In 1999, the Indianapolis plant manufactured 13,000 new pumps and countless parts. The plant recently opened a repair center that services all brands of used industrial pumps in addition to Peerless.

Peerless Pumps are sold in the United States through a network of more than 300 distributors. These pumps are installed locally in Conseco Fieldhouse, the RCA Dome, Methodist Hospital, and Eli Lilly and Company. The brand can also be found at Scotland's Edinburgh Castle and in some of the world's largest buildings, such as the Sears Tower in Chicago, Petronas Towers in Kuala Lumpur, and the Emirates Towers in Dubai.

With such a well-known and pervasive product, Sterling Fluid Systems (USA) Inc. continues to expand its customer base, as well as its profits. By manufacturing with an eye for quality and selling with attention to customer service, the company is finding enduring success.

Today, the 300,000-square-foot Sterling Fluid Systems (USA) Inc. facility in Indianapolis employs nearly 300 people and is capable of testing all sizes of Sterling pumps. It is one of three Peerless Pump plants in North America and one of more than 30 Sterling manufacturing and assembly facilities worldwide (top).

Led by Sterling Group President and Chief Executive Peter Andrews (left) and Sterling Fluid Systems (Middle East) General Manager Steven Keen, Sterling Fluid Systems installed a complex system of high-pressure vertical turbine pumps in the Emirates Tower I, the tallest building in the United Arab Emirates and the 10th-tallest in the world. The Indianapolis plant manufactured the main fire pump packages and the horizontal booster pumps, making it possible for the contract to be delivered on time (bottom).

Monarch Beverage Company Inc.

MONARCH BEVERAGE COMPANY INC. DISTRIBUTES WHOLE-sale beer and wine to central Indiana retail locations from a state-of-the-art warehouse on the city's southwest side. The company prides itself on providing the standard of ideal service to its customers, as well as a principled approach of educating the public about the responsible use of its products.

Edwin T. French Sr. founded Monarch in 1947 with one brand of beer and only six employees. From a Market Street warehouse that was the size of a modest home, French and his staff handled sales and deliveries.

Today, under the leadership of Edwin T. French Jr., Monarch is the leading beer distributor and the third-largest wine distributor in Indiana. Nationwide, it is among the 25 largest wholesalers in terms of case volume sold and has annual sales of about $150 million.

A King among Distributors

Carling Black Label was the only brand Monarch carried in 1947. Today, the company represents approximately 100 beers, including Miller, Coors, Corona, Heineken, and the local, micro-brewed Oaken Barrel. The company's distribution area encompasses 40 counties in central and southeast Indiana, where it supplies restaurants, bars, liquor stores, grocery stores, and drugstores.

Monarch began distributing wine in 1971 and now represents more than 100 brands, including the Gallo and Franzia labels. Its wine distribution territory spans 69 Indiana counties in the southern three-quarters of the state, where Monarch maintains about a 30 percent share of the wholesale market.

Monarch's growth has resulted from aggressive pursuit and acquisitions. It has acquired about 20 smaller distributors since 1975—six in 1999 alone—and has been named distributor for almost every supplier new to the area. In the 1990s, annual sales increased from 650,000 to 10 million cases. The company estimates that its sales of beer will soon exceed 10 million cases, and sales of wine will soon amount to around 800,000 cases.

The Castle among Warehouses

Since 1997, Monarch's 400 employees and its fleet of 115 delivery vehicles have served customers from a new, 300,000-square-foot office and warehouse on the southwest side of the city. The warehouse portion occupies two-thirds of the space and is a picture of cleanliness and efficiency. When Monarch began planning the new facility, several cities outside of Marion County courted the megadistributor, but the company decided to remain in Indianapolis, because it would be close to home and the majority of its customers.

Monarch has about 20 business days of inventory on hand at any given time, which is the equivalent of 750,000 cases of beer. A refrigerated section maintains a 15-day stock of

Monarch Beverage Company Inc. distributes wholesale beer to central Indiana retail locations from a state-of-the-art warehouse on the city's southwest side.

The company represents approximately 765 beers, including Miller, Coors, Corona, Heineken, and the local, micro-brewed Oaken Barrel.

draft beer for restaurants and bars, and drive-through loading bays provide the convenience of nighttime loading for delivery trucks.

In 1996, Monarch formed EF Transit Inc. to assume transportation and warehouse operations, and to allow improved focus on operational issues and opportunities. In addition to Monarch Beverage, EF Transit's customer base includes seven beer distributors, four breweries, and a trailer manufacturer in Terre Haute.

The subsidiary, which delivers to locations in Indiana and Ohio, derives significant benefit from relationships with the Miller and Coors brewing companies as well. Its continual movement of products for Monarch gives it a competitive advantage over other freight companies, and it can easily step in for other distributors and breweries when service levels are in jeopardy, adding significant value for the customer.

A Focus on Social Responsibility

Monarch is acutely aware that it distributes a product with potential for abuse, so it dedicates significant resources—both in dollars and time—toward miti-

gation. It often partners with the corporations whose brands it distributes on promotional efforts to encourage responsible use of the products.

The company also partners with retail customers, such as liquor and grocery stores, to aid in the sponsorship of charitable events for the Leukemia Society and the Juvenile Diabetes Foundation, among others. In addition, it helps nonprofit organizations limit the cost of fund-raising events by donating beer and wine.

In early 2000, the company launched the Monarch Charitable Foundation as a way to increase employee involvement in charitable giving. Monarch provided the seed money, and the foundation accepts employee donations. Employees can then direct how funds will be distributed to qualifying not-for-profit organizations.

Coors Brewing Company recently recognized Monarch's efforts and performance as a distributor in 1999 with its prestigious Founder's Award, which is given to wholesalers who demonstrate unique excellence in distributing the Coors family of products.

Today, Monarch has reached the physical and geographic limits of a single-location wholesaler, and future growth and prosperity will capture a greater share in existing markets. Increasing market share will be accomplished by continuing to provide an ever escalating level of service to customers and by working closely with suppliers and customers to increase demand for the products Monarch represents.

At Monarch's state-of-the-art Indianapolis warehouse, a refrigerated section maintains a 15-day stock of draft beer for restaurants and bars, and drive-through loading bays provide the convenience of nighttime loading for delivery trucks.

Carrier Corporation

D R. WILLIS HAVILAND CARRIER, THE FATHER OF MODERN air-conditioning, was recently named one of the 20 most influential builders and titans of the 20th century by *Time* magazine. Today, the company Carrier founded— Carrier Corporation—is the world's largest manufacturer of heating and cooling systems. Proudly, the Residential and Light Commercial Systems group, an entity of Carrier Corporation's North American operations, is headquartered in Indianapolis.

The Residential and Light Commercial Systems group became a part of the Indianapolis community in 1959, with the purchase of a local manufacturing firm, BDP Co. Located on the city's west side, the 800,000-square-foot campus employs approximately 1,500 people locally in its factory, administrative offices, and world-class research and development center. This group is also responsible for manufacturing and distribution facilities in Tyler, Texas, as well as Collierville and Lewisburg, Tennessee.

Expanding the Reach

Carrier Corporation is one of five businesses owned by United Technologies Corporation (UTC), a provider of high-technology products to the aerospace, building systems, and residential home owner industries through-

out the world. UTC's companies are all industry leaders, including Pratt & Whitney jet engines, Otis elevators, Sikorsky helicopters, and Hamilton Sundstrand aviation controls and components.

Carrier Corporation's Residential and Light Commercial Systems group designs, manufactures, distributes, and markets

gas furnaces, air conditioners, fan coils, heat pumps, electronic air cleaners, humidifiers, thermostats, heat recovery ventilators, and zoning systems under the brand names Carrier, Bryant, and Payne. These leading products are known for their high quality and reliability, and are marketed to home buyers and commercial contractors.

In 1999, Carrier Corporation extended its market share with the acquisition of International Comfort Products (ICP) Corporation, headquartered in Lewisburg, with additional manufacturing locations in Wichita Falls, Texas, and Quebec. ICP manufactures and markets central air-conditioning and heat pump systems, gas and oil furnaces, air handlers, component parts, and accessories under the brand names Heil, Tempstar, Arcoaire, Comfortmaker. Airquest, Keeprite, Lincoln, Dettson, and Clare. With this acquisition, Carrier Corporation will generate productivity improvements through accelerating implementation of advanced manufactur-

World-class quality is built into every Carrier Corporation system by the expertise of more than 1,500 employees in Indianapolis (top).

More than 1 million gas furnaces and fan coils roll off the lines at the 800,000-square-foot Indianapolis facility each year (bottom).

ing practices, product delivery systems, and technology integration.

A Technology Leader

Carrier markets its products as "custom made indoor weather." The unique, world-class research and development center in Indianapolis is capable of simulating environmental tests such as the sub-zero, arctic weather of snow and ice, or Sahara Desert conditions of up to 125 degrees. Researchers also utilize the center's sound room to measure the decibel level at which heating and cooling equipment operates, in an ongoing effort to minimize noise levels. Carrier Corporation employees have been granted more than 50 patents in the last five years in the disciplines of compressors, heat transfer, air management, electronics, and refrigerant management.

Patents in refrigerant management will help bring Carrier Corporation into compliance with the 1990 Clean Air Act and the internationally binding Montreal Protocol. These agreements call for an international phaseout of R-22 refrigerants used in most air-conditioning and heat pump systems. In response, extensive testing led Carrier Corporation to the use of Puron®, a non-chlorine-based refrigerant—first introduced in 1996—that does not damage the earth's protective ozone. Air-conditioning systems using the Puron refrigerant have an outstanding record of reliability and customer satisfaction. Carrier is expanding its Puron product line to offer a wider range of environmentally sound products that make use of this proprietary refrigerant. Puron is also being introduced into European and Japanese markets, as well as in a variety of commercial applications.

A Leader across All Lines

Carrier Corporation has been the world's leading manufacturer and marketer of heating, ventilating, air-conditioning, and refrigeration equipment since its founder invented the basics of modern air-conditioning in 1902. Today, operating in 171 countries, the Carrier brand combines its global expertise with the superior customer responsiveness of its local operations to lead nearly every geographic market. The Carrier brand represents the industry's broadest selection of quiet, compact, energy-efficient, and environmentally friendly heating and cooling systems. The company remains a global leader in every one of its markets.

The history of indoor comfort is a history of Carrier Corporation, and there is more behind the comfort that is often taken for granted on a swelteringly hot day or a freezing cold day than one might think. Carrier Corporation will continue its quest to provide home owners with creative, comfortable heating and cooling solutions. Says Frank Hartman, president of the Residential and Light Commercial Systems group, "Our future success and continued industry leadership are based on our commitment toward investment in research, technology, and people. And our people make the difference."

Carrier heating and cooling systems are installed by a network of independent dealers throughout the country (top).

In 1996, Carrier continued its technological leadership with the introduction of the first residential cooling systems featuring a non-ozone-depleting refrigerant called Puron® (bottom).

Paul Harris Stores, Inc.

IT HAS BEEN A REMARKABLE ADVENTURE IN RETAILING FOR PAUL Harris Stores, Inc.—from its founding in the 1950s by two Indianapolis men, to its dramatic national expansion and record sales in recent years, to its purchase of the J. Peterman Company. And the excitement of the journey continues. ■ The Paul Harris private-label clothing collections are marketed to fit every

aspect of a woman's lifestyle. Key words that drive the Paul Harris merchandising effort include versatile, comfortable, active, coordinated, seasonal, and smart. And with 1999's purchase of the J. Peterman Company, the adjectives upscale and eclectic can be added to the Paul Harris vocabulary. Parodied on the hit television show Seinfeld, the J. Peterman Company brand offers elegant and uncommon merchandise for men, women, and the home.

Currently, Paul Harris Stores, Inc. has more than 331 stores in 31 states, including 34 in Indiana and 11 in the Indianapolis metropolitan area. Nearly half of all stores have opened since 1997, including the chain's first Paul Harris flagship store in 1998. Both the J. Peterman and the Paul Harris flagships have set up shop in the historic Merchant's Bank Building

at Meridian and Washington streets in downtown Indianapolis. The Chicago Paul Harris flagship opened the following year along the famous Magnificent Mile.

The 11 J. Peterman Company stores showcase timeless apparel for men and women, unique gifts, and extraordinary objects. In the famous J. Peterman style of ad-

venture and intrigue, a stroll through the store is a journey through various destinations such as Bar and Cigar, the Bath, and the Library.

From Local Entrepreneurs to National Retailers

Earl Harris and Gerald Paul founded Paul Harris in 1952, selling men's shirts. They

"It is all about the customer," President and General Merchandising Manager Glenn S. Lyon says. "We want her to walk into a Paul Harris store and be in her comfort zone. She doesn't have to turn anywhere else for her wardrobe needs."

"It is our goal to exceed customer expectations, beyond the logos and imagery," says Executive Vice President Sally M. Tassani, "to deliver a superior selection of quality merchandise at a competitive price."

eventually expanded merchandise to include other menswear, women's apparel, and a children's line before focusing exclusively on private-label women's clothing and accessories.

Paul retired as chairman in 1994. Current President and General Merchandising Manager Glenn S. Lyon joined Paul Harris in March 2000. With a remarkable, 25-year background in women's specialty retailing, merchandise development, and sales, Lyon joined a strong executive team spearheaded by Sally M. Tassani, executive vice president, and Keith L. Himmel Jr., vice president of finance, controller, and corporate secretary.

The company includes Paul Harris, Paul Harris Direct, and J. Peterman Company stores, and J. Peterman's on-line Owner's Manual. The J. Peterman Company—purchased out of bankruptcy in early 1999—was saved from liquidation and certain oblivion. The former Lexington, Kentucky-based operation is now included in the Indianapolis Paul Harris corporate headquarters.

In 1999, Paul Harris sales reached $264 million—a 9.2 percent increase from 1998 and the highest ever recorded by Paul Harris. Notably, Paul Harris had a record December for 1999, representing the best month in the history of the company.

New merchandise lines demonstrated remarkable growth in 1999. For example, the Paul Harris Sport line was up 45.4 percent, and denim grew 31.7 percent.

Paul Harris collections have expanded size offerings, now carrying sizes two to 16, as well as extra-large sizes and limited petite offerings. The collections are designed to mix and match, with separates made from the same dye lots to ensure color consistency.

A New Era

In his new position as president and general merchandising manager, Lyon has set his immediate focus on building the merchandising function through customer lifestyle. "It is all about the customer," Lyon says. "We want her to walk into a Paul Harris store and be in her comfort zone. She doesn't have to turn anywhere else for her wardrobe needs."

Future goals for Paul Harris include expanding on a branding strategy introduced in 1998. Under the concept, Paul Harris merchandise keeps pace with the demands of the company's target audience—busy women. This theme is woven through the store signage and other materials.

"It is our goal to exceed customer expectations, beyond the logos and imagery," says

Tassani, "to deliver a superior selection of quality merchandise at a competitive price."

Paul Harris understands the increasing casualness of the American wardrobe. Industry research suggests that few retailers at the moderate price point are meeting the relaxed, business-casual need. Paul Harris seeks to fulfill that need for its customer.

"Fashion will propel us," says Lyon. "We will make it easy for our core customer because we will give her what she is demanding—today's styles and fashions appropriately translated for her lifestyle."

Lyon's vision for Paul Harris also includes leveraging the J. Peterman brand through various channels. "With the acquisition of the J. Peterman Company, we are in the enviable position of owning a brand with great customer recognition, esteem, and cachet," says Lyon. "I see this as a growth opportunity."

Paul Harris has also recently redesigned its two Web sites, www.paulharris.com and www.jpeterman.com. "This multichanneled initiative can heighten the in-store shopping experience," says Lyon. "E-commerce offers both Paul Harris and J. Peterman some new, exciting avenues for our customers, as well as exposure to new markets."

Defense Finance and Accounting Service-Indianapolis Center (DFAS)

DEFENSE FINANCE AND ACCOUNTING SERVICE (DFAS), although its name is not always recognized by most Indianapolis residents, has a long and important tradition in the city. Many are probably much more familiar with its former name, the U.S. Army Finance and Accounting Center. Until 1991, Fort Benjamin Harrison, located in the northeast corner of Indianapolis, housed the Finance Center, known throughout the Department of Defense as the Home of the Army Dollar.

At that time, the Department of Defense converted the center and the workforce into the Defense Finance and Accounting Service-Indianapolis Center. With headquarters located in Washington, D.C., DFAS has four other major centers: Denver; Columbus and Cleveland, Ohio; and Kansas City, Missouri. The agency employs approximately 18,000 personnel worldwide with more than 2,500 employees at the Indianapolis Center.

The Defense Finance and Accounting Service-Indianapolis Center (DFAS) is a planned community of people, systems, and technology aligned to improve the Department of Defense's finance and accounting operations (top).

The mission of DFAS is to provide finance and accounting services to the Department of Defense during times of peace or conflict (bottom).

Mission

DFAS's mission is to provide finance and accounting services to the Department of Defense during times of peace or conflict. Its goal is to offer accurate, timely, and effective customer support at a low cost.

DFAS generates real value by integrating the best finance and accounting operations from the army, air force, navy, Marine Corps, and the Defense Logistics Agency into a single, efficient organization. This includes nearly $300 billion in purchasing and payroll services for more than 6 million military and civilian personnel, payment of millions of invoices and transportation bills, and financial management of the multibillion-dollar foreign military sales program.

With its broad talent of professional, technical, and administrative staff, DFAS is continuously pursuing innovative ways of integrating technologies and consolidating efforts to provide fast, efficient service. The organization is a planned community of people, systems, and technology aligned to improve the Department of Defense's finance and accounting operations. The mission of the men and women involved in this community is to create the next generation of procedures and standards that will shape the future of defense finance and accounting.

Community Involvement

As an agency, DFAS cares about its employees' needs and concerns, and in turn, its people care about their community.

The General Services Administration, which recently acquired the Maj. Gen. Emmett J. Bean Federal Center, covers more than 14 acres and is the third-largest federal building in the United States.

DFAS is proud of its employees for their dedication, talents, and expertise. In addition, it is one of the largest employers of deaf, hearing-impaired, and physically challenged employees in the city.

The agency is also involved with the community, dedicating time, effort, and money. To continue the great tradition that Fort Benjamin Harrison began, DFAS provides more than 200 road guards to the Indianapolis Life 500 Festival Mini-Marathon. Employees also work with a myriad of other programs and events, such as the March of Dimes' Walk America, the American Cancer Society's Relay for Life, the Children's Guardian Home, and many other nonprofit groups.

Education is very important to DFAS employees. Their involvement in the Partners in Education Program includes being pen pals, tutors, and classroom readers. Employees read to the first- or second-graders and then go to lunch with them. This is fondly referred to as the "chat and chew" program. DFAS has also assisted elementary, middle, and high school students by donating more than 1,100 computers to schools across the country.

DFAS donates its time throughout the year, but annually, it also contributes money through the Combined Federal Campaign. In 1999, more than $179,000 was donated—a dollar amount that the agency can proudly say increases each year, even as its workforce numbers decrease.

Looking to the Future

DFAS has adopted a plan for change that has had impact throughout the Department of Defense. More importantly, it has surveyed, adapted, and applied to its operation some of the proven approaches of modern business. DFAS is not an insulated community, and its management is focused on new trends in local, economic, social, political, and technological environments. As a result, the agency uses the latest applied technologies in finance and accounting in the Department of Defense.

DFAS has an in-house learning center that focuses on specialized and general training and education for its employees. It also has a successful intern program that recruits and trains talented, motivated employees and college graduates, laying the groundwork for building the agency's future leaders.

The General Services Administration recently acquired the Maj. Gen. Emmett J. Bean Federal Center, and is in the process of a multimillion-dollar renovation. This will be the first major renovation and refurbishment since its construction in 1953. The building itself covers more than 14 acres and is the third-largest federal building in the United States. In addition to the renovation, a new state-of-the-art child care center for children of DFAS employees has broken ground and will be completed in the summer of 2000.

The DFAS story is one about progress and innovation, about adapting to changing times and needs, about pride in the community, and about a high quality of service to customers. Most of all, it is a story still being written.

The men and women involved in DFAS are people whose mission is to create the next generation of procedures and standards, which will shape the future of defense finance and accounting.

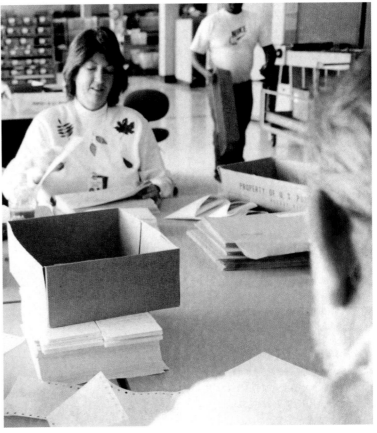

Moorfeed Corporation

MORE AND MORE CONSUMER PRODUCTS—FROM COMPUTER keyboards, inkjet cartridges, automobiles, and automatic dishwashers, to hairspray bottles, lipstick tubes, and razors—are less expensive to manufacture today because of the use of parts-feeding equipment. Indianapolis' Moorfeed Corporation has played a significant role in the birth of this industry, and today remains the oldest manufacturer dedicated solely to parts-feeding equipment and systems worldwide. With annual sales in excess of $14 million and more than 25 patents in its field of expertise, Moorfeed is an industry leader.

The company grew out of a small machine shop called Moore Equipment Company, which was opened in the late 1940s by Robert P. Moore. Moore got his start building labeling equipment for Eli Lilly and Company. That led to experimentation with industrial parts-feeding equipment, which at the time was made from aluminum. Durability was a problem, and Moore set out to improve the process. His shop began making the equipment from stainless steel, and that made the difference. The company was incorporated in 1960 as Moorfeed Corporation, and has grown into a producer of custom-designed and -built parts-feeding systems, part-positioning and -placing devices, and system control.

Current President and Owner Domenic Angelicchio joined the firm part-time in 1963 while still in college. He liked the industry so much that he changed his major to mechanical engineering and began working full-time at Moorfeed while attending Purdue University. Angelicchio acquired the company in 1973.

Moorfeed moved from near downtown in 1978 to its current 60,000-square-foot facility on Indianapolis' northeast side. In 1993, the company opened its second location, a 12,000-square-foot manufacturing facility in Largo, Florida, to serve its southeast markets.

Pioneer in Product Refinement

Throughout the 1970s, demand for increased assembly rates focused Moorfeed's attention on developing higher-speed equipment, which then relied on vibration technology. In the early 1980s, Moorfeed developed a patented process to increase equipment speed through the use of centrifugal force. Although most assembly feed equipment produced today still uses vibration, the use of centrifugal force continues to expand, with some Moorfeed systems feeding as many as 4,000 parts per minute. The company has also pioneered vision systems integration, using cameras to detect, reposition, and/or remove improperly oriented parts from the parts-feeding system of the assembly line.

Ironically, much of the work needed to design and produce automation machinery, a combination of art and science, is performed by hand by Moorfeed craftsmen. The company has more than 150 employees, most of whom work out of the Indianapolis plant. Fully 90 percent of all equipment produced is designed and built for particular applications, including parts-positioning devices, pick-and-place units, computer-logic controls, and bulk material-handling equipment.

Since Moorfeed equipment sets the industry standard for easy setup, stability, reliability, and flexibility, its Fortune 1000 customers often request assistance in designing their products, as a way to facilitate automation. If an assembly process requires higher feed rates, faster speeds, multiple lines, or difficult orientations, Moorfeed's highly skilled labor force can engineer solutions.

"There will be those who try to copy some of our design concepts," says Angelicchio. "But they cannot copy our creative problem-solving energy that compels us continually to raise the standard of excellence in our field." That is the reason Moorfeed is the global leader in parts-feeding automation.

Domenic Angelicchio, president and owner of Moorfeed Corporation, demonstrates one of the company's patented high-speed systems, which presents candy bars to a packaging operation at the rate of 1,100 pieces per minute.

Leading the Way

345

1954 UNITED SIGNATURE FOODS, LLC

1954 WISH TV8

1960 IBM CORPORATION

1960 SIMON PROPERTY GROUP

1962 SHIEL SEXTON COMPANY INC.

1963 CARR METAL PRODUCTS, INC.

1963 IVY TECH STATE COLLEGE - CENTRAL INDIANA

1967 PACERS SPORTS & ENTERTAINMENT CORPORATION

1968 BINDLEY WESTERN INDUSTRIES, INC.

1969 GOELZER INVESTMENT MANAGEMENT

1969 GOELZER INVESTMENT BANKING

1970 D.B. MANN DEVELOPMENT

1970 HERITAGE ENVIRONMENTAL SERVICES

1971 THE INDIANA HAND CENTER

1973 ASSOCIATED BUILDERS AND CONTRACTORS OF INDIANA

1973 CROSSMAN COMMUNITIES, INC.

1973 DIVERSIFIED SYSTEMS INC.

1973 TOBIAS INSURANCE GROUP, INC.

United Signature Foods, LLC

UNITED SIGNATURE FOODS, LLC IS ONE OF THE COUNTRY'S LARGEST manufacturers of products for the food service industry. It is a flexible manufacturer that specializes in high-quality, high-value products. The company enjoys an industry position of leadership and respect earned through more than 100 years of innovation and trend setting. ■ United Signature Foods

has three manufacturing facilities, with a combined total of 730,000 square feet of space in Indianapolis, Los Angeles, and San Francisco. Quality product lines include soups, soup bases, salad dressings, mayonnaise, dry and frozen sauces, and frozen appetizers. Developed by an industry-respected research and development team, manufactured under strict quality assurance practices, and marketed nationwide by a seasoned sales force, many United Signature Foods' products can be enjoyed in dining establishments locally and nationwide.

United Signature Foods' product lines include more than 400 food products, focusing on private label, custom formulations, and branded products within the broad line distribution, retail/club stores, and chain account channels. Branded products include Kettle Rich® frozen soups and soup bases; Signature Harvest™ dressings, mayonnaise, and sauces; LaRequesta™ salsas; Trail

Blazer™ barbecue sauces; and Nancy's® frozen appetizers.

A History of Commitment

One of three production facilities, United Signature Foods' Indianapolis manufacturing is located on the southeast side of Indianapolis. The plant began operations in 1910 as Columbia Conserve Company, until it was purchased by one of its primary customers, John Sexton and

Company of Chicago, in 1953. John Sexton was a family-owned coffee, tea, and spice company that traced its roots back to 1883. Under the Sexton ownership, the company moved into a full-line distributor to restaurants, schools, hospitals, and nursing homes.

In 1968, Beatrice Foods purchased Sexton, operating it as a wholly owned subsidiary until 1983, when it sold the company to S.E. Rykoff & Company of Los Angeles. The company, then known as Rykoff-Sexton, Inc., moved its Chicago research and development laboratories to Indianapolis and expanded into the production of frozen products. Through another series of mergers and acquisitions, the company became the manufacturing division of U.S. Foodservice, the second-largest food service distributor in the country. In August 1998, U.S. Foodservice sold that manufacturing division, which is now United Signature Foods.

In June 1999, United Signature Foods acquired Nancy's Specialty Foods, manufacturer of high-quality, frozen appetizers sold to club stores, including

United Signature Foods, LLC is one of the country's largest manufacturers of products for the food service industry. It is a flexible manufacturer that specializes in high-quality, high-value products.

Sam's and Costco; retail stores such as Marsh Supermarkets; and food service distributors. The company continues to invest in and expand its production facilities and offices in order to remain an industry leader.

Quality, Service, and Integrity

United Signature Foods provides some of the highest-quality products, exceptional value, and outstanding service in the industry. The company's commitment to quality has earned it a nationwide reputation for products made with only the finest, freshest ingredients— and lots of them.

Service is critical to United Signature Foods' customers. Its management, sales, and marketing teams; customer service department; and production staffs are committed to exceeding their customers' expectations in this area.

A company's greatest strength is its people, and this is especially true at United Signature Foods. Just as the company is dedicated to its people, employees at every level are dedicated to what they do and how they do it. There are a number of employees whose commitment is evident by their longevity with the organization—of the 225 employees at the India-

napolis plant, 30 have more than 30 years of service, including four who have more than 40 years of service. United Signature Foods' employees are all partners who share in the company vision.

A Vision for the Future

United Signature Foods is a highly regarded developer, manufacturer, and marketing partner to U.S.-based food service and retail customers, offering a portfolio of high-end-quality, excellent-value food products.

To its customers, it constantly strives to meet this vision with a total service execution that exceeds their expectations. To consumers, the company for the

most part is unknown, as it does not market directly to consumers or patrons, but indirectly through its customers to build joint businesses. To employees, United Signature Foods is an excellent place to work and grow as both individuals and team members, where contributions are respected and justly rewarded. The company believes strongly in the values derived from the diversity of its employees.

As the new century begins, United Signature Foods is renewing its commitment to its employees, suppliers, and customers, and is looking forward to continuing as an integral part of the Indianapolis business community.

The company continues to invest in and expand its production facilities and offices in order to remain an industry leader.

WISH-TV 8

WITH TWO OF INDIANAPOLIS' MOST RECOGNIZED anchors—Mike Ahern and Debby Knox—and a long list of television firsts, there's little wonder why WISH-TV 8 is central Indiana's news leader. It is consistently Indiana's most watched television station, and in February 1996, was the number one-rated CBS affiliate in the country.

WISH-TV 8 signed on the air in Indianapolis on July 1, 1954, at 6 p.m., almost 13 years after the initial broadcast of WISH Radio. On the initial broadcast, a 15-minute program introduced the staff, numbering then about 65, with 11 local owners.

The station quickly established a reputation for being on the scene of breaking news. In 1963, the station broadcast live coverage of the tragic Indianapolis Coliseum explosion—the first news event of its kind to be broadcast live in the city. And in 1964, an ambitious photographer sneaked into the Beatles concert and shot exclusive footage of the world-famous group.

Today, the staff numbers more than 170 people working in news, sales, programming, creative services, production, engineering, traffic, and accounting. WISH-TV 8 is owned by LIN Television, which operates 12 stations across the country.

Recognizable People

Perhaps central to the station's success is its anchor team of Mike Ahern and Debby Knox. A graduate of Indianapolis' Cathedral High School and the University of Notre Dame, Ahern joined WISH in 1967. Before moving to WISH-TV, Ahern's voice could be heard on WIRE Radio, where as a news reporter and sports director, he instituted mobile news coverage. He has received numerous awards, including a CASPER for coverage of the Blizzard of '78, three CASPERs for WISH-TV's news magazine *30 Minutes*, and recognition from the Indianapolis Press Club for best documentary, best enterprise feature, and best historical feature. Readers of both the *Indianapolis Star* and the *Indianapolis Monthly* have named Ahern Best News Anchor for the past 10 years.

Knox joined Ahern at the anchor desk in 1980. Holding both a bachelor's and a master's degree from the University of Michigan, she worked at stations in Elkhart and South Bend before coming to Indianapolis and WISH-TV 8. Knox has won many awards for health reporting, including one from the Society of Professional Journalists for an investigation of doctors on drugs. Another investigative report on the Central Indiana Regional Blood Center garnered her four major awards, including a CASPER, and was instrumental in the enactment of state legislation to protect the blood

Bruce McConnell (right), one of the original owners, and his son Bob, the station's first general manager, helped make WISH-TV 8 a television pioneer. The station signed on the air in Indianapolis on July 1, 1954.

E. ANTHONY VALAINIS

supply. Knox's medical reports have won three Indiana State Medical Journalism awards, along with Associated Press and United Press International awards.

WISH-TV Vice President and News Director Lee Giles is the longest-running news director at any local television station in the country. He has served as news director since May 1968. Giles joined WISH-TV in 1963 as the station's first editorial director and has served as anchor, state house reporter, and managing editor. In 1993, Giles was inducted into the Indiana Journalism Hall of Fame.

Indiana's First 24-Hour News and Weather Station

News 8 provides viewers with the most news programming of any local station, beginning each weekday morning with a three-hour broadcast. In 1990, WISH-TV launched its 24-hour news service, providing live updates every hour throughout the day. In addition, its Local Weather Station on cable provides viewers with around-the-clock weather forecasts and information.

WISH-TV 8 is on the cutting edge of news and weather reporting technology. News 8 gets viewers closer to breaking events with *Live Chopper 8*. Capable

of traveling up to 150 miles per hour, the Bell 206L-3 Long-Ranger helicopter is equipped with four onboard cameras.

The Flir Ultramedia III, exclusive to this market, is *Live Chopper 8*'s main camera lens, featuring 360 degrees of rotation, gyrostabilization, and up to 96 times zoom capability. "At 500 feet, we can read a license plate," says Scott Blumenthal, station president and general manager. "The steadiest, closest picture is what it's all about. When viewers see coverage from our chopper, it's like they're on the scene with us." The lens is so powerful it is also able to provide color pictures even at night.

With a team of meteorologists and the state-of-the-art Forecast Center 8, WISH-TV has the team and tools to keep viewers ahead of approaching storms. Doppler radar is a meteorologist's best tool for tracking severe weather, forecasting a storm's intensity, and detecting tornado development; WISH-TV's Super Doppler 8 is far more powerful than the average Doppler radar and is equipped with advanced features such as street-level mapping and lightning-strike detection.

Dual Doppler 8, the only system of its kind in the Midwest, links the power of Super Doppler

8 to a sister radar site 175 miles away. This gives the WISH-TV forecasters a nearly 300-mile, live look at threatening skies, and allows the station to track approaching storms hours in advance.

Television First

WISH-TV has always been a television pioneer both locally and nationally. In 1956, it was one of the first to install a video tape machine, and in 1983, was the first station in the country with Sony Betacam cameras, which are now the industry standard. Beginning in March 1999, WISH-TV was one of the first stations in the country to broadcast in digital for high-definition television (HDTV). In September 1999, it began broadcasting CBS network programming in HDTV.

"We've always tried to be on the cutting edge, and HDTV is the biggest TV technological development since color," says Blumenthal. "We're not only the first in our market to broadcast digitally, but one of the first in the nation."

As WISH-TV 8 focuses on the new millennium, the station's award-winning anchors and its emphasis on cutting-edge technology will keep it highly ranked in Indianapolis and in the nation.

WISH-TV's *Live Chopper 8* has a camera lens featuring 360 degrees of rotation, gyro-stabilization, and up to 96 times zoom capability (left).

WISH-TV News 8's Debby Knox and Mike Ahern are two of Indianapolis' most recognized anchors (right).

IBM Corporation

THE FASTEST-GROWING SEGMENT OF IBM CORPORATION IS not hardware anymore—it's services and solutions. And with 1,000 employees, two recent acquisitions, and an extensive client list, the Indianapolis office of IBM is one of the largest technology companies in central Indiana. ■ IBM was formed in 1911, and through the years, the company has transformed itself from a manufacturer of mechanical business machines to a producer of large mainframe computer systems to the commercial inventor of the personal computer and the largest information technology services company in the world. With 1998 net income of $6.3 billion on $81.7 billion in revenue, IBM remains the largest holder of technology-related patents nationwide and a leader in technology innovation.

On a local scale, that innovation demonstrates itself by creating value through people. In 1992, local IBM employees occupied 11 floors in the Bank One Building, but faced layoffs. To help prevent loss of jobs, the group became the first in the IBM family to implement an aggressive telecommuting strategy. Four hundred employees began working from home offices, reducing office space in the bank building to two floors and saving $5 million a year.

The result has been a culture that evaluates performance by results and growth in employment opportunity. IBM closed out its Bank One Tower office in fall 1999, and consolidated employees in a new building at the Precedent Office Park. The new site supports telecommuting with shared cubicles that can be reserved, team and conference rooms for meetings, a productivity center for copying, and programmable phones.

IBM has created additional value through the acquisition of two central Indiana software companies, doubling its local employee base. In 1997, the firm acquired Professional Data Management, which develops software for insurance companies, and renamed it LifePro. In 1998, IBM purchased Software Artistry, which develops help desk and customer relationship management software, and merged it into Tivoli.

Impacting the Community

IBM prides itself on its community involvement. In 1998 alone, corporate contributions totaled $116 million. Employees added another $44 million through matching gift programs, and they volunteered approximately 4 million hours of service to local causes as well.

In Indianapolis, IBM sponsors a Junior Achievement program called Exchange City for area fifth graders. Employees donate their time and the company donates the technology to create an automated model city on Virginia Avenue near downtown. Supplementary classroom materials give students six weeks of preparation for the day their class visits and runs the city.

In addition, IBM employees are Partners in Education at Indianapolis Public School 14, where they plan picnics and holiday parties, and sponsor many other activities. The company also donates about $50,000 to $75,000 worth of hardware and software equipment to area nonprofits every year.

IBM's key commitment to communities, though, is its contribution to a better economic environment that creates more jobs, and the future looks promising. "As companies get past year 2000 compliance, more resources will free up to explore e-business opportunities," says Michael W. Wiley, Indianapolis general manager. "Because IBM offers the broadest range of products and services, we believe we're the business other businesses will turn to to help them implement e-business."

IBM Corporation's building at Precedent Office Park in Indianapolis supports telecommuting with shared cubicles that can be reserved, team and conference rooms for meetings, and the latest networking and connectivity technology.

Ivy Tech State College -Central Indiana

WITH MORE THAN 8,000 STUDENTS AND 30 PROGRAM areas of study, Ivy Tech State College-Central Indiana is part of a statewide system that is the third-largest institution of higher education in the state. The college awards the associate's degree, the associate of applied science degree, and the

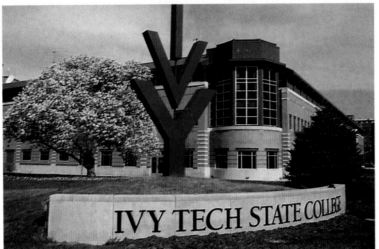

technical and career certificate. Approximately 98 percent of Ivy Tech graduates stay in central Indiana to live and work.

Instruction is based on practicality, allowing graduates to apply their classroom instruction within the central Indiana workforce. Ivy Tech instructors have worked or are presently employed in the fields they teach, in order to keep current and to provide students with exceptional insight.

"One of the greatest misconceptions about Ivy Tech is that we are simply a vocational school where students learn trades," says Dr. Meredith Carter, vice president/chancellor for Ivy Tech-Central Indiana. "Throughout its 36-year history, Ivy Tech has had one consistent mission— to help people develop a higher standard of living through both education and training. Some of our top programs include nursing, respiratory care, business administration, accounting, hospitality administration, and computers. The college also offers customized training and workforce development support for local business and industry."

Classes are offered seven days a week, and students can take courses at the main campus located at Fall Creek Parkway and Meridian Street, or at 17 sites throughout central Indiana including Avon High School, Ben Davis High School, Carmel Junior High School, Decatur Central High School, Greenfield Central High School, Belzer Middle School, Lawrence North High School, Lebanon High School, Meadows Area College in the Community, Mooresville High School, Noblesville High School, Perry Meridian Middle School, Pike High School, Blue River Career Center in Shelby-

ville, and Walker Career Center. Tuition at Ivy Tech is only $66.20 per credit hour, making it Indiana's best educational value.

Ivy Tech also offers short- or long-term customized training programs that enable central Indiana businesses to take courses in the workplace or at the main campus. Subject areas include first aid, stress management, sanitation, office skills, communications, computer training, Zenger Miller training courses, manufacturing technologies, and basic workplace education.

"We stress convenience and affordability in addition to practicality," says Carter. "Many of our students work full-time, but attend school part-time. Often, our students are single parents, so we want to offer opportunities close to home and work at an affordable price."

Additionally, Ivy Tech Foundation provides thousands of dollars in scholarships annually to those students who qualify. Ivy Tech courses and programs transfer to 35 four-year colleges and universities, including Ball State University (BSU), Indiana University-Purdue/University at Indianapolis (IUPUI), Indiana

State University (ISU), and University of Indianapolis (U of I), to name a few.

"We're seeing a significant number of students who come to Ivy Tech to take courses that will transfer to a residential college," says Carter. "Those students, whether transferring within Indiana or around the country, find that many of their courses will transfer, and a bachelor's degree or higher is the end result."

By listening and responding to central Indiana business and industry, while also serving residents in central Indiana with education and training programs, Ivy Tech is providing a strong link to economic development. "Ivy Tech is proud to be a partner in this endeavor," says Carter.

With more than 8,000 students and 30 program areas of study, Ivy Tech State College-Central Indiana is part of a statewide system that is the third-largest institution of higher education in the state. Approximately 98 percent of Ivy Tech graduates stay in central Indiana to live and work.

Ivy Tech-Central Indiana students receive practical instruction that is applicable to central Indiana's workforce.

Simon Property Group

HEADQUARTERED IN INDIANAPOLIS, SIMON PROPERTY GROUP is the country's largest owner of malls and shopping centers, and works to offer the best shopping possible— from the Forum Shops at Caesars in Las Vegas, to the Mall of America in Minneapolis, to Circle Centre in Indianapolis, to Roosevelt Field in New York. The company's

Circle Centre is a shopping and entertainment megaplex that has been the cornerstone for the revitalization of downtown Indianapolis (right).

This new food court was a key component of the renovation and expansion of Simon Property Group's Castleton Square in Indianapolis (botttom).

mission is to provide shoppers with a high-quality, friendly, and value-added shopping experience wherever they travel.

Simon traces its start in Indianapolis to Melvin Simon, a New York native stationed at Fort Benjamin Harrison in the late 1950s. When Simon's enlistment in the army was up, he found a job leasing space in strip malls. Brothers Herbert and Fred soon joined him, and the partners opened their first fully owned shopping center, Southgate Plaza in Bloomington, in 1960.

The Simon brothers invested in the enclosed mall trend early on, opening their first enclosed center in 1964 in Fort Collins, Colorado. Later that same year, they built Mounds Mall in

Anderson as the first enclosed Simon mall in the Hoosier State.

In 1993, the company completed its initial public offering and began trading on the New York Stock Exchange. Simon has since grown its portfolio threefold to become the largest publicly traded retail real estate company in North America.

Simon now owns or has an interest in more than 250 properties, amounting to 180 million square feet of gross leasable area in 36 states. Simon-owned or -managed malls attract more than 2.3 billion shopping visits annually by 100 million distinct shoppers. Total revenue in 1999 neared the $2 billion mark.

Leveraging a Reputation

Among its retail tenants, Simon has long been known for relationship building, innovation, and quality of shopping experience. The next logical step was to brand that reputation in a memorable way for shoppers. To that end, Simon introduced gift certificates in 1996, good at any of its properties nationwide, and MALLPeRKS in 1997, the industry's only national mall-shopper loyalty program. Both programs remain successful today. In 1998, gift certificates sold to the tune of $105 million, and the number of shoppers enrolled in MALLPeRKS doubled to more than 2 million.

In early 1999, Simon rolled out its next phase of branding: the Simon name coupled with the name of the mall on entry doors, parking lot banners, and signs within the malls. There's also another, more visible commitment in every Simon center—a pledge signed by each member of the mall staff "to provide superior shopping, with special amenities and incentives, in a meticulously maintained environment,

while being a responsible corporate citizen."

The company launched a signature lifestyle magazine in a unique joint venture with Time Inc. Custom Publishing. Available in Simon centers nationwide and fittingly titled *S*, the publication includes articles from Time's brands— *Sports Illustrated, Money, Parenting*, and *InStyle*— rewritten to fit Simon shopper demographics. Each monthly issue of *S* has a four-page Mall Talk section with local information on mall events, community happenings, and new store openings. With distribution at 2.2 million issues monthly, Simon is now Time Inc. Custom Publishing's largest client.

"Our research shows that most shoppers no longer just want the quick, efficient shopping trips of a few years ago," says David Simon, CEO. "They want shopping to be a little more fun. *S* magazine responds to that need, making it possible for them to take the fun of their Simon shopping experience home with them."

Leaving a Legacy

In 1998, the Simon organization established the Simon Youth Foundation, a not-for-profit organization dedicated to providing educational and career development opportunities for young people nationwide through a combination of unique efforts. First, it provides students with the opportunity to learn and receive a high school diploma in a nontraditional setting—the shopping mall. Students at these Education Resource Centers (ERCs) may also participate in internships at mall retail stores. Simon plans to install ERCs at its properties across the country. Eleven were in operation or under development by the end of 1999, including one in Indianapolis.

A natural extension of the program is Simon's Peacemaker

Corps, which is being developed with the help of the U.S. Department of Housing and Urban Development and Friends of the United Nations. It will teach young people skills for conflict resolution, violence mitigation, and tolerance.

Spawning Revitalization

Simon owns the six major malls in Indianapolis and continues to reaffirm its investment with major expansion and redevelopment programs. In 1997, Lafayette Square was completely renovated, featuring the addition of Waccamaw and a new food court with an expanded L.S. Ayres. In 1998, a major redevelopment of Castleton Square was completed with additional

small shop space, a new Galyan's store, a Von Maur department store, and an expanded L.S. Ayres.

Simon Property Group is perhaps most admired locally for its dedication to the development of a downtown mall— Circle Centre—which opened in 1995. The Simon family started talking about building a downtown mall in 1979, but it took many years and a unique partnership with the city's largest corporations to make it a reality.

"Circle Centre has absolutely been the catalyst for revitalization of downtown," says David Simon. "And that's really what we want for all of our properties—to be the right experience for their market, and to make every store profitable."

Mall of America in Minneapolis, Minnesota, is the largest enclosed shopping and entertainment complex in the United States.

Shiel Sexton Company Inc.

SHIEL SEXTON COMPANY INC.'S COMMITMENT TO ITS MISSION "TO develop a truly great construction company" has put it at the top of local construction services firms. Central to being truly great is the company's absolute refusal to lose a customer. ■ "Our underlying goal has always been 100 percent customer satisfaction. Our project management teams are focused on learning and responding to the unique requirements of each of our customers," says Andrew K. Shiel, who became president of Shiel Sexton Company in 1989 upon the retirement of his father, company cofounder Richard C. Shiel. "The best way to achieve 100 percent customer satisfaction is to be a specialist in our customers' business. That's why we concentrate on attracting, retaining, and training the industry's best talent in each of the market sectors in which we operate."

Customer-Focused

It's a philosophy that works. Since 1992, the company has doubled its workforce to 210 and tripled sales to a projected $150 million for 1999. Most of Shiel Sexton's customers are locally based, but the company often handles projects for clients all over the Midwest and beyond. "Our goal is to satisfy our clients' contracting needs wherever they may be," Shiel explains.

Key relationships developed in the 1970s with Marsh Supermarkets and Roche Diagnostics Corporation (formerly Boehringer Mannheim Corporation) have contributed to that growth and provide examples of Shiel's philosophy in action. Shiel Sexton built Marsh's corporate headquarters in Fishers, just north of Indianapolis, and many of its supermarkets throughout the state. It also constructed one of Roche's first Indianapolis buildings and has continued to construct the company's facilities ever since.

The EMMIS Communications headquarters on Monument Circle is a more recent Shiel Sexton project and one of the most visible to date. The recent Federal Express expansion at Indianapolis International Airport is the firm's largest single project. Currently, Shiel Sexton is working on another landmark corporate headquarters for Anthem Inc. (Anthem Blue Cross Blue Shield).

In addition to Shiel Sexton's prominence in commercial construction, the company is building on recent successes in health care and education. The Education Group recently completed the first new Catholic urban school in the United States in 40 years, Holy Angels School, which opened to students in fall 1999. In fall 1997, the company completed St. Simon school in the Geist Reservoir vicinity in northeast Indianapolis. The chief financial officer for the Indianapolis archdiocese was quoted in the *Indianapolis Business Journal* as saying that Shiel Sexton was awarded the contract because "they did their homework. They understood the customer better than anyone else." Other current clients include DePauw and Butler universities and Cathedral and Chatard high schools.

The Healthcare Group recently completed the Com-

Clockwise from top:
In 1999, Shiel Sexton Company Inc. completed construction on EMMIS Communications' world headquarters, which houses seven radio stations as well as the publishing offices for *Indianapolis Monthly*. A total of 25 state-of-the-art radio studios are located in the building, with two located directly on the ground floor facing Monument Circle.

Marsh Supermarkets Inc.'s corporate headquarters in Fishers, Indiana, is only one of the numerous buildings Shiel Sexton has constructed for Marsh Supermarkets since its first project for the company in 1974.

Shiel Sexton constructed the F.W. Olin Biological Sciences Building, as well as many other projects, for DePauw University in Greencastle, Indiana.

prehensive Advanced Medical Cardiology Unit and the linear accelerator project for Clarian Health.

When cofounder Timothy J. Sexton retired in 1996, Shiel used the opportunity to better position the company for a successful future by expanding the role of partner Michael T. Dilts, president, and by bringing on board a new partner, Brian J. Sullivan, executive vice president. "Allowing nonfamily to participate in management and ownership of the firm is a very significant change for us," Shiel concedes, "but it is critical for succession planning and growth."

A work philosophy that values family and community remains evident. The management team encourages both, maintaining that such involvement makes more well-rounded employees. Many Shiel Sexton employees coach sports teams and are fundraisers and volunteers for their children's schools. Employees can be found ringing bells for the Salvation Army during the Christmas season and supporting the company's many not-for-profit customers.

Motivation

One of the company's guiding principles says a lot about the company's culture: The firm believes work should be fun and personally satisfying. "We recognized a long time ago the relationship between enjoying your job and performance. That's why we go to great lengths to understand employees as individuals, and to create an environment that is fun and supportive," notes Shiel. "There are a lot of things that can be done with benefits, technology, and the office itself."

In February 2000, the company moved its headquarters to a renovated downtown building that will be close to the Indianapolis Central Canal, a major new public amenity.

Judging by the multitude of satisfied clients and the physical legacy of the buildings throughout the area, Shiel Sexton has made a lasting contribution to both the industry and the local community.

Clockwise from top:
(From left) Michael T. Dilts, Brian J. Sullivan, and Andrew K. Shiel, owners of Shiel Sexton, are committed to the corporate mission, "to develop a truly great construction company."

Renovated in 1996, the historic Murat Centre gave Indianapolis a new stage to host concerts, Broadway shows, and a variety of other live performances.

The renovation of the Children's Museum of Indianapolis included the addition of restaurants, a dining area, and a museum store.

Carr Metal Products, Inc.

FOR MORE THAN THREE DECADES, CARR METAL PRODUCTS, INC. (CMP) has quietly been developing and manufacturing products that enhance the quality of life. The early days of the company were defined by the partnership between E.L. Carr and Bernie B. Berry Jr., who had combined their tool and die experience. After Carr died, Berry purchased the assets of the company and pursued new avenues of opportunity.

Armed with design skill and a degree from Purdue University, Berry set forth to chart a course for Carr Metal Products. His creative talents led to many endeavors in various commercial and industrial environments. A common thread through these opportunities was the concept of providing customers with engineered solutions and precision manufacturing.

The company prospered through this commitment, which brought on the early stages of growth, thus requiring additional space and employees. During these years, Berry continued his passion for innovative solutions, and many of these ideas were protected through patents. Berry's son, Berry III, graduated from Purdue University in 1975 and decided to take an apprenticeship in his father's company. In 1985, CMP announced that Bernie B. Berry III would become president, and as such would direct the company's activities and growth strategies.

Adopting new technology for processing precision sheet metal parts faster and more accurately made Carr Metal Products, Inc. (CMP) one of the first companies in Indiana to enter into new laser-cutting technology.

New Horizons

Carr Metal Products realized that superior customer service alone was not the key to continued growth in the sheet metal fabricating market. Berry III decided to explore new technology for processing precision sheet metal parts faster and more accurately. This exploration made Carr Metal Products one of the first companies in Indiana to employ a computerized turret press and enter into new laser-cutting technology. The acquisition of this high-speed, precision punching and cutting equipment positioned Carr Metal Products advantageously for future opportunities. In conjunction with the fabricating equipment enhancements, Carr Metal Products also invested in the newly developed computer aided design (CAD) system to design and fabricate products efficiently.

Investments in technology and quality systems are evident everywhere within the company, from the manufacturing floor to the Quality Control Department. Carr Metal Products was one of the first 10 companies in the country to purchase a computer-

Carr Metal Products develops and manufactures products that enhance the quality of life.

controlled flat sheet inspection system. This equipment allows the Inspection Department to compare the sheet metal component to the original CAD drawing, greatly reducing inspection times. The company has introduced computerized, three-dimensional inspection to its final inspection process, providing 100 percent inspection of all its medical products.

In early 1994, Berry III realized that the company's quality management system was antiquated and would have to be replaced. The company elected to pursue a quality system that was just emerging in the United States—ISO 9000. The ISO quality management system is internationally recognized. Carr Metal Products began a very aggressive ISO 9001 implementation schedule, and was awarded certification in December 1994, joining a group of registered companies in the United States totaling fewer than 5,000.

Market Creation

Northern Indiana is often considered the orthopedic capital of the world. Carr Metal Products' strategic location in Indianapolis led to an opportunity for the company to assist its customers in the design and manufacture of a new concept—special sterilizing cases and trays. Sterilization procedures for processing medical instruments and implantable material was routinely performed by placing the components in a stainless steel basket and wrapping them in sterile cloths; the sterile packages would then be opened in the operating room. The combined development effort launched a new technology and a fundamental shift in the operating procedures of the past.

Carr Metal Products pioneered the concept of screen-printing the graphic representations of instruments and part numbers for positive identification. This, coupled with an order of use layout, has become a standard in the industry. The benefits of this type of packaging include the ability to perform a quick visual scan confirming that all essential components are present. It also assures an improved efficiency in performing procedures.

Calling Indianapolis Home

Carr Metal Products is a worldwide leader in the design, development, and manufacture of precision sheet metal and plastic fabrications. Carr Metal Product's continued growth has seen the company expand from a one-room operation to a manufacturing complex that spans two modern buildings and 100,000 square feet.

The company believes Indianapolis offers a strategic advantage. The city's diverse labor resources have contributed to Carr Metal Product's outstanding employee base of excellent craftsmen. Says Berry III, "Indianapolis is the crossroads of America and as such, allows Carr Metal Products to provide close support to our in-state orthopedic customers north of us and industrial customers—such as Cummins— to the south or any point east to west. I believe our city and the talents of the people in this city are often underestimated. These men and women are Carr Metal Products greatest asset. Carr Metal Products is proud to call Indianapolis home."

Carr Metal Products uses the latest technology in most areas of fabrication, including laser cutting.

Carr Metal Products was one of the first 10 companies in the country to purchase a computer-controlled flat sheet inspection system (left).

The company has introduced computerized, three-dimensional inspection to its final inspection process, providing 100 percent inspection of all its medical products (right).

Pacers Sports &
Entertainment Corporation

IN A STATE WHERE BASKETBALL RULES, THE POWER OF THE HOME COURT advantage is a strong one indeed. When the Indiana Pacers moved to Conseco Fieldhouse in fall 1999, the team gained the competitive edge to play at full force. ■ "The state of Indiana has a unique history and tradition in basketball," says Donnie Walsh, Pacers Sports & Entertainment Corporation president. "We built Conseco Fieldhouse to reflect that history and tradition."

More than a few visitors have noted the arena's resemblance to Butler University's Hinkle Fieldhouse, built in 1928 and long considered the temple of Indiana college and high school basketball. Now, Hoosier professional basketball has an equally impressive house of worship at a time when performance of and pride in the NBA Pacers have never been better.

The Road to Excellence

The Indiana Pacers have had three homes in their history and have played in two leagues. When the franchise was founded in 1967, it was as a charter member in the American Basketball Association (ABA). Its home court was the Indiana State Fairgrounds Coliseum.

During its nine-year tenure in the ABA, the club posted seven winning seasons and captured three ABA championships, moving to its second home in Market Square Arena in 1974. When the ABA merged with the NBA in 1976, the Pacers were one of four ABA franchises to cross over.

The team became one of the NBA's top clubs in the mid-1990s. When favorite son Larry Bird retired from professional play with the Boston Celtics and returned home as head coach of the Pacers in 1997, the Pacers won 58 games and reached the Eastern Conference finals. The Pacers have gone to the finals four times in a six-year period.

Home, Sweet Home

Ground was broken for the franchise's current home in 1997. The $183 million, 750,000-square-foot Conseco Fieldhouse is at once a tribute to Indiana's basketball heritage and its engineering technology, exceeding all requirements of the Americans with Disabilities Act. With 18,500 seats, including 69 suites and 2,400 club seats, the facility has all the amenities—from 71 rest rooms with a total of 570 fixtures to 54 concession stands with 106 points of sale.

Some 1,200 workers labored more than two years to build the 14-story, 6.2-acre facility, using 600,000 bricks, 1,800 pieces of limestone totaling 660 tons, 2,600 tons of roof steel, 58,000 square feet of glass, and 38,000 miles of cable. Features such as the glass curtain walls, the grand staircase, and 3,860-pound, hand-carved basketball in the Home Court Team Store are reminiscent of an upscale shopping mall.

That's not surprising, considering Pacers owners Melvin and Herbert Simon are also co-chairmen of Simon Property Group, an Indianapolis-based real estate development and management company that owns or has interest in nearly 230 shopping centers nationwide, including the six major malls in the city.

"Local owners who are personally involved in downtown redevelopment will make all the difference as Pacers Sports & Entertainment fields a Women's NBA team in summer 2000 and considers other opportunities for growth," Walsh says.

Team spirit has spurred community development over the years, resulting in an even greater home court advantage. For fans and investors alike, the Pacers have proven to be a true asset for the state of Indiana, and Indianapolis in particular.

When the Indiana Pacers moved to Conseco Fieldhouse in fall 1999, the team gained the competitive edge to play at full force. With 18,500 seats, including 69 suites and 2,400 club seats, the $183 million, 750,000-square-foot Conseco Fieldhouse is at once a tribute to Indiana's basketball heritage and its engineering technology.

FOUNDED IN 1971, THE INDIANA HAND CENTER IS A WORLD LEADER in the treatment and rehabilitation of the hand, wrist, elbow, and shoulder. The center's 42,000-square-foot main office adjacent to St.Vincent Hospital includes 18 patient examination rooms, an outpatient surgery center, and occupational and physical therapy services. The medical

staff treats patients at five other Indianapolis locations, as well as at additional offices throughout central Indiana.

Hand surgeons include James B. Steichen, M.D.; William B. Kleinman, M.D.; Hill Hastings II, M.D.; Richard S. Idler, M.D.; Thomas J. Fischer, M.D.; James J. Creighton Jr., M.D.; Alexander D. Mih, M.D.; Robert M. Baltera, M.D.; Jeffrey A. Greenberg, M.D.; and Thomas W. Kiesler, M.D.

The Indiana Hand Center surgeons have pioneered innovative techniques and developed equipment used around the world in the care and treatment of the upper extremity. Specialists treat conditions ranging from severe birth defects to hand, wrist, elbow, or shoulder dysfunction caused by work environment, arthritis, or severe injury caused by accidents of all varieties.

The Indiana Hand Center surgeons are world recognized not only for their expertise in medical care, but also for their innovation in the development of specialized surgical equipment and procedures. They lecture and teach techniques to physicians and medical students throughout the world. In addition, the physicians have collectively published more than 700 scientific papers or book chapters and nine textbooks.

In order to provide patients with disease and treatment educational information, The Indiana Hand Center has created an award-winning Web site, located at www.indianahandcenter.com.

Fellowship Program

In addition, The Indiana Hand Center physicians share their expertise and knowledge through a fellowship program accredited by the Accreditation Council for Graduate Medical Education.

Through this program, six fully trained orthopedic or plastic surgeons are selected annually to receive advanced specialty training in upper extremity and microvascular surgery. The fellowship program is one year in length. To date, there are more than 120 Indiana Hand Center Fellows practicing upper extremity medicine throughout the world.

Rehabilitation

The Indiana Hand Center is also home of The Hand Rehabilitation Center, a leading provider of physical and occupational therapy. This program helps individuals use conservative treatment and/or regain strength and flexibility after medical treatment. Most of the therapists are certified hand therapists, having received advanced treatment in physical therapy of the upper extremity.

Workers' Compensation

More than one-third of The Indiana Hand Center's patients are workers who have been injured on the job. The center has a sophisticated workers' compensation program that works with employers, case managers, and patients to return employees to their jobs as quickly as possible. The Center for Working Hands provides occupational rehabili-

tation in a worklike environment, helping patients learn how to complete their tasks without additional injury.

The Indiana Hand Center is recognized throughout the world as a leading provider of medical care for the entire arm—from the shoulder to the fingertips.

The Indiana Hand Center provides complete care for conditions ranging from common dysfunctions to complex injuries.

Bindley Western Industries, Inc.

WHEN THE PRESIDENT OF THE UNITED STATES GETS prescription medication, it likely comes from Bindley Western Industries, Inc. (BWI), an Indianapolis-based distributor of pharmaceuticals and related health care products throughout the country. Its customers are retail drugstores, chain warehouses, health care providers, and various federal and state agencies.

With nearly 9 percent of the total market share, BWI is the fifth-largest distributor of pharmaceuticals in the United States. Since its founding in 1968, the company has experienced compounded annual growth of 20 percent. Annual sales are more than $8 billion, with about 40 percent of company revenue generated from bulk deliveries to chain warehouses and 60 percent from deliveries directly to stores and other health care providers.

The company's inventory list today exceeds 50,000 items and includes nonperishable foods and health and beauty aids as well as pharmaceuticals. In 1998, the company spun off a Florida subsidiary, Priority Healthcare Corporation, which provides specialty pharmaceuticals and disease treatment services to office-based physicians, outpatient renal dialysis centers, and home care markets.

Entrepreneurship and Keen Understanding

Chairman and CEO William E. Bindley started the company in 1968 in Terre Haute with $50,000 of his own money and a keen understanding of cash flow. He elected not to go into the family business, known as E.H. Bindley & Company, a century-old drug wholesaler, because he wanted to do something new. Drugstore chains were just beginning to develop, and Bindley was interested in providing dock-to-dock distribution services to them. Because his family's business focused on independent store owners, he wouldn't be in competition.

"I wasn't able to borrow any money from the bank," he says. "They just didn't understand my business plan." With his family's blessing and his headquarters located in the basement of one of the family's warehouses, Bindley scraped together the money he needed by selling the equity in his Terre Haute home and some other development property.

Indiana drugstore legend Bud Hook, father of the Hook's Drug Store chain that eventually joined with CVS Corporation, also helped Bindley. "Bud let me get inside Hook's and do a study of how they were buying and warehousing pharma-

Bindley Western Industries, Inc. (BWI) began public trading on the New York Stock Exchange in 1995. Representing the company on that first day are (from left) Richard Grasso, chairman and CEO, New York Stock Exchange; William Bindley, chairman and CEO, BWI; and Thomas Salentine, executive vice president and CFO, BWI.

BWI's state-of-the-art communications center is located at the company's headquarters building in Indianapolis (left).

Customer orders are picked, packed, and shipped for next-day delivery thoughout the night at BWI's 18 distribution facilities (right).

ceuticals," he says. "I came up with a program where I could buy products at better prices and provide better turnaround and better service." That's where managing the margins came in. Instead of venture capital to finance his plan, he turned to what he called vendor capital. "Vendor capital is free. I knew if I got paid by my customers faster than I had to pay my vendors, I would have the use of that money between those payment dates. So, the more I sold, the more cash I would have. That's exactly how I financed the business until it went public in 1983."

The company began marketing to independent drugstores after Bindley's father retired and sold the family business in 1979. It currently markets a point-of-sale program called First Choice for Value to more than 1,000 independent pharmacies; the program includes private-label products, signage, product jackets, newspaper circulars, and anything else the store might need to compete with the chains.

Valued Employees, Valuing Customers

Bindley attributes BWI's success, in part, to an emphasis on service and strong relation-ships with customers, which often opens the door to new business. He says he learned that from his father. But automation and its impact on efficiency make a difference as well. Leading-edge computerization at the company's 18 locations throughout the country provides the tools to replenish inventories without costly warehousing. Ordering is done from either a handheld electronic order entry device or BWI's personalized, PC-based customer order system, and payment is handled through electronic funds transfer. System accuracy means that BWI doesn't need to stock vast quantities at great expense, but instead can turn over a smaller inventory much more often compared to the industry average of eight.

"We have the lowest general administration costs of any of our competitors," says Keith Burks, president since 1990. "That level of service pays for itself in happy customers and fosters an environment where customers develop positive relationships with distribution employees. When it comes to competing, we've tried to differentiate ourselves by being a large company with a lot of resources that is also more personal, flexible, and customer-focused."

The company understands the link between happy employees and happy customers, and has used stock options as incentives, with insiders owning about 29 percent of shares. According to Burks, BWI is one company in which employees can build a career, no matter where they start. He began his career at BWI in 1977 in Terre Haute, working part-time in the warehouse while going to college, and even helped move boxes when the company transferred its operations to Indianapolis in 1979.

Burks, who became president in 1990 at the age of 31, predicts continued growth for BWI, citing Health Care Financing Administration statistics that predict a 9.6 percent increase in prescription drug spending from 1996 to 2007, to $171 billion, and a 6.8 percent increase in health care spending, to $2.1 trillion. "Our overriding mission has always been to lower the cost of health care while improving patient care. When we can do that while also enhancing shareholder value and building customer and vendor partnerships, we'll expand our reach," says Burks.

Goelzer Investment Management

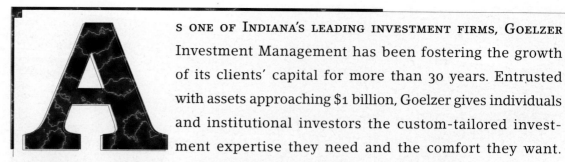

A S ONE OF INDIANA'S LEADING INVESTMENT FIRMS, GOELZER Investment Management has been fostering the growth of its clients' capital for more than 30 years. Entrusted with assets approaching $1 billion, Goelzer gives individuals and institutional investors the custom-tailored investment expertise they need and the comfort they want.

Don W. Goelzer founded the firm in 1969. Since then, the name Goelzer has proved to be synonymous with trust, prudent investment advice, professionalism, and the highest level of personalized service.

A Tradition of Trust

Goelzer was initially established as an Indianapolis-based investment banking firm providing traditional brokerage, business valuations, and related financial advisory services. Early to respond to the financial needs of clients who require advanced portfolio management services, the firm became a registered investment adviser in 1981.

The firm continues to build on its founding principle—developing trust and forging long-term relationships with clients. Goelzer's disciplined investment process and client-focused portfolio strategies have provided more than 450 clients in 28 states with capital preservation and growth while avoiding undue risk.

Goelzer supports clients with a financially strong and well-capitalized corporate structure. This solid foundation gives the firm outstanding investment management capabilities and ensures superior service to advisory clients. Goelzer's continuity and stability have allowed the firm to weather many market cycles with consistency, delivering excellent investment performance. Dedication to professionalism and confidentiality has given Goelzer a reputation for unquestioned reliability and integrity in the investment industry.

Personal Involvement

Viewing each client relationship as a partnership, Goelzer has made exceptional, personalized service the cornerstone of the firm's success. This service begins with a personalized analysis designed to help both Goelzer's investment professionals and the client understand individual financial goals and desires. This protocol allows Goelzer to work intimately with each client to establish well-defined investment goals and objectives.

Each client represents an individual relationship, and every portfolio is customized to conform to the client's investment objectives and risk tolerances. The firm believes the manner in which a portfolio manager personally handles individual accounts—along with proficiency in proactive client contact—is the key to a successful advisory relationship.

A Wealth of Knowledge

Goelzer's professionals combine more than 300 years of investment experience with an extensive research process and sound investment philosophy. The firm's unique blend of history, stability, and seasoned professionals positions Goelzer for success in today's volatile investment environment. Sound decision-making processes and in-depth economic analysis provide a solid competitive edge for the company's clients.

Goelzer works within the framework of a well-defined investment policy established by its Investment Policy Committee, which is comprised of senior investment officers and portfolio managers. The committee makes sound investment decisions by combining the investment knowledge of its professionals with extensive internal and external research.

As the 21st century unfolds, Goelzer is positioned to increase its professional staff to accommodate new growth, thus providing exceptional investment advice and personalized service to its clients. The firm will continue to build wealth for clients using whatever new opportunities the future brings, never forgetting its commitment to preserving and growing its clients' capital.

Personalized attention for each Goelzer Investment Management client starts with an experienced senior investment officer or portfolio manager (top).

Goelzer Investment Management works within the framework of a well-defined policy established by its Investment Policy Committee, which is comprised of senior investment officers and portfolio managers, including (seated from left) Fred Cuthbert, Walter Gross, Brett McKamey, Don Goelzer, (standing from left) George Cassiere, Neal Smith, and Greg Goelzer (bottom).

LESLIE MCGUIRE PHOTOGRAPHY

LESLIE MCGUIRE PHOTOGRAPHY

GOELZER INVESTMENT BANKING HAS BEEN CONDUCTING investment banking activities, including performing business valuations, structuring transactions, selling businesses, and raising capital, since Don W. Goelzer founded the firm in 1969. Today, it is among the Midwest's most active business valuation firms. Business and partnership valuations are completed for clients in a variety of industries for tax, corporate finance, and litigation matters. Goelzer also acts as financial adviser to numerous established employee stock ownership plans (ESOP), as well as those in the process of being formed. Like many of its clients, Goelzer is also an employee-owned company.

A Rich History of Experience

The firm has a formidable history of representing companies and their shareholders in diverse investment banking roles. During the past several years, Goelzer has assisted numerous private companies in an effort to merge with or be acquired by public companies. It has also facilitated other sales of businesses, leveraged buyouts, leveraged ESOPs, and recapitalizations. Additionally, Goelzer raises debt and equity for companies to support internal growth. The firm is also a leading provider of fairness opinions supporting transactions.

An impartial, unbiased opinion is often essential in cases requiring a subjective value judgment. Goelzer goes to great lengths to ensure confidentiality and maintain an objective posture in addressing the needs of clients.

Additionally, the firm's professionals bring a wealth of experience to bear in addressing client needs. Cumulatively, professional members of the Goelzer Investment Banking team have been providing valuation and financial advisory services to the business community for more than a century.

Full-Service Investment Banking

Goelzer provides a wide variety of investment banking, business valuation, ESOP, and corporate financial advisory services. The firm's experience and knowledge help clients consider a corporate finance transaction, identify alternatives, and analyze the risk/reward profile of each option. Goelzer also advises corporations on divestitures, management incentive programs, financing alternatives, and exit strategies.

The company is highly regarded and active in the area of estate and gift tax valuations, and routinely renders opinions of value for other tax matters. Goelzer's valuations have supported and facilitated the consummation of numerous and diverse corporate finance transactions. Moreover, attorneys, arbitrators, and mediators have repeatedly entrusted Goelzer to aid them and their clients in their respective litigation or mediation matters.

Goelzer is an expert in the use of ESOPs as a benefit plan, an ownership transition device, and a corporate finance tool. The firm has worked with scores of companies that have consummated ESOP transactions in recent years. Goelzer's in-depth knowledge of the laws and current issues facing the ESOP community enables the firm's clients to develop innovative ESOP structures.

Goelzer has demonstrated the ability to get to the heart of an issue, organize the challenge into a readily understandable report, and offer answers and solutions based on solid analytical skills gained through many years of experience.

Goelzer is located in the Bank One Center in downtown Indianapolis, overlooking historic Monument Circle (left).

George Cassiere (left) and Don Goelzer serve as managing directors of Goelzer Investment Banking (right).

D.B. Mann Development

OFFERING A COMPLETE APPROACH TO REAL ESTATE DEVELOPMENT and management, D.B. Mann Development has created a niche in the central Indiana commercial real-estate industry. The firm provides a total package that combines acquisition, design, development, construction, leasing, sales, and property management. Established in 1970 as a commercial real estate development company, D.B. Mann has expanded its expertise to include office, retail, industrial, and single-family residential development. Today, the firm has more than 1 million square feet of commercial space under its ownership and has been responsible for a dozen quality residential communities in the Greater Indianapolis area.

A History of Family Ownership

The firm started as Mann Realty Company, a family-owned partnership operated by Jerry and Edna Mann and their children Terri, Dave, and Brian. ATEC Associates, another Mann-owned business, specializing in geotechnical, materials, and environmental engineering, sparked Jerry Mann's com-

D.B. Mann Development residential developments are designed around a central community park, and usually include amenities such as a swimming pool, a cabana, a playground, and tennis and basketball courts. The developments provide housing opportunities in a broad spectrum of markets, including single-family homes from entry-level to $450,000, custom homes.

mercial construction ambition. Mann Realty Company aided ATEC's growth by constructing and leasing back commercial buildings for its business use. The company's first speculative project was Hawthorn Park in Indianapolis, one of the area's first mixed-use office-warehouse parks, constructed in 1972.

The Manns' oldest son, Dave, joined the firm in the early 1980s, prompting a company name change to D.B. Mann Development and the company's full-time concentration in the real estate development industry. Son Brian and daughter Terri also joined the firm as full-time partners in the 1990s. ATEC was subsequently sold in 1996, although D.B. Mann still owns and leases buildings back to the new owner.

The company still reflects a family atmosphere in its management style and its concern for its tenants and clients. D.B. Mann has long-term relationships with many original tenants that date back to the 1970s. The flexibility of D.B. Mann's properties allows companies to grow, expand, and change without the hassle of a major relocation. The company continues to build more buildings and diversify its properties, making it possible to fulfill its tenants' expansion and growth needs. "If D.B. Mann owns the property, as a tenant you are never far from a decision maker," says Brian Mann. "You are always dealing with the owners, and we value the long-term benefit of keeping tenants happy."

Specialists in Office-Warehouse Parks

D.B. Mann specializes in office and low-rise industrial flexible-space buildings, organized in parks or developments. Most often, these are single-story spaces with to-the-door parking, private entrances, custom-built interiors, and truck docks. Mann was one of the first commercial developers in Indianapolis to make buildings of this type look less industrial, promoting the flex space concept for offices through the use of more glass, tile accents, and glass canopies.

The firm's strategy has been to secure highly visible sites with superior transportation access and to offer general contractor services in the construction of buildings and the finishing of interiors to client specifications. Some of D.B. Mann's recent office/flex projects are Parkside, Pendleton Trade Center, and Bash Business Center, which include facilities for Union Federal Savings Bank, United Parcel Service, Sears, Community Hospital, and Topics Newspapers.

In the late 1980s, D.B. Mann entered the retail sector of commercial development by introducing Pyramid Place Shoppes in College Park. Its success spurred the company's growth into larger regional centers. Recent retail projects include Sunnyside Shoppes, Pyramid North, and Fishers Trade Center with tenants such as Kroger, Kmart, McDonald's, and Blockbuster Video. For 2000, indications are for continued growth in the explosive Indianapolis retail market.

Residential Development

In 1985, D.B. Mann developed its first residential development, Pine Springs, located in Lawrence, Indiana. Since entering the residential development arena, the firm has acquired, planned, or developed more than 1,000 acres of land and more than 3,500 dwelling units with communities in Indianapolis, Fishers, Decatur, and Noblesville. The company's residential developments have been designed to provide housing opportunities in a broad spectrum of markets. Projects include single-family homes from entry-level to $450,000, custom homes. Residential developments are designed around a central community park, and usually include amenities such as a swimming pool, a cabana, a playground, and tennis and basketball courts.

Currently, D.B. Mann is working on Summerbrook, a 450-acre, mixed-use community in Madison County near the Interstate 69 Exit 14 interchange. Summerbrook is a planned community, with residential, retail, commercial, and light industrial uses as part of the project. The concept of the design is to allow people to live and work in close proximity. Approximately 250 acres having

interstate frontage are primarily commercial and industrial, with an area reserved for community services, such as a fire station, a library, and community meeting rooms.

Creating the Future

"Wherever our projects take us, we strive to meet the concerns of the local community, because we know that our developments will be around for a long time, long after we're gone," says Dave Mann. "We're not just developing home sites and office parks, we're creating communities where people will live and work for many generations to come. We will continue to grow because we take our business very personally and try to make our developments a community advantage for all. I am very proud of that fact."

D.B. Mann's recent projects include Parkside, Pendleton Trade Center, and Stony Ridge.

Heritage Environmental Services

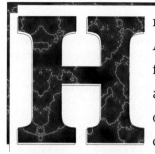

HERITAGE ENVIRONMENTAL SERVICES WAS QUIETLY CLEANING UP America long before environmental stewardship became fashionable or even mandated. Today, the company operates a nationwide network of service facilities for the management of bulk and containerized wastes, and offers services that include environmental engineering and consulting, property cleanup, industrial maintenance, laboratory testing, waste transport, and on-site waste management.

An Idea That Paid Off

The firm began operating out of its west Indianapolis facility more than 20 years ago, but its origins go back 30 years to when it emerged as a division of a Columbus, Indiana, road-building company that was established in 1968. That company was looking for ways to use its key employees during winter months when road projects tapered off. After investigating several options, the company turned to oil recovery, using oil it reclaimed in winter activities to fuel asphalt plants in the summer when road-building work increased. The growing environmental awareness in society motivated Heritage to treat its waste more extensively than the law required, and that brought about the realization that this treatment was a service other companies would pay Heritage to perform. The company found there was a real opportunity for ingenuity in this field; tapping this market was the challenge that followed.

Today, Heritage recovers more than 50 million gallons of used oil each year. It is the largest privately held, comprehensive environmental company in the United States, and its commercial laboratory is the largest in the Midwest and one of the largest in the nation. The laboratory is nationally recognized and provides industrial, municipal, and engineering clients with precise assessments of drinking water, wastewater, waste oils, and other solid and hazardous wastes. Nearly half of Heritage's 1,000 employees work out of the 75-acre Indianapolis location.

Heritage has the best compliance record in the business and sets the industry standard for judging environmental service. It remains the only U. S. waste company with multiple sites and no substantive environmental issues—quite a feat, considering that Heritage routinely cleans up after the world's top industrial companies and largest waste generators.

Creative Solutions

About 50 percent of Heritage's $150 million in revenues in 1999 came from waste treatment and disposal. Even so, its future strategy focuses on finding more creative ways to solve industry problems.

The company already has a number of patented waste

Heritage Environmental Services' flagship treatment facility is located in Indianapolis.

A field services division provides demolition, decontamination, property cleanup, industrial cleaning, and ground-water remediation services at customer sites.

treatment methods—most notably, a proprietary process for neutralizing cyanide prior to disposal—but finds the greatest opportunity when it can minimize use of its landfill. "The real opportunities in this industry involve getting people out of the landfill business completely, because it is the only way to limit long-term liability," explains President Ken Price.

In other words, the company is finding ways to reuse or reprocess waste streams. For example, Heritage is working on a method to recover zinc from electric arc furnace dust produced by the steel industry. This is the single largest dry waste stream generated in the United States; however, most recycling methods for it have failed to gain acceptance because of the high cost. While straight treatment and disposal is still the most affordable option, Heritage is working on a method it believes will change that.

"All our customers want to be environmentalists, but there's a financial limit," Price says. "The process we're developing is more than cost competitive with treatment and disposal. The lab work is finished, and we're in the process of doing a pilot program."

Innovation and Full Service

Heritage routinely puts a large percentage of its gross sales back into research and development, outpacing most other environmental service companies. It also differentiates itself from competitors through single point-of-contact project chemists with an average experience level of more than 20 years, state-of-the-art instrumentation, and a computer system that provides customers with round-the-clock, on-line data access and reporting flexibility.

Through its transport division, Heritage provides complete waste transfer services across the nation with a fleet of more than 200 vehicles that are equipped to move liquids, corrosives, solids, and containers. Its Heritage Crystal Clean division provides commercial and industrial parts washer services, including small-quantity drum pickup.

A field services division provides demolition, decontamination, property cleanup, industrial cleaning, and groundwater remediation services at customer sites. "Even though more and more waste generators have developed the ability to treat their own wastes, if it starts to take the focus away from the real business operation, companies can call us in as outsourcers to manage those on-site facilities," Price explains. "With our technology, expertise, and research group, we can bring some very dynamic programs to a customer site while also reducing costs to our clients."

On-site services include emergency response for plant explosions, truck rollovers, train derailments, spills, and other incidents. A research and development arm supports all aspects of field services, with the aim of developing marketable products from wastes, offsetting cleanup costs.

"The majority of remediation projects do not result in a market-ready product, and the ones that do are in early development stages and not ready for public disclosure," Price emphasizes. "However, those currently in development may eventually allow the responsible party to, in effect, clean up a site for free."

Harnessing the environmental stewardship of large waste-producing companies and providing a range of services and solutions noted for their ingenuity, Heritage Environmental Services can capitalize on the creation of a cleaner and safer environment now and in the years to come.

As part of the company's full roster of services, Heritage technicians unpack chemicals for processing.

Associated Builders and Contractors of Indiana

ASSOCIATED BUILDERS AND CONTRACTORS (ABC) IS THE ONLY national construction management association devoted exclusively to promoting and defending the open/merit shop form of construction. It represents more than 20,000 construction and construction-related firms in more than 80 chapters across the United States. Headquartered in Indianapolis, the Indiana chapter includes 450 firms. Indiana ABC members are organized into six councils according to geography, and include general contractors and construction managers, specialty and trade subcontractors, suppliers of construction materials, and professional firms.

"Collectively, ABC members promote cost-effectiveness and productivity in the construction industry through elimination of costly work rules," says J. R. Gaylor, Indiana executive director. "They also fight for the awarding of contracts based on the lowest responsible bid and/or the merit of the bidder."

The Merit Shop Philosophy

ABC was established in 1950, when seven Maryland contractors met to counter organizing by local unions. They invented the term merit shop to describe their philosophy of free enterprise, which emphasized the right of the construction firm to manage and the right of employees to be rewarded based on achievement.

The organization has become one of the fastest-growing construction associations in the country. While only 30 percent of the nation's construction was performed merit shop in 1970, the method currently accounts for more than 75 percent of all construction in the United States. Although only six of the top 400 construction firms nationwide were ABC members in 1970, today more than half are members.

With the support of national and state staffs, ABC provides representation at all levels of government. Full-time government relations experts in Washington, D.C., monitor legislation that could affect the construction industry and work to secure pro-merit shop regulations.

ABC initiated its Indiana chapter in 1973 in Fort Wayne. The state headquarters moved to Indianapolis in 1976, but maintains a staffed office in Fort Wayne as well. State meetings are held monthly within the six Indiana regions in order to keep members informed about developments in legislation, labor relations, safety, and education.

Members have access to legal counsel on labor relations, membership directory and referral, comprehensive group health insurance for employees and their families, and administered pension plans, as well as the quarterly *Hoosier Contractor* magazine and the bimonthly *Merit Messenger* newsletter.

Emphasis on Education

Through the National Center for Construction Education, ABC is one of the country's leading providers of craft training. The U.S. Department of Labor's Bureau of Apprenticeship and Training has certified Indiana ABC programs in 14 different crafts.

In Indiana classes, the highest enrollments are in electrical, carpentry, metal building assembly, plumbing, pipe fitting, sheet metal, and roofing, as well as heating, ventilation, and air-conditioning. Classes are held at five training sites across the state, and most programs involve four years of combined classroom learning and on-the-job training. ABC provides journeyman instructors for the class-

The Associated Builders and Contractors (ABC) of Indiana state board of directors includes (seated, from left) Chuck Bodenhafer, Bodenhafer Insurance & Investments; Doug Trolson, chapter attorney, Hoffman, Drewry, Hancock, Simmons; Barb Phillips, Gaylor Electric; State President Phil Mussallem, Electrical Staffing, Inc.; Ken Hedlund, state treasurer, Somerset Financial Services; (second row, from left) Don Wiles, Harrison & Moberly; Richard Lamb, Reddinger Constructors, Inc.; Randy Borror, Liberty Construction, Inc.; Harry Milli, Certified Floorcovering Services, Inc.; Jim Steinberger, Steinberger Construction, Inc.; Dean Hall, R. Dean Hall, Inc.; (third row, from left) Karl Meyer, Meyer Najem Corporation; Ken Neumeister, Liberty Construction, Inc.; Larry Clugh, Clugh Trucking, Inc.; John Roop, Capitol City Fence Co., Inc.; John Maidlow, Lehman's Inc. of Anderson; Kevin Berger, Easterday Construction Co., Inc.; and Scott Hoeppner, Hoeppner Construction Corporation.

ABC is one of the country's leading providers of craft training.

room portion and works with member contractors to arrange on-the-job experiences.

A new initiative called School to Career takes the first-year classroom portion of the program to high school juniors and seniors. Schools can adopt the ABC curriculum, or students can take classes at an ABC night school. The association works with students to place them in paid work experience in the summer or with co-op programs during the school year. Either way, they graduate from high school ready to start the second year of training.

Thirty-five vocational programs throughout the state are already participating in School to Career. All told, ABC is training about 1,100 apprentices at any given time. More than 80 percent of those who begin ABC programs complete them.

Promoting a Career Path

ABC also provides management training classes, offering everything from four-hour seminars to extensive, 10-week courses in subjects such as job-site supervision, blueprint reading, critical path scheduling, employee motivation, and project management. These courses articulate a career path for apprentices interested in construction supervision and promote the construction industry as a source of financially rewarding careers.

ABC is the only organization to receive a safety award from the National Construction and Safety Roundtable twice for its programs. ABC's Construction Site Safety Technician program involves 100 hours of training on more than 50 safety-related topics, while its Construction Site Safety Supervisor program involves 40 hours of training designed to enhance a supervisor's ability to manage a crew safely and to oversee crew compliance with safety standards.

ABC also encourages drug testing, runs a variety of seminars on Occupational Safety and Health Administration stan-

dards, and trains all apprentices in first aid and cardiopulmonary resuscitation. ABC's code of ethics and Accredited Quality Contractor programs encourage quality work and professionalism.

In 1994, ABC members showed their commitment to the community, safe construction, and fire safety by building and donating to the Indianapolis Fire Department the Survive Alive house. This facility creates a simulated fire environment where children can learn how to survive in a fire emergency. ABC members continue to maintain all repairs and equipment for the house as well.

"We help our members grow, whether they are large, international companies or small, local firms," Gaylor says. "We also help the industry grow by ensuring merit contractors can compete freely in the marketplace. We work with our members not only to build better companies, but to build better lives."

Crossmann Communities, Inc.

MOST FIRST-TIME HOME BUYERS DREAM OF FINDING A NEW home that is both affordable and quality built. Since its beginning in 1973, Crossmann Communities, Inc. has helped thousands of families realize that dream. ■ Ranked as the largest new-home builder in Indianapolis, Crossmann's three product lines—

New American Homes, Deluxe Homes, and Trimark Homes—offer affordably priced entry-level and first move-up homes. In recent years, Crossmann has delivered more new homes in Indianapolis, Lafayette, and Fort Wayne than any other builder in Indiana.

The company's success rests on a targeted approach to building. Crossmann concentrates efforts in areas where there is significant, long-term demand for homes. Standardized products and high volume make the company's construction process more efficient, resulting in top quality at the most affordable prices.

Keys to Success

"Part of being successful stems from the people with whom you surround yourself," says President and Chief Operating Officer Richard H. Crosser. "Our contractors and suppliers are long-term, loyal partners. Many of our contractors work exclusively for our company and have been doing so for many years."

Crossmann stands behind the quality of its homes and is committed to customer service. Buyers are encouraged to visit their homes during the construction process. Inspections are conducted before buyers take possession and again at periodic intervals after they've lived in the home. Included with each new Crossmann home is a 10-year warranty from an independent warranty company. In addition, Crossmann Customer Service vans can be seen all around the Indianapolis metro area; when a new home owner needs help, the vans are ready to respond to every call.

Realizing many buyers have financial concerns, Crossmann Communities offers several unique solutions. The Nehemiah Program requires no money down from a new home buyer. Also, the Guaranteed Sale Plan offers families a way to begin building a new home before selling their current home by putting their existing equity to work.

Sales consultants for all Crossmann product lines are top-notch professionals who work closely with each customer. Flexible financing through the company's own mortgage company means sales consultants always have up-to-date information and can help each

Since its beginning in 1973, Crossmann Communities, Inc. has helped thousands of families realize the dream of owning a new home that is both affordable and quality built.

family find the right financing program.

Growth and Planning Point to Success

In 1993, Crossmann Communities became publicly owned with an initial stock offering of 2.22 million shares, the sale of which netted nearly $22 million. Designed to increase growth potential, the stock offering ultimately gave Crossmann an opportunity to launch major expansion efforts.

The company expanded in the Midwest and the Southeast, targeting cities with characteristics that make them attractive to new employers, which in turn creates a need for housing. Besides Indiana, Crossmann currently offers homes in Ohio, Kentucky, Tennessee, North Carolina, and South Carolina.

The company also acquires raw land for future building. Once land has been purchased, Crossmann begins development, including site planning and engineering, as well as construction of roads; sewer, water, and drainage facilities; and other amenities.

Crossmann's objective is not just to build homes, but to build community neighborhoods. For this reason the management team strives to maintain an inventory of developed home sites sufficient for building months in advance.

Successful Products, Successful Team

Three distinct Crossmann product lines are aimed at entry-level and first-time move-up buyers, who are often pleasantly surprised by the quality and value of the homes. "Features that would have exclusively been in a custom home 20 years ago are today standard in our first-time home buyer homes," says Chairman and CEO John B. Scheumann.

The New American Homes line is an entry-level product that offers many floor plans, with prices starting in the $80,000 range. Although two-story homes are available, New American Homes is best known for building affordable, ranch-style homes—ideal for families or singles just starting out—with three to four bedrooms, two bathrooms, and two-car garages. Deluxe Homes also features primarily ranch-style homes, but with some upgraded specifications, features, and options. The Deluxe Homes line starts at $90,000. The Trimark Homes product line offers a more upscale product with even more options and custom features, as well as a greater selection

Crossmann stands behind the quality of its homes and is committed to customer service.

of two-story floor plans, with prices starting at $100,000.

"Successful companies are built from the bottom up," says Crosser. "A lot of planning and teamwork are keys to Crossmann Communities' success. The input of the sales force, as well as of many of the 300-plus employees, is always valued by management."

Crossmann was ranked by *Builder* magazine as the 16th-largest builder in the United States in 1999, and the number one builder by the *Indianapolis Business Journal*. Of Indianapolis, Crosser notes, "City government is extremely cooperative and has provided encouragement to new businesses relocating to this city. As a result, we have experienced tremendous job growth, and the real estate industry has benefited substantially. We think our corporate home of Indianapolis is the greatest city in the country."

When a new homeowner needs assistance, the Crossman customer service vans are ready to respond.

Diversified Systems Inc.

BECAUSE TIME IS OF THE ESSENCE IN MOST BUSINESS PRACTICES today, Diversified Systems Inc. (dsi) distinguishes itself as the customer's single source for bringing better products to market faster. Since 1973, the company has provided comprehensive engineering services that bring innovative concepts to reality through technologically advanced, cost-effective electronics solutions that give customers the ability to capitalize on open windows of opportunity.

A variety of services, integrated at one facility, provide every function needed in the electronics design and manufacturing process. During each step in the process, dsi can apply electronic technology, troubleshoot problems, streamline production processes, or find a more cost-effective way to achieve the customer's goals.

Unique from the Start

Company President Stanley Bentley and Vice President of Operations Dave Jessup started dsi while both were working in other jobs in the industry. The company began as a traditional engineering and design firm, but the partners soon shifted to providing a product: manufacturing and assembling printed circuit boards.

The business operated with a small day crew and a larger evening crew through most of the 1970s, but by 1980, it had grown too large to manage part-time. "To really attack the market properly, we needed more equipment, which meant a bank loan," Bentley says. So in 1980, the two men began focusing their full attention on dsi.

A third partner, Paul Madden, joined as vice president of finance a few years later, and the company's more than 450 employees were consolidated from three facilities to one 25-acre site in 1995.

Bentley says dsi's offerings set it apart from the competition early on. Typically, one company manufactures the circuit boards and another assembles them, but dsi does both. "Throw in our patented, 24-hour assembly and rapid prototyping abilities, and you begin to see why we believe we have no true competitors."

With full turnkey manufacturing capability all under one roof, dsi is uniquely positioned to offer leading-edge technology and production-quality assemblies faster than anyone else. dsi carries out many functions concurrently and tracks orders using a unique infrared locating system, which allows the company to turn a computer-engineered file into an assembled, working product in just three to five days. Added in 1996, this part of the business took two years to develop and launch. Now, the firm ships about four to six of these orders every day.

Some examples of products dsi has prototyped include an airborne systems heart monitor and a high-definition television transmitter. The company also has worked on a police gun handgrip that provides detailed data for training purposes, such as how the weapon was used, date, time, direction, and frequency of firing.

A Broad Client Base

dsi designs, prototypes, and manufactures circuit boards

Diversified Systems Inc. (dsi) designs, prototypes, and manufactures circuit boards and other products for a variety of internationally based clients.

and other products for a variety of internationally based clients. Most of its work involves creating high-end, rather than consumer-grade, products for the automotive, medical, aerospace, communications, transportation, robotics, and security industries.

Although most of dsi's clients are not based in Indiana, the company likes to tell the story of a major Indiana manufacturer who searched all over the world for a company with the design, production, and service capabilities it required, then found the only capable company, dsi, located fewer than 100 miles away.

For the automotive industry, dsi has worked on critical systems, such as antilock brakes, engines, and air-bag controllers. The firm has been involved in the creation of laboratory instrumentation for the medical industry, Internet and network products for the telecommunications industry, and automated machine tools for industrial manufacturing. Quality certifications of dsi include QS 9000 and ISO 9002, and the firm follows Institute of Printed Circuits standards as well.

Once dsi identifies a customer, the company invests time in building a relationship before any business ever takes place. dsi even offers free technology overview courses to help customers understand its systems and production methods.

"I like to say we have long courtships and lasting marriages," Bentley says. "We want to set up an environment where commerce can happen, and sometimes that takes a year or better. We present what we do and open all our books to potential clients, so it does, indeed, take on the nature of a marriage. But because of that careful courtship, we don't lose customers." This conservative approach has led to a compounded annual growth rate of 20 to 25 percent since 1990.

dsi provides comprehensive engineering services that bring innovative concepts to reality through technologically advanced, cost-effective electronics solutions that give customers the ability to capitalize on open windows of opportunity (top).

With full turnkey manufacturing capability all under one roof, dsi is uniquely positioned to offer leading-edge technology and rapid, production-quality assemblies (bottom).

Exceptional Work Environment

dsi strives to maintain a work environment that will attract and retain the best employees in the industry. Its workforce is 50 percent female, and it offers flextime, job sharing, telecommuting, and extensive training opportunities.

In late 1999, Easter Seals Crossroads opened an on-site, 11,000-square-foot day care at dsi. dsi's partnership with the well-known and respected organization is a tremendous benefit to employees, who enjoy a discount off the published day care service rate. They can visit their children on breaks and have the peace of mind that comes with knowing their children are within walking distance of their work areas.

"Our business demands exceptional people, so we make sure they have whatever tools they need to do their job," Bentley says. "I find enormous satisfaction in watching the results obtained when creative license is allowed to flourish in an environment that encourages thinking outside the box."

Tobias Insurance Group, Inc.

IN TWO AND A HALF DECADES, TOBIAS INSURANCE GROUP, INC. HAS grown to become one of the largest Commercial/Industrial Insurance Brokers in the Midwest. Founded by Nick Rutigliano in 1973, Tobias has become a fully integrated insurance broker. "Great clients and the Midwest's thriving business community have made our first 25 years pass in seemingly no time at all," says Rutigliano.

Tobias has a highly skilled staff of insurance professionals who continue to build a larger, more diverse clientele. As displayed in its operating principle, Tobias has been executing the skills of listening, learning, and creating.

These principles are the foundation on which Tobias was established. This foundation, which Rutigliano continues to adhere to today, includes client advocacy; analysis, options, and advice; and client choice.

Client advocacy dictates that Tobias apply its knowledge, experience, and market leverage in representing its clients during negotiations of program terms,

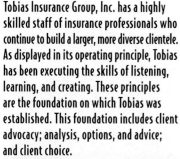

Tobias Insurance Group, Inc. has a highly skilled staff of insurance professionals who continue to build a larger, more diverse clientele. As displayed in its operating principle, Tobias has been executing the skills of listening, learning, and creating. These principles are the foundation on which Tobias was established. This foundation includes client advocacy; analysis, options, and advice; and client choice.

premiums, and claim settlements.

Analysis, options, and advice are the innovation and engineering tools Tobias brings to each situation.

Client choice reminds everyone at Tobias that they need to exceed the client's expectations. Accomplishing this mission earns the company the opportunity to be of service again.

Tobias helps clients daily to make a difference in the quality of life in the Midwest and across the country. When its insurance specialists collaborate and help their clients make a bid on a large public works construction project or develop an insurance program to start an environmental cleanup, Tobias is making a difference.

Beyond the Property and Casualty Insurance arena, Tobias has developed major divisions in Employee Benefits, Surety, and Risk Management consulting. The company examines each critical situation and responds with multiple options. This has helped it to become a recommended problem solver in its field.

Tobias develops Risk Management tools to help clients best control their destinies. Whether

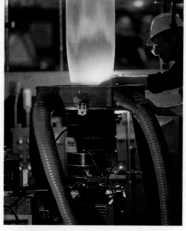

it is a multinational firm that can benefit from a Captive or a multistate exposure that can benefit from a Large Deductible program, Tobias can deliver the resources, depth, and experience to develop the solutions its clients deserve.

While most firms are trying to develop products to sell on the Internet, Tobias provides clients with Internet access to report, view, and track claim information 24 hours a day, seven days a week. Multistate Workers' Compensation forms and Occupational Safety and Health Administration log forms are directly available to clients and can be effortlessly maintained.

Tobias designs client-customized programs that individually suit each company's insurance needs. "Tobias has been mastering the skills of listening, learning, and creating," says Rutigliano. "This key concept makes our clients the nucleus of our existence."

1974   RESORT CONDOMINIUMS INTERNATIONAL

1974   ROCHE DIAGNOSTICS CORPORATION

1975   BILL ESTES AUTOMOTIVE

1975   BSA DESIGN

1975   MANPOWER PROFESSIONAL

1976   BRENWICK DEVELOPMENT COMPANY

1977   LAUTH PROPERTY GROUP

1977   MARTIN UNIVERSITY

1977   DELTA FAUCET COMPANY

1979   CONSECO, INC.

1979   EMMIS COMMUNICATIONS CORPORATION

1980   MAYS CHEMICAL COMPANY

1981   MACMILLAN USA

1982   CENTILLION DATA SYSTEMS/
        E.NOVA, LLC

1983   COMMUNITY CANCER CARE INC.

1983   INDIANAPOLIS ECONOMIC DEVELOPMENT
        CORPORATION

1983   INDIANAPOLIS PRIVATE INDUSTRY COUNCIL

1983   SPRINT CORPORATION

Resort Condominiums International

INCE RESORT CONDOMINIUMS INTERNATIONAL (RCI) INTRODUCED the concept of vacation exchange to the time-share industry in 1974, it has made more than 15 million dream vacations come true. Today, RCI is the exchange provider of choice for the time-share industry, offering a broad range of innovative products and services to more than 3,500 affiliated resorts and more than 2.5 million members. The firm's resorts make up 70 percent of all time-shares worldwide, and are located in nearly 100 countries. RCI confirms nearly 2 million exchanges annually—accounting for 80 percent of all vacation exchanges—sending some 6.5 million people on vacation.

Catalyst for an Industry

Using a shoe box and some index cards, Christel and Jon DeHaan started RCI in their suburban Indianapolis kitchen in 1974. At the time, the time-share industry wasn't growing because owners were stuck going to the same locations at the same times, year after year. The DeHaans began calling resorts and signing them up, keeping track of results with their low-tech tabletop filing system.

By the end of 1975, the firm had published its first resort directory, signed up 35 resorts and 1,000 member families, and confirmed 236 exchanges. The exchange concept caught on quickly, with RCI opening international offices in Mexico City in 1976, the United Kingdom in 1977, and Japan in 1981.

The firm's success did not go unnoticed. *Inc.* magazine named RCI one of the 500 fastest-growing privately owned businesses in the country during the years 1983, 1984, and 1985, followed by the firm recording its one-millionth member in 1989 and its one-millionth exchange in 1992. Hospitality Franchise Systems bought RCI and its related travel-service companies from Christel DeHaan in 1996.

Single-Source Service Provider

Today, RCI is committed to providing greater value to resort clients and members through an expanding lineup of solutions-based products and services. RCI is the industry's only single-source provider of time-share services support in what has become a $6 billion global industry with more than 5,000 resorts.

RCI provides an array of travel products and services to members and resort affiliates, including airfare and car rental. The firm also offers a wide range of services exclusively to the time-share industry. For developers just beginning a resort project, RCI assists in market research and analysis, feasibility, and project planning. The company guides developers through the details of development as well, including purchase negotiations, resort unit and amenity design criteria, and contractor and Realtor selection. RCI also develops sales materials, trains sales staff, and establishes evaluation and measurement systems for affiliates who request them.

Operations and management are other areas where RCI offers its expertise to resorts. The company develops, installs, and services customized, integrated software that handles resort functions, such as reservations. RCI also has a network of Preferred Alliances vendors who provide resort-related products and services to the firm's affiliates.

RCI publishes glossy, four-color magazines for both of its customer segments: *Endless Vacation* for members and *Premier* for affiliated resorts and the time-share industry. Each is distributed six times a year. The company is also testing a points-based exchange service that provides members additional benefits. An expanded-service Web site is being launched in 2000.

Vacation at Work

About half of RCI's 4,000 employees in 32 countries work in one of the company's 25 call centers, handling an average of 24,000 calls daily. More than 250 employees staff RCI's corporate headquarters on Indianapolis' north side, while another 950 work in the company's recently renovated Vacation Plaza call center nearby.

RCI opened Vacation Plaza in June 1998 after a $28 million purchase and renovation turned the existing, 200,000-square-foot facility into a high-tech, tropically decorated haven. A $7 million investment in technology contributed to an increase in productivity of more than 10 percent overall, with gains of as much as 20 percent in some areas.

The Vacation Plaza facility utilizes Windows-based personal-computer workstations and automatic number identification that links with real-time screen synchronization of member records. Instead of desktop telephones, vacation counselors use "soft phones" that integrate telephone and PC operations. Special equipment routes calls to the most available call center worldwide, while scheduling software helps management forecast workload and match schedules to anticipated call volumes.

A flexible, casual-dress work environment contributes to the feeling that Vacation Plaza is a

workplace getaway. Part-time employment options are available, with full benefits offered at 30 hours. The company staffs additional state-of-the-art call centers in Cork, Mexico City, and St. John.

A cafeteria at the call center location is open for breakfast, lunch, and dinner, while an employee cafeteria at the corporate offices offers breakfast and lunch. All Indianapolis RCI employees receive a generous vacation package that includes the opportunity to stay at affiliated resorts where excess weeks are available.

As Cortney Haber, an RCI workforce management employee, says of her vacation at RCI-affiliated Sun City, "Total luxury. I never could stay at a place like that or afford a vacation like this were it not for time-sharing."

The company also provides access to an on-site fitness center, insurance benefits, tuition reimbursement, a 401(k) retirement plan, and partially subsidized day care.

Building a Better Industry and Community

RCI is the only company aggressively pursuing growth in all time-share-industry seg-

RCI has about 4,000 employees in 32 countries. In 1998, they arranged more than 1.8 million vacation exchanges.

ments, and uses an evaluation and designation system as an incentive for resorts to exceed quality standards. More than 600 affiliates have been named Gold Crown resorts and nearly 450 more have achieved Resort of International Distinction status. Premium-level exchanges account for about one-third of all RCI exchanges annually. The company supports its community as well. Indianapolis employees have been active with Habitat for Humanity, and the company often donates time-share vacation packages to charities for use in fund-raising auctions, proving that making vacation dreams come true is still the heart of RCI.

RCI has more than 3,500 affiliated resorts in nearly 100 countries. In fact, a person would have to take a vacation every week for 60 years to visit all of the resorts in the RCI family.

Roche Diagnostics Corporation

LOCATED ON THE FAR NORTH SIDE OF INDIANAPOLIS IN A campuslike setting, Roche Diagnostics Corporation is home to the North American headquarters for the diagnostics business of the global health care leader F. Hoffmann-La Roche. Roche products and services address prevention, diagnosis, and treatment of diseases, thus enhancing well-being and quality of life.

Roche is a research-based health care organization with principal businesses in pharmaceuticals, diagnostics, vitamins, fragrances, and flavors—all of which are world leaders in their respective markets. Roche is active in the discovery, development, manufacture, and marketing of novel health care solutions. The formula for the company's success includes a rich combination of talented people, cutting-edge technology, constant innovation, and total dedication to customer needs.

More Than a Century of Innovation

Founded in 1896 in Basel, Switzerland, Roche has grown from a small drug laboratory into a multinational company with more than $19 billion in annual sales. Fritz Hoffmann founded the company on what was then a revolutionary idea—that medicines could be produced on an industrial scale outside the pharmacy and sold internationally.

As one of Indianapolis' premier employers, Roche Diagnostics Corporation is actively involved with many community-related activities. Roche is one of the companies behind a local initiative to encourage economic development through high technology.

Throughout the years, and still today, Roche has remained involved in a number of breakthrough efforts in the pharmaceutical business, including treatments for cancer, HIV, bacterial infections, transplant rejection, depression, neurodegenerative diseases, metabolic disorders, inflammation, and cardiovascular disease. Since pioneering vitamin C synthesis in 1934, Roche has become the world's biggest producer of vitamins, second only to nature itself. Following Roche's acquisition of Boehringer Mannheim in 1998, the company is now the industry leader for in vitro diagnostics testing. Whether searching for new molecules or surveying consumer trends, the company maintains a creative environment that thrives on progress and change.

Worldwide, Roche employs more than 67,000 people and sells products in more than 150 countries. Roche's multinational presence reinforces the ability to compete on the global market and anticipate marketplace needs in all regions of the world. The company maintains its success through a major commitment to research and development. Every year, Roche invests more than 15 percent of worldwide sales revenues—one of the highest rates in the industry—back into the discovery and development of new products.

Integrated Health Care Solutions: Managing All Aspects of Disease

Since its founding, Roche has earned an international reputation for its major medical advances. The company pursues novel approaches in the search for new and better health care products and services. A prime example is the way Roche is forging closer links between diagnosis and treatment in the emerging field of integrated health care solutions.

Roche's business spans all aspects of health care. The integrated health care approach is offering more and more ways of identifying and targeting diseases early, when their damaging effects can be prevented. Roche seeks to address every stage of health care delivery, from predisposition analysis, targeted screening, diagnosis, and therapy to regular follow-ups and therapeutic monitoring. Integrated health care delivery requires close cooperation between scientists working in genetics, research, diagnostics, and therapeutics.

Although a single medicine often may be all it takes to help a patient, successful treatment requires far more—such as a diagnostics test and a tailor-made treatment option to go with it, or drug therapy coupled with a test to monitor the patient's response. Medically, the patient benefits, and economically, there are advantages for the health care sector as a whole. Roche combines strengths in diagnostics and therapeutics to a degree unrivaled by any other company.

World-Champion Diagnostics

Health care providers worldwide recognize the power of diagnostics to reduce the cost and increase the efficiency of total health management, and Roche intends to make a significant contribution to both. With a broad range of innovative diagnostic tests and systems that play a pivotal role in the groundbreaking area of integrated health care solutions, Roche Diagnostics products cover the early detection, targeted screening, evaluation, and monitoring of diseases. The company is active in all market segments, from scientific research and clinical laboratory systems to patient self-monitoring. It has been said that there is not a laboratory in the world without at least one Roche Diagnostics product.

Roche Diagnostics is one of the world's leading producers of systems for researching the causes of and predispositions to disease. For those doing research, Roche annually launches more than 100 products for analyzing disease in such fields as oncology, immunology, cardiology, and diabetes. The company has also produced Nobel Prize-winning research into polymerase chain reaction (PCR), establishing it as an industry standard for scientific and commercial applications. Roche Diagnostics' PCR-based products make it possible to monitor disease progression and response to therapy, and will eventually be used to predict disease predisposition and individualize patient care.

Roche Diagnostics is a forerunner in providing diagnostic laboratory systems with instruments to measure hundreds of parameters in blood, serum, or urine. Conversely, the company is working to bring the laboratory to the patient through simple, reliable test systems. Products include diabetes and cardiovascular tests and monitoring devices, health management software, patient-education programs, and diagnostic kits for self-testing.

Global Center of Excellence in Indianapolis

Maintaining leadership in the diagnostics market today means fulfilling customer expectations at the very highest level. By bringing together extensive know-how at five global Centers of Excellence, Roche Diagnostics is able to provide innovative, economical, and timesaving solutions for biomedical research, laboratory diagnostics, and patient self-monitoring.

More than 2,500 people work at Roche Diagnostics Corporation's Indianapolis campus. The site, which was originally established in 1974, is now one of the five global Centers of Excellence and has a major research and manufacturing focus associated with drug abuse testing and therapeutic drug monitoring. The Indianapolis headquarters also is a key manufacturing site for Roche's blood glucose monitoring strips, and is responsible for the marketing, sales, service, and distribution of all Roche Diagnostics' products sold within North America.

With a wealth of experience, coupled with state-of-the-art facilities and a highly skilled, motivated, and dedicated workforce, the employees of Roche Diagnostics Corporation play a key role within the global Roche organization. As one of the most innovative, comprehensive, and dynamic health care companies in the world, the many products and services provided by Roche are continually helping to enhance the overall quality of life.

Clockwise from top:
The Accu-Chek Advantage blood glucose monitoring system applies advanced, highly accurate sensor technology to diabetes testing. Blood glucose meters for diabetes monitoring and other self-testing systems enable patients to successfully manage their chronic conditions—thus, substantially improving their quality of life.

The MODULAR system is highly adaptable to the needs of large-volume hospitals and clinical laboratories.

Roche has been guided by a fundamental commitment to research and development that has earned the company an international reputation for major medical advances.

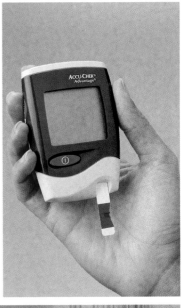

Bill Estes Automotive

FOR MORE THAN 25 YEARS, BILL ESTES CHEVROLET HAS BEEN living up to its mission of bringing central Indiana a "Better Way to Drive." A sign of this philosophy's success was evident in 1999 when the dealership was recognized as Indiana's largest Chevrolet dealership based on car and truck volume, and the 10th largest nationwide among more than 4,000 Chevy franchises.

Along with celebrating its 25th anniversary in 2000, Bill Estes Automotive also opened the new Bill Estes Dodge, located just west of the Chevrolet dealership in Indianapolis, and a brand-new, 25,000-square-foot home for Bill Estes Ford in Brownsburg, Indiana.

Family Ties

Bill Estes comes by his automotive interest naturally. His father, E.M. "Pete" Estes, was president of General Motors from 1978 through 1984. Pete Estes worked his way up the General Motors (GM) career ladder: Beginning as an engineer for Pontiac and Oldsmobile, he was eventually appointed head of Pontiac, then of Chevrolet, before assuming the role of president of GM.

As a young engineer for Oldsmobile, Pete Estes developed the famous Rocket V8 engine, then teamed with GM design legends Semon Knudsen and John DeLorean to develop two of GM's most popular cars, the Pontiac GTO and the Camaro, GM's "Mustang Fighter." The rest of the Estes family played a part by helping name the Camaro at the dinner table, right before production began in 1966.

"I remember my father pulling a piece of paper out of his pocket at dinner one night," Bill Estes recalls. "On it were potential names created by a consultant, including Camaro, Stinger, Panther, and Navarro. My mother and I both liked Camaro best, and it went on to test well before focus groups."

Shortly after graduation from the University of North Carolina, Bill Estes decided he

wanted to remain involved in the family business, but in dealership management rather than in manufacturing. "No doubt about it, my father's reputation helped secure my first job at a dealership," Estes admits, "but I've worked twice as hard to prove myself because of it."

Making His Own Mark

Beginning in 1975, all the hard work paid off when Bill Estes opened his Chevrolet dealership with 22 employees selling 40 to 50 vehicles a month. By 1990, growing sales called for more space, and Bill Estes Chevrolet moved a few blocks south of its original location to its current 15-acre site on Indianapolis' northwest side. The dealership now employs more than 200 people in sales, service, and management, and averages 350-plus vehicles sold every month.

Interested buyers may now choose from more than 1,000 new vehicles in inventory, including a large selection of Chevy pickups, vans, SUVs, and commercial trucks. Sales of these vehicles continue to outstrip car sales two to one, in contrast to buying trends when Bill Estes Chevrolet first opened.

"When customers see the Bill Estes name on an automotive franchise," says Bill Estes, owner of Bill Estes Automotive, "they know they'll find a 'Better Way to Drive.' And we're working every day to make our dealerships better."

In 1999, Bill Estes Chevrolet was recognized as Indiana's largest Chevrolet dealership based on car and truck volume, and the 10th largest nationwide among more than 4,000 Chevy franchises.

Bill Estes Automotive provides the highest-quality customer service possible, with the goal of creating long-term relationships with car buyers.

The sales process begins what Bill Estes hopes will be a long-term relationship with every customer. To this end, Bill Estes Chevrolet is presently ranked as one of the top 10 Chevrolet dealerships in customer satisfaction nationwide, as determined by GM's customer satisfaction index (CSI), and it prides itself on continually providing extraordinary customer service.

To demonstrate this commitment, Bill Estes Chevrolet features late night service hours, with service bays open every weekday from 7:30 A.M. until midnight. The service department is also open on Saturdays from 9 A.M. until 1:30 P.M. Bill Estes says he extended service hours to, "offer more convenience to our customers and to finish up the 20 to 40 service orders left over at the end of each day."

The popularity of late night service hours was immediate, as it allows customers to drop off their vehicles after work, head home for dinner, and return for their cars later that evening. To meet demand, Bill Estes Chevrolet increased evening staffing from minimal levels to that of daytime staffing.

Other area dealerships now send their customers to Bill Estes Chevrolet for emergency evening service. And every Christmas season, the Bill Estes service technicians assume the roles of Santa's helpers and provide free toy assembly for harried parents.

Always a Better Way

Pete Estes passed away in 1989, but his influence on his son is evident. Bill Estes attributes his success to having a strong role model in his father, who taught him how to treat customers right. He also credits listening to customers, which helps find ways to make their sales and service experiences easier and more enjoyable.

"My father always told me to do it the right way, and that's how I've built my business," he says. "You simply treat the customer right. It works whether you're designing the new Camaros or selling them. When customers see the Bill Estes name on an automotive franchise, they know they'll find a 'Better Way to Drive.' And we're working every day to make our dealerships better."

BSA Design

HAVING RECENTLY CELEBRATED ITS 25TH ANNIVERSARY, BSA Design is today Indiana's leading architectural and engineering design firm in the health care industry, as noted by both *Engineering News-Record* and *Modern Healthcare* magazines. The firm has successfully weathered the ever changing faces of health care and continued to design better healing environments for the people of Indianapolis.

Its unique design style is incorporated into many health care facilities in Indianapolis and the surrounding areas, gracing Community Hospitals of Indianapolis, St. Vincent Hospital and Health Services, and Clarian Health Partners, to name just a few.

In the last decade, the firm has been diversifying its market to provide innovative design solutions for a variety of complex technical environments. "The history in health care has prepared us for just about anything," says Monte Hoover, president since 1995. "Health care applications are the most demanding in terms of architecture and engineering, and therefore have allowed us to extend our market reach in a way that makes sense."

The Client's Champion

While more than half of BSA's work still involves health care, the firm is also involved in education, academic and technology research, government, utility, industrial, and commercial projects. For instance, in its 210th project for Indiana University, BSA has designed the new Sciences and Physical Plant Building at the Indiana University (IU) Kokomo regional campus. The challenge presented to BSA Design was not simply to design a new and better space for the students, administration, and faculty, but rather to design one that encourages the interrelationships between these groups by creating a "connection." BSA has designed an environment that fosters camaraderie and relationships unique to a college campus, and dispels the idea that IU Kokomo is strictly a commuter campus. The Sciences and Physical Plant Building is a 79,000-gross-square-foot structure intended to house the departments of biology, chemistry, physics, geology, allied health, and math/information sciences, and will be complete in the fall of 2000.

BSA's relationship with its clients is unique compared to

Clockwise from top:
Having recently celebrated its 25th anniversary, BSA Design is today Indian's leading architectural and engineering firm in the health care industry, as noted by both *Engineering News-Record and Modern Healthcare* magazine. The firm has successfully weathered the every changing faces of health care and continued to design better healing environments for the people of Indianapolis.

The Clarian Health Partners Cardiac Comprehensive Critical Care unit, which opened at Indianapolis' Methodist Hospital in February 1999, is the first of its kind in the country. Designed by the people who use it every day—primarily nursing and patient user groups—the facility features rooms that incorporate a family area within the health care space.

BSA designed the new Sciences and Physical Plant Building at Indiana University Kokomo to enhance the collegiate feel and to encourage student interaction on campus.

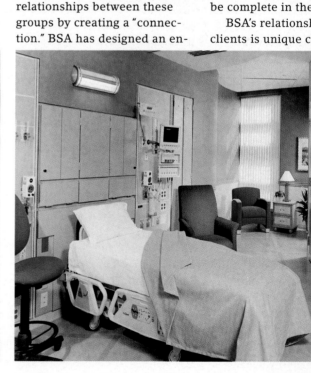

other A/E firms, stemming from the principle that each project be led by a Client Champion who works to understand and accommodate the client's needs before the project gets underway. "Understanding requires careful and thorough listening, and we take the time to partner with our clients, gaining a deep and intimate knowledge of their business, as well as their industry," Hoover says. "Only then can we begin to analyze complex facility problems, formulate clear solutions, improve efficiency, maximize returns on investments, and ensure client satisfaction." The system has proven successful with a repeat client rate of more than 90 percent.

Strong relationships and engaging the client in the earliest stages of design were key ingredients in the development of the Clarian Health Partners Cardiac Comprehensive Critical Care unit, which opened at Indianapolis' Methodist Hospital in February 1999. The first of its kind in the country, the unit was designed by the people who use it every day—primarily nursing and patient user groups. The facility employs architecture and interior design in its medical environment to create a vision of wellness care that supersedes illness care, where the patient, not the procedure, is the focus. An integral component to this line of thought is the understanding that the patient's environment plays an essential role in the healing process. Studies show that use of color, light, and texture has had a profound effect on the alleviation of fear and anxiety in the patient, and enhances recovery time.

BSA's design concept for this unit stemmed from research that demonstrated the negative results of moving patients from room to room in order to accommodate their levels of acuteness. So the firm designed rooms that would serve patients at each stage of their recovery, thus minimizing transportation

between units. While the resulting $6.2 million facility won't replace highly specialized critical care units, it will serve a predetermined, predictable patient population on a clear pathway for health and, with its residential look and functionality, is a model for patient care.

Superior Quality of Work

Whether the need is for seamless facility planning, design implementation, or ongoing support, BSA is respected for the superior quality of its work, strong client relationships, and signature solutions that meet both functionality and budgetary requirements.

Other recent successes include a world-class clinical trial unit for Eli Lilly and Company, opened in 1998; it will host the final phase of testing for Lilly pharmaceutical products. The relocation of the Lilly Clinic atop the Adult Outpatient Center, on the Indiana University-Purdue University Indianapolis (IUPUI) campus, establishes a prominent new expansion to Eli Lilly's clinical research and reinforces its mission of global pharmaceutical development.

While Indiana secures BSA's largest volume of work, the firm has done numerous projects throughout the Midwest and across the border into Mexico. In 1999, the firm completed a state-of-the-art manufacturing plant—the first manufacturing facility to be built/located outside the United States for BSA's Seymour, Indiana-based client. Located in Queretaro, Mexico, this facility will supply lighting products to automotive manufacturers in Mexico. BSA Design teamed up with a Mexico-based architectural firm to provide design services for this facility.

Project leadership is a key area where the firm anticipates more growth. CEO Don Altemeyer is currently heading a team overseeing design and construction of a new terminal at Indianapolis International

Airport. "We're serving as an executive architect," he explains, "acting on behalf of the city to keep the project organized, on time, and on budget. While we're not doing the design, we are overseeing a dozen different consultants contributing to the project."

This area of project leadership, as well as the Client Champion approach discussed earlier, has created the opportunity for broader firm ownership. Currently, with 20 principals and 16 associate principals, all client projects are led by an owner of the firm. These project managers are each responsible both to the client and to the firm for successful project delivery.

"Our philosophy has always been that in order to serve the client adequately, you have to limit the number of clients per employee," explains Altemeyer. "We see our philosophy of employee ownership as a key growth strategy."

Clockwise from top:
Located on the Indiana University-Purdue University Indianapolis campus is the Lilly Clinic situated atop the existing Adult Outpatient Center.

The atrium of the Indiana University Medical Center on the campus is an inviting gateway into the newly renovated School of Medicine.

The firm's unique design style graces the Ruth Lilly Conference Center across from St. Vincent Hospital's main campus.

Manpower Professional

MANPOWER PROFESSIONAL BRINGS A UNIQUE TWIST to contract staffing by providing businesses with a single point of contact worldwide for finding professionals in the technical disciplines. It's the fastest-growing segment of Manpower, the leading staffing service in the world and although it may work in conjunction with traditional Manpower affiliates to fulfill a client's total staffing needs, the workers from Manpower Professional specialize in areas such as engineering, finance, information technology, publications, science, telecommunications, and other professional areas.

A Reliable Resource

The Indianapolis office of Manpower Professional has been helping area businesses solve their temporary technical staffing needs for more than 25 years. When it began finding engineers for local concerns in 1975, it was one of the first branches of its kind in the Manpower family.

Today, it is one of the top five Manpower Professional centers in the nation, with a 400 percent increase in sales volume since 1996. Its territory covers the entire state of Indiana and part of Michigan, and the expertise of its workers goes beyond engineering. In addition to placing highly skilled technical and professional workers in contract staffing positions, Manpower Professional helps businesses locate and screen candidates for direct hire openings.

The firm also manages all contract workers at a business location, setting up a satellite office to keep positions filled and work moving. Currently, the Indianapolis office oversees satellite offices at client facilities in Benton Harbor, Michigan; Evansville; and Kokomo. Clients run the gamut from manufacturing and automotive businesses to service-oriented industries such as government agencies, hospitals, insurance, and banking.

Finding the Best People

To assure the largest possible pool of qualified professionals, Manpower Professional recruits aggressively through its own Web site, other Internet sites, newspapers, national trade publications, job fairs, referral bonus programs, and referrals.

NetExpress, the firm's proprietary Internet job-posting tool, brings in more than 60,000 résumés per month in response to specific job postings. TechBase, Manpower Professional's networked candidate management system, gives it the ability to select professionals from hundreds of thousands of candidates, locally or globally.

No one takes a more comprehensive approach to staffing—from qualifying résumés to making a systematic, accurate match of specialist to assignment. Manpower Professional performs an in-depth analysis of the work environment and job requirements to assure the best match between client and contractor. Soon after a business requests workers, it receives referrals of qualified candidates from which it can select the right person for that particular project.

Making the System Work

Manpower Professional's Global Learning Center supports its information technology workers with free training on compact disc or the Internet. With a library of more than 1,000 courses, it can reengineer the skills of a contract specialist to meet specific client requirements. It also uses a comprehensive screening process, called TECKCHK, to assess programmers' skill levels.

"*InfoWeek* magazine named Manpower, as a company, one of the top 150 users of technology in the country," says Connie Whisner, Indianapolis Manpower Professional manager. "We put that same innovation to work in helping our clients find the right professional and technical worker to meet their needs."

Members of the staff at Manpower Professional—formerly Manpower Technical—in Indianapolis include (from left) Marilyn Roach, Kim Partain, Brenda Cockrell, Leesa Cooper, Jill Keltner, and Connie Whisner.

MASCO CORPORATION MAY NOT BE A HOUSEHOLD NAME, BUT most households use either its Delta® or its Peerless® faucet—two of the company's leading brands. ■ Masco's history and that of its legendary faucets, however go back much further. Founder Alex Manoogian perfected and introduced the revolutionary, single-

Delta Faucet Company

handle Delta faucet in 1954. Initially, everyone scoffed at the idea of a faucet with only one handle, but Manoogian hired his own salesmen to distribute his faucets out of the trunks of their cars—giving away more than they sold at first. The faucet eventually won over critics because its washerless design, made with only one moving part, performed more reliably.

Household Market Leader

Today, Manoogian's son, Richard, is chairman and chief executive officer of Masco, which includes brand-name building products such as Kraft Maid and Merillat cabinets, Baldwin door hardware, and Aqua Glass shower enclosures. Delta Faucet Company manufactures more than 50,000 faucets every day.

Headquartered in Indianapolis since 1977, Delta Faucet sells to plumbing wholesalers and home improvement retailers, who sell to plumbers, contractors, remodelers, builders, and consumers. In a recent *Professional Builder* brand study, it led all

other brands for awareness, use, and preference. Peerless Faucet, added in 1971 to meet the needs of the growing do-it-yourself and buy-it-yourself markets, is the top seller in home and retail centers because it is easy to install.

Both brands contribute to the company's steady growth in faucet sales. In 1999, faucet sales were $937 million—an increase of 6 percent over the

previous year. During the past five years, faucet sales have increased at an average annual rate of 7 percent.

Masters of Quality and Innovation

Many of the materials in Delta or Peerless faucets are manufactured by a sister company, which helps maintain quality. Delta and Peerless specialize in the precision machining of brass bar stock to create valves and other faucet parts. In fact, the company uses more than 65 tons per day, making it the largest user of brass bar stock in the United States. Through brands that also include Delta Commercial, Cambridge Brass®, and the luxury line Delta Select®, the company offers 4,000 faucet models in 53 countries at virtually every price point in styles to suit every decor and taste.

More recently, Delta and Peerless made industry headlines with Brilliance® brass and pearl nickel finishes. Introduced in 1996, Brilliance is so abrasion resistant it can be cleaned and scoured with most household products. The space-age finish, for which the company holds 20 patents, is achieved by bombarding faucets with electrically charged atoms to bond layers of metal. The result is a finish unaffected by hard water and guaranteed never to corrode, tarnish, or discolor.

The quality and innovation that produced the first single-handle faucet and the Brilliance finish remain key strategies in expanding Masco's influence worldwide. Already the number one faucet manufacturer in the United States, Delta and Peerless brands are destined to become household names worldwide.

Delta Faucet Company made industry headlines with space-age Brilliance® brass and pearl nickel finishes, which are so abrasion resistant they can be cleaned and scoured with most household products (top).

Using more than 65 tons of brass per day, Delta and Peerless specialize in the precision machining of brass bar stock to create valves and other faucet parts (bottom).

Brenwick Development Company

IN THE 24 YEARS SINCE A SHOVELFUL OF DIRT WAS TURNED TO START Zionsville's Countrywood neighborhood, Brenwick Development Company has created some of the most popular neighborhoods in the Indianapolis area, including Ashbrooke, Waterstone, Austin Oaks, and Prairie View. ■ Led by George Sweet and Tom Huston, winners of a 1998 Entrepreneur of the Year Award for their efforts, Brenwick prides itself on creating leading-edge communities that enhance the quality of life, the character of a community, and the value of home investment. Brenwick is focused on exceptional land planning, development of a superior product, and exceptional customer service. That experience and commitment can now be seen in Brenwick's newest and most innovative neighborhood, The Village of WestClay.

In planning The Village of WestClay, Sweet and Huston, both native Hoosiers, drew on their appreciation of traditional neighborhoods and classic Indiana towns. They spent a great deal of time studying the land plans of cherished Indiana communities, such as Madison and the historic neighborhoods of Indianapolis. They saw how traditional architecture enhanced those places and beautiful southern cities such as Savannah, Georgia, and Charleston and Beaufort, South Carolina. They also studied new, yet traditional communities like Disney's Celebration in Orlando, the Kentlands in Gaithersburg, and Newpointe in Beaufort.

Brenwick has taken the best

ideas from each, adapted them to the needs and lifestyles of today's home owners, and built on them to create The Village of WestClay. The community, located in southwestern Hamilton County, is perhaps the ideal example of what Brenwick calls "the art of creating neighborhoods."

More than a subdivision, the Village of WestClay is founded on the values that established so many great neighborhoods before the great suburbanization after World War II. The Village of WestClay will have the characteristics of the best of those neighborhoods, with neighbor-

hood shopping, restaurants, small offices, apartments, town homes, and single-family custom homes, all centered around a town square with civic buildings placed prominently within the neighborhood. Planned for all generations, The Village of WestClay aims to be secure, environmentally sensitive, architecturally enriching, health enhancing, workforce productive, and family friendly.

The Village of WestClay is unified by a common design theme reminiscent of architectural styles found in prosperous Indiana towns at the turn of

Planned for all generations, The Village of WestClay aims to be secure, environmentally sensitive, architecturally enriching, health enhancing, workforce productive, and family friendly.

the 20th century. Homes and buildings in the Village of WestClay will boast traditional designs, including Federal, Gothic, Italianate, and Greek Revival. Custom-built homes, reflecting these styles, will surround a village center with its meeting house, chapel, upscale town homes, apartments, small offices, restaurants, and shops. The goal is to capture a moment in time, convincingly reflective of the natural growth of a community during a 75-year period.

Essential to the design of the Village of WestClay is the integration of life activities within the community's nearly 700 acres. Civic and social spaces will be the major focal points reflecting historic architecture. In fact, nearly one-quarter of the Village of WestClay will serve as common area open space. Pocket parks, lakes, fountains, playgrounds, ball fields, a nature preserve, a bandstand gazebo, a croquet court, and nearly 10 miles of walking trails provide places for recreation and meditation. They further emphasize the spirit of community the neighborhood promotes.

The first homes in the Village of WestClay are featured in a home show planned for July 2000. In collaboration with *Indianapolis Monthly* magazine, the show will serve as the Indianapolis Millennium Village of Dreams. Included are eight Village homes on Meeting House

Homes and buildings in the Village of WestClay will boast traditional designs, including Federal, Gothic, Italianate, and Greek Revival. Custom-built Village and Estate homes, reflecting these styles, will surround a village center with its meeting house, chapel, upscale town homes, apartments, small offices, restaurants, and shops.

Road constructed by builders who were selected as Brenwick's exclusive Village Builders. Each of these builders participated in a four-day training seminar on traditional architecture and traditional neighborhood developments. The show will also include 14 homes on Broad Street, The Village's version of historical Meridian Street, Washington Boulevard, and the Lockerbie area.

Brenwick has carved out a unique legacy in Indiana neighborhood development. Its creative approach to planned communities concentrates on how physical elements shape spaces, evoke emotions, protect privacy, and promote social interaction. The "art of creating neighborhoods" comes in visualizing a lifestyle and carefully constructing a complete environment to nurture it.

Lauth Property Group

AS THE STATE'S LARGEST PRIVATELY HELD REAL ESTATE development and construction company, Lauth Property Group strives to cultivate relationships. The company credits the entrepreneurial spirit of its employees with keeping it nimble and attuned to customer needs. ■ Lauth Property Group was founded in 1977 as a property man-

agement and retail property developer. Today, the firm develops all types of commercial properties and offers construction, build-to-suit, and fee management services with a solutions-oriented approach. This means putting the customer requirements first, then using individual team and intellectual resources, skills, and creativity to develop unique solutions.

Solutions-Oriented Approach

The firm has consciously resisted the push to go public. Much of Lauth Property Group's success is attributable to remaining privately owned with the flexibility to focus on the needs of the firm's clients rather than on its shareholders, stock price, analyst estimates, and other pitfalls of investor relations.

It is a formula that works for the three owners—a management team consisting of Chief Executive Officer Bob Lauth, President Greg Gurnik, and Chief Financial Officer Larry Palmer. The company has amassed more than $1 billion worth of construction and development experience, and has several million square feet of projects in development at any one time.

"Our success depends upon fully understanding a client's requirements. Every relationship is a long-term commitment," says Lauth. "We save our clients money because we work hard to understand their needs, and we don't recommend vendors, products, or solutions that aren't high quality and high reliability."

Lauth Property Group is also well known for its negotiation skills and its ability to find cost savings in almost every project. In some cases, the firm finds economic development incentives that benefit its clients. It is typical for the firm to save clients a significant percentage of the total project cost and a comparable amount of time in the completion of a new facility through its value-engineering approach. This gives clients more time and resources to spend on managing their core business. "Our goal is to deliver solutions that our clients can stake their reputations on, because we have staked our reputation on them," says Lauth.

Lauth Property Group is responsible for such notewor-

Founded in 1977, Lauth Property Group is now the state's largest privately held real estate development and construction company.

thy Indianapolis projects as USA Group's downtown offices, Bindley Western Industries' corporate headquarters on the northwest side, Intech Park also on the northwest side, Crosspoint Plaza office park on the northeast side, and Eaglepoint Business Park in nearby Brownsburg. But the firm has also designed, developed, and constructed projects in 23 states.

Cutting-Edge Technology

As the developer of Intech Park, the city's showcase technology business park at Interstate 465 and West 71st Street, Lauth Property Group understands the infrastructure needs of today's technology-dependent businesses. The 210-acre Intech Park is an innovative marriage of a natural, parklike setting with a high-technology infrastructure. A dual-feed power supply; a fiber-optic network that ensures multiple paths into each building and adequate bandwidth; integrated voice and data communications systems; video-conferencing; and a parkwide Intranet are just a few of the park's many technology features. A high-speed Internet backbone offers dedicated Internet access and Web site design, management, and hosting. Tenants benefit from a single point of contact—one source for coordinating their technology needs on one bill.

The park accommodates more than 2 million square feet of office and research and development space in 18 to 25 buildings arranged in a campuslike setting. The development includes an incubator for start-up businesses, restaurants, hotels, banking, day care, and other support services for the convenience of the employees and customers of the 175 or so corporations that call Intech Park home. In addition to its technology infrastructure, the park features extensive landscaping, waterways, walking trails, recreation facilities, and a conference center.

Working Example

An example of Lauth Property Group's development capabilities can be found in the firm's headquarters on College Avenue in Indianapolis. Built in 1999, the two-story atrium entryway of the building makes an immediate impression, as does the marriage of open systems, indirect lighting, multiple meeting spaces of various sizes, and laptop plug-ins throughout. The building was envisioned as a working example of functionality, high technology, and good looks for a reasonable cost.

The company's telephone system has a wireless feature that facilitates staff mobility throughout the building and grounds. Wireless phones have the same numbers as corresponding desk phones, so employees are easily reachable. In addition, the system allows voice mail messages to be read at employee desktops, and faxes can be sent and received at the desktop as well.

"We're most proud of the professionalism and the skill of our people, so we like to

do things that make their jobs easier," Gurnik says. "The phones reflect how our people work—operating as individual business units, taking what they feel capable of handling, taking responsibility rather than waiting for it to be handed out. It's an environment that breaks down bureaucracy, allows a lot of interaction across company divisions, and keeps us all on our toes, attentive to what the customer needs."

"Our success depends upon fully understanding a client's requirements. Every relationship is a long-term commitment," says Chief Executive Officer Bob Lauth.

Lauth Property Group is known for its negotiation skills and its ability to find cost savings in almost every project.

Martin University

WHEN REVEREND FATHER BONIFACE HARDIN, O.S.B., founded Martin University in 1977, he started a unique institution focused on creative approaches to learning, directed at adult, low-income, and minority students. His efforts have been an unqualified success: In fewer than 25 years, Martin has expanded its undergraduate degree programs to 26, added two master's programs, and conferred degrees on nearly 1,000 students.

Hardin, who has served as president since the school opened, named the university after Dr. Martin Luther King Jr. and St. Martin de Porres, both of whom cared deeply and publicly about serving the physical, spiritual, mental, and intellectual needs of people, especially the poor. Two years after its founding, the university was incorporated; in 1980, it received candidacy status with the North Central Association of Colleges and Schools. Martin was granted regional accreditation in 1987 and became a university in 1990, the same year it received permission from the North Central Association to offer its master's programs. Its first master's degree was conferred in 1993, the year it began holding two graduation ceremonies per year.

Martin's main campus, which includes nine buildings, is located today in the inner-city neighborhood of Brightwood. The original campus at 35th Street and College Avenue is still used for outreach activities, such as educational programs targeted at the African-American community. On August 9, 1999, the anniversary of the school's founding, a groundbreaking ceremony was held for the institution's first new building, an educational center. Located at 22nd and Station streets at the university's Avondale campus, it is scheduled for completion in 2001 and will include additional classrooms, faculty offices, student-centered services, and community outreach programs. The Lilly Endowment, Inc. awarded Martin University $5 million for the new educational center. A capital campaign was initiated to raise the additional $5 million needed for the construction of the center.

A Diverse Student Body

Martin's undergraduate graduation class size has increased from one in 1981 to more than 60 today. The average age of a Martin student is 38. The school's multicultural curriculum offers bachelor of arts and science degrees in majors that include religious studies, business, marketing, behavioral sciences, chemistry, biology, and genetic counseling.

A relatively new major, humane exchange, educates students about humane interaction and its ability to foster leadership for change in society. A degree in humane exchange prepares students for work in human services, and emphasizes ethical practices, social change, knowledge, and understanding of concepts surrounding discriminatory attitudes and practices, advocacy, mediation, and other issues related to humane interaction. Graduate degrees in community psychology and

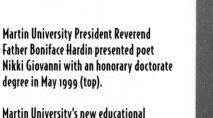

Martin University President Reverend Father Boniface Hardin presented poet Nikki Giovanni with an honorary doctorate degree in May 1999 (top).

Martin University's new educational center will house offices, classrooms, a gathertorium (a 1,000-seat auditorium for graduations, cultural events, and other programs open to the community), and a glass-and-metal globe (bottom).

SCHMIDT ASSOCIATED ARCHITECTS

urban ministry studies are available as well.

About 20 percent of Martin graduates go on to other universities and obtain graduate degrees. Alumni have attended such institutions as Oxford University in the United Kingdom, University of Iowa School of Medicine, Indiana University and its law school, Purdue University, and Valparaiso University, becoming lawyers, judges, teachers, nurses, public administrators, and business owners. The vast majority—90 percent—remain in Indianapolis, working in local companies and organizations and volunteering in their local churches and community agencies. About half of Martin's graduates work in full-time community service and related professions.

Since 1988, Martin has also brought educational opportunities to inmates at the Indiana's Women's Prison through its Lady Elizabeth campus. As of May 1999, more than 25 student inmates had graduated from Martin with bachelor's degrees. The university also opens its doors to seniors and children who wish to attend computer courses and summer-school programs and to the general public for economic- and political-empowerment seminars.

Top-Notch Faculty

Twenty of Martin's 40 faculty members hold doctoral degrees, and 20 hold master's degrees.

Many faculty, along with many of the 43 administrative support staff, have global ties to a variety of countries, as well as to a variety of religions ranging from Judaism to Christianity to Islam. Faculty and staff as a whole represent 15 nationalities and speak 30 languages.

While the university does not have a sports program, it does mount several dramatic and musical productions every year. Recent student performhave included *An Evening with Edgar Allan Poe*, Euripides' *Medea*, and the first-ever musical dramatization of *Beowulf*, written by two faculty members. Since 1993, Martin has presented an annual theatrical production on the life of Frederick Douglass, a former slave whose work as an abolitionist led to his appointment as U.S. Minister to Haiti. Other cultural programs include well-known speakers, new plays, musical performances by faculty and students, and musical and literary presentations by visiting artists. Members of the Indianapolis Chamber Winds are artists-in-residence.

Community service is an important part of Martin University's charter as well. The school's Health Education and Counseling Center provides services—particularly for substance abuse and social-psychological problems in the community—to underserved minorities. The university's Institute for Urban Ministries provides, particularly for

the African-American community, continuing studies and needs assessments of urban churches, as well as lecture programs and a visiting scholars program. Martin University faculty and staff provide a wide range of enrichment activities for hundreds of children in kindergarten through 12th grade during the summer College Preparatory Program.

Martin has plans for the development of a doctoral program in humane exchange. "We're always in the state of becoming, always meeting unmet needs," Hardin says. "If we're not willing to change, then we have no business existing. We have to really be ready to meet the needs of the times and of the future."

Clockwise from top left:
Always a festive occasion, graduation is held twice a year at Martin University.

Dr. Bobbie Beckwith, a university trustee emeritus who received one of Martin University's honorary doctorates, took part in the planting on August 9, 1999, that celebrated the groundbreaking for the new educational center.

Twenty of Martin's 40 faculty members hold doctoral degrees, and 20 hold master's degrees. Many faculty, along with many of the 43 administrative support staff, have global ties to a variety of countries, as well as to a variety of religions ranging from Judaism to Christianity to Islam. Faculty and staff as a whole represent 15 nationalities and speak 30 languages.

Conseco, Inc.

CONSECO, INC. IS A FINANCIAL SERVICES ORGANIZATION headquartered in Carmel, just north of Indianapolis. The company, with more than $100 billion of managed assets, is a leading source for insurance, investment, and lending products, helping 12.5 million customers nationwide step up to a better, more secure future. ▪ Conseco's 16,000 employee associates are spread over eight major locations and hundreds of smaller offices across the country. But central Indiana is still the company's home, with more than 3,500 of its associates working on the 170-acre Carmel campus. Conseco's insurance products—from life and health insurance to retirement annuities—are sold by 160,000 agents and by a direct marketing company. Conseco mutual funds are sold through more than 100 broker/dealers. And Conseco's consumer and commercial lending products are sold through more than 20,000 dealers and 200 sales offices.

More than 3,500 Conseco, Inc. associates work at the 170-acre headquarters in Carmel, located just north of Indianapolis.

Lean, Agile, and Focused

In 1979, Conseco was little more than $10,000 of assets and an idea. The insurance industry had been dominated by inside-the-box managers, the products of a century of slow evolution. Then the industry changed. There emerged new competitors who were more innovative and more responsive. As a result, consumers, given more choices from more sources, became more demanding.

It was during this tumultuous period that Conseco was founded. "We set out from the beginning to be different from our peers," says Stephen C. Hilbert, founder and chairman.

"Our core strategies were to offer products that were good not only for the company and its distribution partners, but for the consumer; and to be lean, agile, and focused, with an entrepreneurial, owner/operator culture. We've been fanatics about following those strategies ever since, and we've produced some remarkable results along the way."

Conseco became an operating company in 1982, completed its initial public offering in 1985, and listed its shares on the New York Stock Exchange in 1986. It was named to the Fortune 500 in 1996 and to the Standard & Poor's 500 in 1997. Since 1982, the firm has completed 20

acquisitions—the largest of which was the 1998 merger with Green Tree Financial Corp. (later renamed Conseco Finance Corp).

The Conseco insurance companies have more than $130 billion of life insurance in force. They are industry leaders in universal life sales, long-term care insurance, agent-produced Medicare supplement insurance, heart/stroke insurance, and equity-indexed annuities.

Conseco Finance, with nationwide operations and more than $45 billion of managed receivables, is one of America's largest consumer finance companies, with leading market positions in retail home equity mortgages, home improvement mortgages, and consumer loans for manufactured housing.

A Step Up Culture

Step Up is not only Conseco's advertising slogan, it is also the essence of the company's culture, its brand promise. "We want to help our customers step up and take control of their financial futures," Hilbert says. "And, as individuals, we're always intent on the next level of performance and new opportunities."

Three major sponsorships are helping Conseco establish its brand. Its status as the official financial services provider of NASCAR, sponsor of Team Conseco on the Winston Cup circuit, and primary sponsor of Team Menard for the 2000 Indy Racing League (IRL) season allow the firm to connect in a truly unique way with the values and interests of its customers, representatives, and associates.

Conseco is attracting even more national attention as the naming rights sponsor for Conseco Fieldhouse, the much acclaimed, retro-style arena that serves as the home of the NBA Indiana Pacers. Conseco has a 20-year naming agreement for the new, 18,500-seat facility, which opened in downtown Indianapolis in November 1999.

"Both opportunities are a unique fit with our vision to be the premier provider of financial

services products to the people of middle America," Hilbert explains. "These are people who want to care for their families, build homes, send their children to college, and generally look forward to the future with optimism rather than uncertainty."

Conseco also contributes generously to United Way, Junior Achievement, the arts, sports, education, municipal projects like Circle Centre Mall, and many other civic enterprises. Likewise, the company encourages its associates to give of their own time and resources to local community service projects.

"Indiana has been a wonderful place for Conseco to do business for more than two decades, and we try to say thank-you every chance we get," says Hilbert. "Our associates, nurtured by their families and friends here in central Indiana, have built one of America's leading financial services companies. Their incredible work ethic and can-do spirit are the backbone of the company. We're enormously proud of our people, our city, and our state, and we are truly grateful for the public and private partnership that has been such a big part of our success."

Stephen C. Hilbert has led Conseco's evolution from a collection of small insurance companies in 1982 to a top Fortune 500 financial service leader.

EMMIS Communications Corporation

NE OF THE NATION'S MOST RESPECTED AND DIVERSIFIED communications companies, EMMIS Communications Corporation owns and operates radio, television, and magazine entities in large and medium-sized markets throughout the United States and Europe. Five of its radio stations—WENS, WNAP, WIBC,

Clockwise from left:
EMMIS Communications Corporation and its Indianapolis entities—*Indianapolis Monthly*, WENS-FM 97.1, WNAP-FM 93.1, WIBC-AM 1070, WTLC-AM 1310, and WTLC-FM 105.7, plus radio networks AgriAmerica and Network Indiana—moved into their new Monument Circle home in December 1998.

EMMIS' Eleven Commandments reflect the company's corporate philosophy and attitude: be passionate about what you do, believe in yourself, and have fun.

Jeffrey H. Smulyan, chairman and CEO of EMMIS Communications, founded the company in his hometown in 1980.

WTLC-AM, and WTLC-FM—entertain and inform central Indiana audiences, as does its *Indianapolis Monthly* magazine.

EMMIS also has radio stations in major markets such as Los Angeles, Chicago, and New York, as well as St. Louis and Terre Haute, and also owns the Network Indiana and AgriAmerica radio news services. Its publishing holdings include *Atlanta*, *Cincinnati*, *Texas Monthly*, and *Country Sampler* magazines. Television holdings include a CBS affiliate, a WB affiliate, and four Fox affiliates, with plans to pick up more. International holdings include Sláger Rádió in Hungary and FM News and Radio 10 in Buenos Aires.

The company, which issued its initial public offering in 1994, posted 1999 net revenues of $232.84 million. Communications Equity Associates lists EMMIS as the 11th most valuable communications group in the nation, and *Inc.* magazine has identified it as one of the fastest-growing companies in America.

Ernst & Young chose EMMIS Chairman and CEO Jeffrey H. Smulyan as Entrepreneur of the Year in 1995, and the radio industry newspaper *R&R* calls Smulyan one of the 10 most influential radio executives of the past two decades. *Radio Ink*, an industry magazine, rates him the 16th most powerful person among radio's more than 4,000 owners, calling him "one of the most astute players in the radio business and one of the most highly respected."

The EMMIS name comes from the Hebrew word for truth. It is not surprising, then, that at the heart of EMMIS are its Eleven Commandments. These commandments encourage employees to apply out-of-the-box thinking to their work by admitting mistakes, being flexible, believing in themselves, holding onto their integrity, having fun, and—above all—taking care of their audiences.

Constructing a Corporate Philosophy

According to British architect Sir Geoffrey Jellicoe, "architecture is to make us know and remember who we are," and the message comes through loud and clear at EMMIS. The EMMIS logo, with its skewed letter *e* breaking out of a box, reflects the organization's emphasis on thinking outside traditional parameters, and tops the firm's central, seven-story tower.

Limestone, glass, and aluminum perhaps never conveyed so much meaning as in the

E. ANTHONY VALAINIS

E. ANTHONY VALAINIS

INDIANAPOLIS MONTHLY STAFF

EMMIS building, completed in 1998, on the southwest quadrant of Indianapolis' Monument Circle. *Radio Ink* also describes the new, $35 million, 142,000-square-foot EMMIS headquarters as "arguably the best radio facility in the country." From the company name and logo positioned on the tower, to interior embellishments, to the Eleven Commandments prominently displayed within, the building embodies the firm's corporate culture.

"With our new home, we sought to create a world headquarters that brought all of our Indianapolis entities and employees into one building," Smulyan says. "More than that, we wanted to create an innovative working environment to reflect the company's fun, creativity, and synergy."

At street level, a pair of on-air showcase radio studios allow passersby to watch radio in action, with high-tech, digital equipment and a video wall highlighting the day's news events in full view. A portion of the building occupied by the staff of *Indianapolis Monthly* fits behind a four-story landmark facade of the defunct *Indianapolis Journal*. Inside the building, the radio-wave motif shows up in everything from the grain of the wood paneling to the undulating gleam of exposed, polished steel inlaid in the floors. Even the uneven spacing of the win-

WENS STAFF

dows is meant to represent an FM radio dial.

The Number One Priority

Throughout its history, EMMIS has constantly explored innovative formats. It created the nation's first 24-hour sports radio station and the first adult classic soul station, both in New York; the first rhythmic Top 40 station in Los Angeles; and the first adult alternative station in Chicago.

As EMMIS adds properties, it strives to make them all unique, thanks to Smulyan's basic philosophy. "This business is a local business," he says. "Each station has to be involved in the lives of listeners and in the life of its community on a daily basis."

In 1997, EMMIS put that theory to the test outside the United States, when it became

the only American company awarded a national license to operate a radio station in Hungary. Once again putting its audience first, EMMIS surveyed Hungarians before deciding on the format for the new station. The overwhelming preference, European and American oldies—many of which had been outlawed during years of Communist rule—became the official format. Within four months, Sláger Rádió was the number one station in Hungary; now it reaches 4 million of the country's 11 million citizens.

"The lesson in Budapest was the same as in the United States," Smulyan says. "Understand the needs of your listeners and advertisers, and strive to serve them every day. We taught our all-Hungarian staff the EMMIS style of broadcasting, and they taught us how it can apply in

Clockwise from left:
WTLC-AM and WTLC-FM have long histories of service to the African-American community of central Indiana. In 1999, station leadership presented a check for $12,841.86 raised during the station's Million Penny March, a one-day fund-raiser for the Flanner House community service center.

Through promotions such as Free Lunch Fridays for Breast Cancer Awareness Month, *Indianapolis Monthly* and other EMMIS entities support organizations throughout the city from its offices on Monument Circle.

97.1 WENS, the best mix of the '70s, '80s, and today, sponsors SkyConcert along the banks of the White River every September. More than 400,000 people are drawn to the downtown area for a day of food, beverages, music, and family activities capped off by a fireworks show set to music.

Hungary. Together, we coined a saying: 'All culture is local; all behavior is universal.' We believe that lesson will serve us well as we further develop our international division."

Poised for Growth

Smulyan has built the EMMIS empire by buying assets only when significant value can be created. He often discovers value where others fail to look—a strategy that has EMMIS poised for growth. "We are going to make opportunistic acquisitions," Smulyan says. "If we see a property we think we can improve significantly and we have an idea, we will buy it."

St. Louis' KSHE is a good example of the EMMIS strategy. The station's ratings were in the middle of the pack in 1983, with a 6.3 percent market share and a classic rock-and-roll format. Despite a solid audience, the station was not generating revenue, and routinely traded advertising time for goods and services in lieu of payment. The core audience had a reputation for a counterculture, rebellious attitude, personified in a mascot named Sweet Meat, a tough-

looking pig with a joint hanging from its lips. Advertisers were leery of the station, even though media buys were cheaper than at similarly ranked mainstream stations.

When EMMIS took on operations of KSHE, it ended advertiser trades and worked to woo media buyers by moving the station's reputation more to the center without alienating an entrenched, loyal audience. To convince media buyers that their perception of listeners was inaccurate, EMMIS borrowed a concept from *Rolling Stone* magazine and created a brochure contrasting how listeners were

◄ E. ANTHONY VALAINIS

perceived with who they actually were. One female listener who was highlighted looked like a Grateful Dead groupie, but was actually a physician. A highlighted male listener looked like a Hell's Angel member, but was, in reality, a Superior Court judge. Focus group data supported the reality-versus-perception campaign.

A television campaign attacked on a second front. One of the ads showed a thirty-something father coming home from work, hugging his young daughter, kissing his wife, and then retreating to his den. Loosening his tie with one hand while cranking up KSHE with the other, this seemingly docile dad starts dancing and playing air guitar. The daughter peeks in, then yells to the mother, "Mom, he's doing it again!" The spot ends with the tag line "KSHE, because you're never to old to Rock and Roll!"

Sweet Meat got a makeover as well. He lost the joint and the stubble of beard, and started wearing aviator shades. A costume was created, and "the kinder looking" Sweet Meat began visiting children in hospitals and appearing at community,

EMMIS CORPORATE STAFF

Indianapolis Monthly, the authority on life in central Indiana, has been a part of the EMMIS family since 1988 (top).

Local, state, and national dignitaries gathered to help EMMIS open its worldwide headquarters on Monument Circle. Assisting with the ribbon cutting were (from left) Indiana Governor Frank O'Bannon, Congressman Dan Burton, Smulyan, Senator Evan Bayh, and former Indianapolis Mayor Steve Goldsmith (bottom).

WIBC, the Voice of Indiana, sponsored the McDonald's Salvation Army Radiothon from EMMIS' street-side showcase studios. The 53-hour event raised more than $125,000 for the Battered Women's Shelter of Indianapolis.

charity, and promotional events. New station management was brought in, and KSHE doubled its market share, moving from a three-way tie for fifth place to second place in the market in fewer than two years.

Although not as flashy as its radio counterpart, the publishing division of EMMIS remains a solid performer. The flagship publication, *Indianapolis Monthly*, which set new profitability records in 1999, has established itself as the authority on life in central Indiana. With 150,000 monthly readers, the 22-year-old publication has been named the nation's best magazine of its size by the City and Regional Magazine Association three times since 1995.

Atlanta magazine completed its best year ever in 1999, with a loyal base of 225,000 readers and more than 100 national and regional editorial and design awards. Established, but new to the EMMIS fold, *Texas Monthly* and *Cincinnati* extended the EMMIS reach to more than 400,000 readers. With the addition of *Country Sampler*, a leading crafts publication reaching 2 million readers, EMMIS Publishing entered a growing area of niche publishing.

Attracting the Best Talent

EMMIS maintains an industry reputation as the ultimate employer, attracting the best talent. Doyle Rose, president of the radio division, is listed as *Radio Ink*'s 25th most influential person in radio, and Greg Nathanson, former head of programming and development for Fox Television—where he established a reputation for having a strong rapport with viewers—heads up the EMMIS television division from Los Angeles.

Two of EMMIS' general managers, Judy Ellis in New York and Val Maki in Los Angeles, are among *Radio Ink*'s top 20 women in radio, ranked ninth and 16th, respectively. Chris Woodward-Duncan, EMMIS' senior vice president and Indianapolis market manager, has similarly been honored by the industry for her achievements. In addition, Deborah Paul, publisher and editor in chief of EMMIS Publishing, has become a household name to nearly a generation of *Indianapolis Monthly* readers.

EMMIS' 1,600 employees, including approximately 300 working out of its worldwide headquarters on Monument

Circle, strive to find creative and novel ways to serve their audiences and contribute to their communities. Rather than dictating how and to which causes its entities should give, EMMIS relies on its employees in each community to decide how to contribute.

During 1999, donations of cash, advertising, brainpower, and time added up to a total of more than $5 million in Indianapolis and more than $14 million in the other cities where EMMIS operates. In Indianapolis, for example, WIBC, the Voice of Indiana, contributed $1.75 million in donations and in-kind gifts in 1999 through such events as the Salvation Army radiothon. WENS 97.1 raised more than $350,000 during its 97-hour radiothon for Riley Hospital for Children.

"At EMMIS, we have never lost sight of the fact that we owe all of our success to our customers—the communities we serve," Smulyan says. "We strongly believe in building our company listener by listener, viewer by viewer, reader by reader, advertiser by advertiser, employee by employee, and community by community."

Mays Chemical Company

SINCE 1980, MAYS CHEMICAL COMPANY HAS BEEN BRINGING smart solutions to businesses through excellent quality, competitive pricing, and outstanding service. Owner William G. Mays has used this strategy to build the company from the ground up to more than $140 million in annual sales. ■ Mays Chemical is the 16th-largest chemical dis-

tributor in North America. In addition to corporate offices in Indianapolis, it has facilities in Chicago, Illinois; Taylor, Michigan; and Gurabo, Puerto Rico. Mays' newest facility in Puerto Rico opened to serve Latin American customers in the pharmaceutical, food, and cosmetics industries. Altogether, Mays Chemical employs about 170 people.

The Mays Reach

Mays is a fully integrated chemical distributor, offering chemicals and other related raw materials, cleaning and sanitation products, outsourcing services, consolidation, and materials management programs. It services a diversified customer base in industries such as food and beverage, pharmaceutical, automotive, personal care, electronics, paint and coatings, pulp and paper, and chemical processing.

The company moved to its 165,000-square-foot corporate headquarters on 71st Street in 1994, and maintains a fully equipped and staffed bulk terminal and laboratory at another Indianapolis site. An extensive transportation network enables the firm to ship via truck, railcar, or barge. Because Mays' sales force covers all of North America, its satellite warehouse network is constantly expanding to meet the needs of its customers. Currently, the company stocks products in California, Massachusetts, New Jersey, New York, North Carolina, Ohio, and Texas.

With nearly 250,000 square feet of temperature-regulated space, Mays owns the most modern automated warehouses in the industry. Products are segregated for storage according to their end uses and hazard categories, and both shipping and receiving docks are covered to prevent exposure to the elements.

The Mays Edge

Mays' customized programs are designed to increase customer profitability—reducing costs through improved efficiencies in purchasing, receiving, accounting, transportation, and other functions. The company has succeeded because of its unique focus on the customer. In today's

Mays Chemical Company moved to its 165,000-square-foot corporate headquarters on 71st Street in 1994 (top), and maintains a fully equipped and staffed bulk terminal and laboratory at another Indianapolis site.

Mays' newest facility in Puerto Rico opened to serve Latin American customers in the pharmaceutical, food, and cosmetics industries (left).

Mays has invested heavily in computer resources to position itself in the technological forefront of the industry. It is electronic data interchange (EDI) capable and can electronically track and store material safety data sheets and certificates of analysis to ensure prompt arrival with each order (right).

competitive business environment, companies face increasing challenges with decreasing resources; Mays tries to fill that gap by offering the most services—consolidation, one-stop shopping, logistical management, global product sourcing, and more.

Rather than offering a standardized list of products, Mays works closely with customers to understand all aspects of their procurement processes. The firm then uses expertise gathered through experience, its network of industry contacts, and its vast stores of market information to customize a program coordinating the purchase and delivery of chemicals and related materials.

By distributing bulk, packaged, and laboratory chemicals, Mays offers a product line with breadth and depth unmatched in the industry. Recent expansion into cleaning and sanitation chemical systems demonstrates its commitment to meeting customer needs.

Mays is known for its flexibility and talent for doing what other companies cannot or will not do. That may mean sourcing hard-to-find items, repackaging into nonstandard sizes, and cus-

tom labeling for specific production needs. The company's supplier base is the most extensive in the industry, with multiple sources available for most products to guarantee supply in all market conditions. In addition, Mays can accommodate even the most obscure requests using its global sourcing database and its network of industry contacts.

The firm has invested heavily in computer resources to position itself in the technological forefront of the industry. It is electronic data interchange (EDI) capable and can electronically track and store material safety data sheets and certificates of analysis to ensure prompt arrival with each order.

The Mays Family

Some of Mays' key customers include General Motors, Allison Transmission, Eli Lilly and Company, General Mills, and Miller Brewing. Miller named Mays Chemical its 1998 Supplier of the Year, and General Motors named Mays one of its premier worldwide suppliers in 1998 for the sixth time. Only 182 of more than 30,000 suppliers receive General Motors' coveted QSP Award for quality, service, and price.

All Mays warehouse employees undergo extensive quality training. The company is both QS 9000 and ISO 9002 certified. In addition to a sales staff with an average experience level of more than 12 years and highly trained customer service specialists, the company offers 24-hour emergency service to ensure requests get prompt attention, even after regular business hours.

That commitment extends to employees as well as to the community. Mays encourages its employees to participate in many community organizations. The company is especially involved in supporting United Way, Circle City Classic, Junior Achievement, and Indiana Black Expo.

"It has been exciting to lead this company from its inception in 1980 through consistent growth averaging 10 percent per year, into new markets and value-added areas of service," says Mays. "As we move forward with plans to become the 10th-largest chemical supplier with sales of $200 million or better, our tradition of reinvestment in people, plant, and equipment to improve quality, service, and efficiency will remain paramount."

Mays employees work closely with customers to understand all aspects of their procurement processes. Then, they use expertise gathered through experience, and the firm's network of industry contacts and vast stores of market information to customize a program coordinating the purchase and delivery of chemicals and related materials (left).

Mays encourages its employees to participate in many community organizations, including Junior Achievement Bowlathon (right).

Macmillan USA

VISITORS TO MACMILLAN USA MIGHT THINK IT'S A SILICON Valley company that took a wrong turn on Interstate 70, landing in Indianapolis' northside office corridor by mistake. But Macmillan USA is headquartered in the Circle City by design. The company takes pride in its ability to create an idiosyncratic culture that works to its advantage in the marketplace.

The Macmillan USA lobby itself could be interpreted as an introduction to a crash course on quirkiness, complete with exposed overhead ducting; bare, cement floors; a zebra-patterned area rug; and rubber trees planted in gleaming trash cans. The company's novel office environment complements its plan to remain one of the industry's leading innovators in both print and digital formats.

Macmillan USA competes in a fast-paced industry where speed to market is all-important. First to develop delivery techniques to match market demands, Macmillan USA continues to boast the fastest production cycles in publishing. An electronic manuscript system gives Macmillan USA its edge, translating a manuscript into a bound book in four weeks or less. A multilingual editorial staff and international distribution channels in 117 countries also make it possible for Macmillan to release new titles simultaneously in France, Germany, Japan, and Russia—both in English and the local language.

The Macmillan USA lobby itself could be interpreted as an introduction to a crash course on quirkiness, complete with exposed overhead ducting; bare, cement floors; a zebra-patterned area rug; and rubber trees planted in gleaming trash cans.

Macmillan USA's products, as well as those of its imprints, line the shelves of computer users everywhere.

Macmillan USA is a unit of Pearson Technology Group, the world's largest provider of consumer and professional computer information technology, engineering, and reference content. Pearson Technology Group is a member of the Pearson Education family of companies, which represents the most respected imprints around the world, including Addison Wesley Longman, Allyn & Bacon, Computer Curriculum Corporation, Globe Fearon, Longman, Scott Foresman, Macmillan USA, Peachpit, and Prentice Hall. Pearson Education is the global education publishing business of Pearson plc, the international media group. In addition to Pearson Education, Pearson plc's primary operations include the Financial Times Group, Penguin Group, and Pearson Television.

A Variety of Products

Each of Macmillan USA's imprints—including Que, Sams, Macmillan Lifestyle, Brady-

GAMES, and Macmillan Software—delivers products instructing and informing users of varying skill levels. Together, they sell more than 14 million books worldwide each year. The company features leading-edge products from all its imprints on its Web site, www.macmillanusa.com.

Founded in 1981, Que published the first computer book to sell more than 1 million copies—*Using Lotus 123*. Since then, Que books have taught more than 75 million people how to use computers, building a brand name and reputation that are unmatched in the industry. A trusted name, Que continues to set the standard for superior tutorial and reference products focusing on all major computer and Internet topics for the novice setting up his or her first PC, as well as for the programmer developing leading-edge computer software.

From its early beginning in 1946 as a leading provider of electrical books, Sams Publishing has established a long history of supplying technical minds with critical information. Today, with best-selling titles such as *Sams Teach Yourself HTML 4 in 24 Hours* and *Red Hat Linux 6 Unleashed*, Sams Publishing is one of the largest and most successful computer book publishers in the world, generating more than $45 million in sales and 450 titles in print. Sams Publishing is focused on teaching tomorrow's programmers, developers, and systems administrators the skills they need to build and maintain leading-edge technology—from introductory tutorials to comprehensive reference books.

Macmillan Lifestyle publishes several series that offer quality content for new learners and relearners on a variety of topics. The Complete Idiot's Guide, the flagship brand, has more than 350 titles already in print—in 25 lifestyle categories. Topics include personal finance, business, health/fitness, foreign language, new age, and relationships. The Ten Minute Guide series presents management and personal finance topics in quick and easy lessons designed for the busy professional and aspiring manager. Macmillan Teach Yourself in 24 Hours is a series targeted to people who want a structured, self-paced tutorial method when learning a new topic.

Macmillan USA's Brady-GAMES imprint is a leader in interactive entertainment pub-

lishing, offering value-priced strategy guides for video and PC-based games. BradyGAMES partners with several companies in the gaming market to create strategy guides on the hottest-selling games. A top-notch development staff and stable of expert authors, who are avid gamers, bolster the imprint. This translates into the most complete guides in the marketplace.

Established in the summer of 1996, Macmillan Software was formed to centralize the electronic and digital assets of Macmillan USA. The result was the emergence of a successful software publishing company that develops award-winning, market-leading products in their respective categories. From Web page construction tools to MP3 technology to the award-winning

Linux products, Macmillan Software strives to deliver innovative software that will educate and empower people.

A Family-Friendly Company

Macmillan USA is an organization that has a lot to offer its employees. In addition to the excitement of the publishing world and being on the cutting edge of technology, Macmillan USA has a stellar employee benefits package. Some of the exceptional benefits that are provided include a very generous vacation program, a tuition reimbursement program, a computer purchase program, adoption assistance, an emergency backup child care program, a casual dress code, and summer hours.

During the past few years, Macmillan USA has added many work-life programs for employees, and was recently named by the *Indianapolis Business Journal* as one of the top Family Friendly Companies in Indianapolis.

Clockwise from left:
In addition to the excitement of the publishing world and being on the cutting edge of technology, Macmillan USA offers a stellar employee benefits package.

Macmillan USA strives to create a unique work environment—featuring pool tables, foosball games, and a coffee bar—to encourage employee creativity.

Each of Macmillan USA's imprints—including Que, Sams, Macmillan Lifestyle, Brady-GAMES, and Macmillan Software—delivers products instructing and informing users of varying skill levels.

Centillion Data Systems

HE CENTILLION GROUP OF COMPANIES DEVELOPS, MARKETS, and supports software. As a company name, the word *centillion* is meant to convey that the firm's products manage an immense amount of data. In fact, the numerical designation of centillion is 10^{303}. ■ Today, the company processes hundreds of millions of billing transactions each month. In addition, its affiliates market internationally recognized digital asset management software and an application service provider (ASP) initiative. Centillion solutions offer businesses productivity, accountability, and an efficient way to manage the changes in information technology. The Centillion companies are growth oriented and open to strategic acquisition and technology investment opportunities, both in central Indiana and across the nation.

Utility Origins

Centillion started as a public subsidiary of the Indianapolis Water Company in 1982 under the name Compucom. Current President John Cauffman joined Compucom as director of operations just before it was sold to investors in 1987. In 1989, he oversaw creation of its electronic, personal-computer-based telephone bill analysis tool. The first of its kind in the industry, this product was the forerunner of the Smart Bill® product Centillion markets today. In 1994, the company was granted two patents for the system and methodology used in Smart Bill. That same year, Compucom changed its name to Centillion Data Systems.

Centillion has grown from 12 employees in 1987 to about 110 today. During the same period, annual sales growth has averaged 100 percent, winning the company a place in Indiana University's Growth 100 list of companies for three years running. Centillion now boasts operations in Germany and Sweden, a vibrant network of value-added resellers for its products, and users in Europe and Australia.

Building the EBA Business

Smart Bill is an electronic billing analysis (EBA) tool that allows businesses to enhance customer acquisition and retention. Its effective use can improve cost management and allocation, analyze marketing campaign impact, and manage customer service functions.

Centillion processes hundreds of millions of data transactions per month for its Smart Bill users, usually managing a customer's billing records in less than two days. Converged data is returned to the customer either on diskette, on compact disc, or via the

Centillion Data Systems is headquartered in the historic Sears and Roebuck Building on North Alabama Street, located in the Lockerbie neighborhood.

Internet. The customer then uses these files to produce bills, further analyzing data using the Windows-based Smart Bill software.

The client software produces more than 200 standard reports that present call detail, call summary, and other transactions. It can also filter data to isolate virtually any characteristic, such as geography, day part, or call duration. The system allows the customer to label bills with its own corporate identity and employs system safeguards to ensure confidentiality.

The extent of Centillion's involvement in the process varies depending on the client's needs. For some customers, it produces only the monthly bill, while for others, it hosts the software, allowing the customer to log into its systems through the Internet.

Smart Bill is recognized as the leading EBA software in a world where electronic bill analysis is a growing trend. A recent industry survey indicated that 59 percent of EBA users derive a high level of value from the system. Among users who spend $50,000 or more per month, satisfaction levels are 70 percent.

Managing Assets Digitally

Destiny and JOB, two newer Centillion products, deal with mountains of data as well. Such data could include digitized

files of text, photos, slide presentations, brochures, artwork, audio, or video. Destiny manages these resources by making them available for collaborative activities by a variety of users, whether they work in the same office, across town, or on the other side of the world. Destiny serves a variety of industries, including pharmaceuticals, property management, food manufacturing, industrial manufacturing, and graphic reproduction. With the use of Destiny software, users have the ability to electronically collaborate, organize, access, and distribute all types of digital files using the Internet or client/server technology.

JOB has a slightly different focus and market. It archives and retrieves text and images, and is geared specifically to newspaper publishers, who recognize it as the premier tool in its market.

Centillion can set up either product as a client-server installation, or it can maintain files for clients who access their resources through the Web. Both products are sold in 10 countries and have been translated into several languages.

Looking for Ideas

Cauffman is proud of Centillion's contributions to high-technology business development in Indianapolis. He has participated in the Indianapolis Economic

Development Corporation's Technology Partnership, and has served on advisory committees for several Indiana universities. In summer 1999, the firm hosted seven interns from four different schools.

The company's downtown offices in the historic Lockerbie neighborhood allow room for growth, and Cauffman is keeping his eye open for opportunities. "We're interested in investing in products that create a niche in a growing market," he says. "We're looking for products with the potential to be market leaders. The nature of our investment would then depend on the knowledge needs of the emerging company."

Clockwise from top left:
As a company name, the word *centillion* is meant to convey that the firm's products manage an immense amount of data. In fact, the numerical designation of centillion is 10^{303}.

Centillion solutions offer businesses productivity, accountability, and an efficient way to manage the changes in information technology.

With a local presence and a global reach, Centillion has grown from 12 employees in 1987 to about 110 today. During the same period, annual sales growth has averaged 100 percent, winning the company a place in Indiana University's Growth 100 list of companies for three years running.

e.Nova, LLC

IKE THE BRIGHT STAR THAT IS ITS NAMESAKE, e.NOVA, LLC brings the capabilities of high-level information technology to light for its client base of small and medium-sized businesses. "We call it the new dawn in information solutions," says David L. Bowers, president, "because it allows our customers to concentrate on their core business while we concentrate on the information systems to support them. It's like having a dedicated team of computer experts at your fingertips. As a result, less time is needed to manage technology and more time is available for the business at hand."

Just Connect

e.Nova offers several services to help customers stay connected with the technological changes driving today's business environment. Its delivery division, called e.Avenues, assists small and medium-sized companies with their information management needs.

Instead of working to keep computer hardware and software upgraded and systems maintained, backed up, and protected, customers rely on e.Nova. The company allows businesses to access applications on an off-site server, using a secure, high-speed connection. The server runs the latest hardware and software, uses high-speed communications connections, and receives around-the-clock service and support.

Client files are maintained, secured, automatically backed up daily, and transported to an off-site vault for storage. A state-of-the-art firewall protects client data, and files are routinely scanned for viruses.

Because desktop units do not run applications themselves, businesses aren't constantly faced with the need to upgrade hardware to run new applications. Plus, they have a set, predictable monthly expense for computer systems, access to around-the-clock service, and faster Internet access.

Opening the Lines of Communication

e.Nova's services extend beyond server-based computing. As customers grow and develop new ideas, e.Nova can help with Web site solutions, network strategy, and hardware requirements. The company provides consulting services to help clients determine and develop the solutions that will work for them. Since e.Nova is a licensed reseller of a variety of products, it can help clients choose which ones will meet their needs rather than pushing one particular product line.

Customers can select from among e.Nova's service options to develop an information and communications management plan that works best for them, including phone service. Xila Communications, a division of e.Nova, can provide the network design and implementation, long-distance service, and dial tone clients require. Xila offers full-service wireless solutions with more than 15 years' experience as a telecommunications service provider.

e.Nova has plans for the future that center on the customer. "Our goal is to be flexible and agile enough to change and add services according to the needs of our clients," Bowers says. "We will move and adjust with our customers. They will spend less time dealing with technology and more times focusing on their core businesses."

Like the bright star that is its namesake, e.Nova, LLC brings the capabilities of high-level information technology to light for its client base of small and medium-sized businesses (left).

e.Nova offers several services to help customers stay connected with the technological changes driving today's business environment (right).

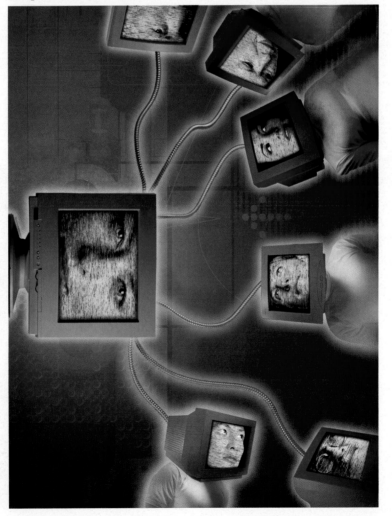

DEVELOPING, IMPLEMENTING, AND MARKETING STATE-OF-the-art oncology programs in community hospitals with varying levels of health care expertise, often in underserved areas of Indiana, is the mission of a health care corporation called Community Cancer Care Inc. (CCC). CCC's health care practitioners see more than 15,000 patients annually, about 15 percent of whom are new patients.

The practice was founded in 1983 by Dr. William Dugan Jr. During his previous tenure as director of the Methodist Hospital Cancer Center, Dugan observed opportunities for cancer patients who had access to specialists early in their diagnoses. From this, he developed a concept that would allow patients in rural communities to receive effective treatment and care without traveling to bigger cities, such as Indianapolis. CCC created a way to manage patients more effectively in local settings and give them more options and opportunities.

Meeting Patient Needs

Dugan still functions as medical director of CCC today. CCC has partnerships with more than 30 hospitals around the state and operates four clinics in Indianapolis. It is the largest provider of medical oncology and hematology services in Indiana. Its treatment programs are available to adult patients with all types of cancer and blood disorders. The CCC outreach program for rural communities makes it possible for patients to receive state-of-the-art care close to home.

The practice includes 20 medical oncologists, a psychiatrist, two psychologists, and a social worker. These physicians and staff members are engaged in standard cancer prevention, detection, and patient treatment efforts, as well as hospice care. CCC's comprehensive community hospital-based programs also include continuing medical education for hospital oncology staff, research, cancer registry, program accreditation, and quality assurance.

CCC makes it possible for 95 percent of patients' care to be delivered through local hospitals. Currently, approximately half of the local programs are accredited through the American College of Surgeons, and CCC is working to accredit even more. Of the 34 accredited oncology programs statewide, 14 are CCC programs, some of which are in very small towns.

Identifying and Managing Symptoms

In 1996, CCC introduced Oncology Symptom Control Research (OSCR), a unique research arm within academia and the private practice sector. The various members of the CCC and local hospital teams work together with the OSCR staff to perform research and manage the symptoms of cancer and its treatment. OSCR makes therapies available for symptoms such as pain, fatigue, nausea, depression, and loss of appetite. The program also conducted the largest symptom control screening related to depression in cancer patients in the United States.

CCC is currently testing a paperless clinical information technology system that will improve overall program communication and enhance accuracy. The system has the capability to record and schedule treatment plans, and can be accessed by CCC's physicians located remotely.

"We try to involve all members of the local health care teams in addressing the physical and emotional needs of patients and their families to improve the quality of life," says Sara Edgerton, chief executive officer. "We also offer ongoing, intensified training to enhance the local health care team's knowledge and awareness of complex diagnoses, treatments, and therapies."

Sara Edgerton, CEO of Community Cancer Care Inc. (CCC), has been dedicated to fighting cancer since the 1970s.

(From left) Drs. Penny Cooper, Dale Theobald, and William Dugan are part of the CCC team. From medical oncology and hematology to symptom management, their diverse knowledge adds to CCC's uniqueness within the private practice sector.

STEVE SADLER / JIM POWELL ADV. PHOTOGRAPHY

Indianapolis Economic Development Corporation

FOR MORE THAN TWO DECADES, THE INDIANAPOLIS REGION HAS been known as the Amateur Sports Capital of the World, but today, that image is evolving to encompass not only sports, but information technology as well. A new slogan—Indianapolis: Wired. Inspired.™—is the focus of a major branding campaign by the Indianapolis Economic Development Corporation (IEDC).

Sparked by the debut of Formula One racing in Indianapolis, the Indianapolis Economic Development Corporation (IEDC) has revitalized a task force to target the motorsports industry.

Established in 1983 as an adjunct of the Indianapolis Chamber of Commerce, the IEDC today operates as a stand-alone, privately funded, not-for-profit organization. Its impact is growing, with a shift to a regional economic development strategy that markets the nine-county central Indiana region as one very impressive package. The Wired. Inspired. campaign helps to give vision to the IEDC's dream to create a technology-based economy generating both wealth and opportunities in The Digital Heartland™ into the 21st century.

The IEDC works to enhance the economy and quality of life that central Indiana residents already enjoy.

The Wired part of the slogan refers to the city's existing

strengths in areas such as software and information technology, medical health, and advanced manufacturing. The Inspired part calls to mind the public/private partnerships for which the city is known nationally, as well as an educational landscape that cultivates the finest technical, engineering, and medical talent in the world.

The cornerstone of the Wired. Inspired. movement is the Technology Partnership of Central Indiana, which grew out of the mayor's high-technology task force. Housed at IEDC, the Technology Partnership implements technology-based economic development strategies in areas such as workforce, capital formation, research and development, and business and regulatory structure. The Technology Partnership will continue to provide leadership on technology issues affecting the region and state, concurrently providing a place for the technology community to network and grow.

Running a Revitalized Race

Sparked by the debut of Formula One (F-1) racing in Indianapolis, the IEDC has revitalized a task force to target the motorsports industry. During the U.S. Grand Prix, Indianapolis will host more than the many race teams and fans who follow F-1 racing. The event will also serve as an economic development showcase for some of the world's biggest corporations in town for the race.

Just as Championship Auto Racing Teams (CART), the Indy Racing League (IRL), and more than 200 racing-related industries' teams are doing business in the Indianapolis region, IEDC is building a case for Formula One investment in the undisputed motorsports capital of the world.

To date, the IEDC's overall strategy has met with great success. Record 1998 results for job retention, job creation, investment, average wage, and expansions/attractions have fallen limply by the wayside as 1999 made its way into the record books. The group was credited with retaining more than 24,000 jobs, creating nearly 11,000 jobs, and garnering private investments of more than $1.8 billion. The average wage of $18.47 per hour for jobs the IEDC helped to create in 1998 paled in comparison to the $29 per hour average of those it helped create in 1999. New businesses and expansions to existing ones were up as well, approaching 50.

As the push for regional cooperation in the Indianapolis area is embraced by the business community and residents, the resulting synergy of the Wired. Inspired. campaign will enhance the economy and quality of life that central Indiana residents already enjoy.

S

PRINT CORPORATION WANTS TO BE KNOWN FOR LEADING THE telecommunications revolution, not just for keeping pace with its competitors. With the first nationwide all-digital fiber-optic network, Sprint serves more than 20 million business and residential customers, and is at the forefront in integrating long distance, local, and wireless communications services.

Sprint traces its roots to the entrepreneurial spirit of two midwesterners who, in 1899, established their own telephone company to compete with the burgeoning Bell system. This system joined with other independents, eventually forming United Telecom in 1984. By 1985, United Telecom had more than 4,700 miles of fiber-optic network in place and lines reaching 30 percent of the nation, and had formed a project partnership with GTE Sprint. In 1991, the two companies merged under the Sprint Corporation name.

Today, Sprint has more than 400 employees statewide and 150 points of distribution in Indianapolis. It remains on the cutting edge of telecommunications technology with one point of contact for its customers.

One Point of Contact

In Indianapolis, Sprint has four major divisions—Sprint Long-Distance Services, Sprint Personal Communications Services (PCS), Sprint equipment division, and Sprint Enterprise Network Services—that work together as one point of contact to help make all of a customer's communications simple and effective.

In 1997, Sprint became the first telephone company to launch an all-digital network in Indiana. Sprint Long-Distance already offered a variety of calling plans to meet the needs of both business and residential customers. The addition of the all-digital network, however, afforded users greater system reliability, especially for data transmission, and greater system flexibility to increase call capacity when needed—both factors of particular interest to businesses transmitting critical data.

Sprint PCS, the company's

wireless services division, provides call clarity comparable to a corded home or office phone, while secure connections through its digital network mean less vulnerability to eavesdropping. A variety of calling plans makes it possible to avoid roaming charges and to have free long distance within the United States from anywhere within the Sprint PCS nationwide network of 280 major metropolitan areas and 4,000 cities and communities.

Additional features include voice mail, caller identification, and call waiting. Sprint PCS is also the first to offer 100 percent digital wireless data service through a handset, allowing customers to use their cell phones to send and receive electronic mail. Like Sprint Long-Distance Services, Sprint PCS is available for businesses, and with Sprint's single point of contact, a company's telephones can be set up centrally to operate the same way in all of its locations.

Sprint's equipment division supports business customers

by providing telecommunications equipment, along with service and maintenance. Products include advanced telephone systems, data network routers, switches, videoconferencing equipment, and voice-mail service to connect desktops with other desktops and integrate computers and telephone systems.

In addition, Sprint Enterprise Network Services provides integration, management, and support services for this distributed computer technology, allowing companies to outsource all or part of the design, implementation, and management of their distributed computer infrastructures.

"The point of contact truly is that it should be simple and effective," explains Randy Cowden, Indianapolis branch manager. "We intend to be the trusted ally of our customers, helping them integrate their communications needs into solutions that serve their lives and the changing world."

With the first nationwide, all-digital fiber-optic network, Sprint Corporation serves more than 20 million business and residential customers, and is at the forefront in integrating long distance, local, and wireless communications services.

Indianapolis Private Industry Council

INITIATING AND FACILITATING COMPREHENSIVE WORKFORCE DEVELOPMENT programs is the hallmark of the Indianapolis Private Industry Council (IPIC). Through its mission of serving as "advisor, advocate, and agenda setter for workforce development" in Marion County, IPIC seeks to creatively link job seekers with employers. This is accomplished through the development of strategic workforce initiatives that are administered by IPIC, carried out through a wide range of community-based organizations, and funded through a unique blending of public and private dollars.

IPIC is known for bringing together diverse groups—service providers, employers, academic institutions, and philanthropic organizations—to discuss best practices, develop key strategies, and design innovative workforce program content. Through these collaborative workforce efforts, IPIC looks to reduce poverty, ensure the long-term vibrancy of neighborhoods, and improve the quality of life for the city's hardest-to-employ citizens. Continually looking beyond Marion County's boundaries, IPIC also focuses on the workforce and labor concerns of the central Indiana region as a whole.

As a policy development and brokering body for workforce initiatives, IPIC is closely aligned with the mayor's office, the Indianapolis Economic Development Corporation (IEDC), and other important community stakeholders. IPIC is governed by an active board of directors, who collectively mirror the Indianapolis business community and include representatives from banking, economic development, education, hospitality, manufacturing, not-for-profit, organized labor, and service industries. Working collectively, both the IPIC board and its corporate staff of workforce professionals ensure that community residents receive needed employment and training services, and that area employers are matched with employees who will sustain, develop, and grow their businesses. Armed with new workforce strategies, partnerships, and initiatives, IPIC is ready to lead the way in developing Marion County's workforce of the 21st century.

A Look to the Past, A Vision of the Future

IPIC was formed in 1983 as the recipient and distribution source for federal Job Training Partnership Act (JTPA) funds in Marion County, the largest service delivery area in the state. Through the use of these funds, the council was charged with delivering workforce services to the local community.

In 1995, IPIC adopted a competitive strategy for delivering job training and workforce development programs. This organizational shift enabled it to focus on broader workforce issues by contracting out employment and training services to local, community-based organizations. By promoting competition among workforce development providers, IPIC created greater efficiency and customer service for job seekers and employers.

In 1998, Congress passed the Workforce Investment Act (WIA), which replaced JTPA and mandated many of the shifts from service provider to policy maker and planner that IPIC had already accomplished. The council today is a business-led organization that operates as one of Indiana's Workforce Investment Boards, receiving and distributing WIA funds in central Indiana.

The Force behind the Work

IPIC has made great strides in linking area citizens with essential employment/training services and career opportunities. It is also continuing to develop innovative programs that enable unemployed, underemployed, and laid-off workers to overcome employment barriers, helping to increase labor availability in Marion County. One

The Indianapolis Private Industry Council (IPIC) is the "advisor, advocate, and agenda setter for workforce development" in Marion County.

IPIC operates under the direction of Kelley D. Gulley, who was appointed president and CEO in 1999.

such project is the expansion of the One-Stop Centers, which were established to offer a greater variety of employment and training services to area citizens—a one-stop shopping concept. At these sites, strategically located around the city, job seekers can participate in interactive job matching, receive federal vouchers for additional training, and access a wide range of employment services. One-Stop Centers also serve as a clearinghouse in connecting job seekers with appropriate agencies that help eliminate barriers to employment, including child care, transportation, language, or substance abuse problems.

Understanding that the youth of today will become the workforce of tomorrow, IPIC has invested its resources in developing a youth employment development network to serve disadvantaged, hard-to-employ youth and young adults at the neighborhood level. This network helps young people between the ages of 15 and 25 make the transition into mainstream, private sector employment by providing culturally specific recruitment, education, training, and job placement services.

IPIC also targets its programs to high-demand industries needing good workers. Through the Leveraging Investments in Neighborhood Communities (LINC) program, individuals receive specialized training to prepare for jobs in the hotel and hospitality industry. Training is offered through a comprehensive network of community-based organizations in targeted neighborhoods throughout Marion County. Graduates of this program help meet specific labor demands of hotel and hospitality employers in the downtown Indianapolis area.

Impacting a Tight Labor Market

With the shortage of labor becoming a growing concern nationally as well as regionally and locally, IPIC has aided in efforts to put welfare recipients to work. The Welfare-to-Work

initiative, created by Congress, provides additional assistance to welfare recipients who have not been successful in leaving welfare through existing reform efforts. IPIC utilizes these federal funds to target and assist hard-to-serve welfare recipients, as well as certain noncustodial parents with similar barriers to employment. This work-first program emphasizes attachment to work as a prerequisite for training and other services needed for long-term success on the job.

IPIC continues to work with employer sectors hardest hit by the tight labor market. Through the development of career ladders and employer programs for recruitment and retention, IPIC helps to place welfare recipients and other job seekers on the road to success. IPIC maintains a close relationship with the employer community by hosting workforce briefings, job fairs, conferences, and other community events.

"IPIC works diligently to understand employers' needs so that employee training programs are not created in a vacuum," says Kelley D. Gulley, president and CEO. "The dollars spent training employees must add value to employees' skills so that they can increase their value to employers and be paid higher wages."

New Technology for a New Workforce

In conjunction with the IEDC and the Polis Center, IPIC provides detailed workforce/labor

data to help employers and job seekers. Workforce Information Now, an Internet-based resource located at www.usworks.com/indymsa, provides access to detailed information from thousands of central Indiana employers, reveals employment trends and forecasts geared toward specific occupations and industries, and matches job seeker skills with available occupations and local training providers.

"IPIC remains committed to providing leadership on matters affecting our community's workforce," says Gulley. "We will continue to pursue new opportunities and to work closely with local and regional partners, helping to bridge the gap between employers seeking qualified workers and individuals seeking training and career opportunities leading to self-sufficiency and advancement."

IPIC bridges the workforce gap between job seekers looking for meaningful training, employment, and advancement, and employers seeking qualified workers to help sustain, develop, and grow their businesses.

IPIC focuses its efforts on youth development, understanding that the youth of today will become the workforce of tomorrow.

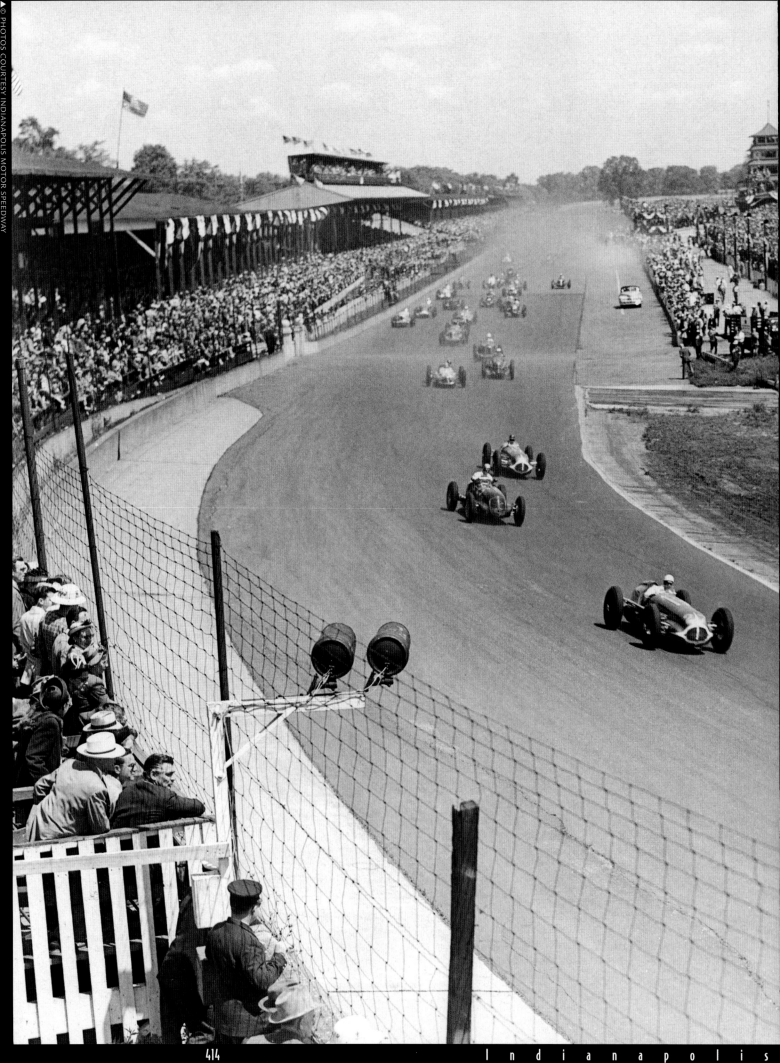

1984 CANTERBURY HOTEL

1984 TOP NOTCH

1984 EDS

1984 INDIANAPOLIS COLTS

1984 FOX WXIN 59/TRIBUNE BROADCASTING

1986 COMCAST CABLEVISION

1986 COVANCE

1986 THE SULLIVAN CORPORATION

1988 FEDEX

1988 KEIHIN INDIANA PRECISION TECHNOLOGY INC.

1988 WEISS COMMUNICATIONS INC.

1989 G.M. CONSTRUCTION, INC.

1989 GSC INDUSTRIES

1989 STANDARD MANAGEMENT CORPORATION

1990 LOCKWOOD GREENE

1990 PROTECTION PLUS INC.

1990 STAR ENVIRONMENTAL INC.

1991 TRINITY HOMES

1992 BOVIS LEND LEASE, INC.

Canterbury Hotel

EFLECTING EUROPEAN TRADITIONS AND THE CHARM OF England, the Canterbury Hotel impresses travelers with its attention to detail and highly personalized service. It is listed on the National Register of Historic Places and has received the AAA Four Diamond Award each year since 1986. ■ In addition,

of more than 3,000 resorts and hotels worldwide, the Canterbury is one of only 110 that can claim distinguished membership to Preferred Hotels and Resorts Worldwide, an independent member organization that sets and maintains the highest-quality standards for fine resorts and hotels worldwide. Impeccable service and outstanding credentials earned the Canterbury its Preferred Hotels and Resorts Worldwide membership in 1986 and continue to draw distinguished travelers.

The Canterbury Hotel's guest rooms feature elegant Queen Anne and Chippendale furnishings, including four-poster beds, marble vanities, and gold-plated fixtures.

Rich in Tradition

The Canterbury Hotel celebrates a long and noteworthy history of hotel keeping. In 1858, prominent Indiana architect Francis Costigan, designer of the J.F.D. Lanier Mansion in Madison, designed, built, and operated the Oriental Hotel in the heart of downtown Indianapolis. Its name was later changed to the Mason House and then to the Oxford Hotel before being razed in 1928 to make room for The Lockerbie, a 12-story, 200-room

hotel designed by architect Bennett Kay.

Eight years later, hotelier Glenn F. Warren changed the name of the property to the Warren Hotel, operating the facility until 1973. Fred C. Tucker Jr., an Indianapolis Realtor, and Donald L. Fortunato, a Chicago businessman, purchased the historic property in 1983 with a vision of transforming it into an intimate luxury hotel with European ambience.

Project architects Browning Day Mullins Dierdorf Inc. created 25 spacious suites and 74 guest rooms, while meticulously preserving the hotel's original 12-story, brick-and-terra-cotta exterior and elegant, two-story atrium.

Rich in Amenities

Today, the Canterbury Hotel seems more home than hotel. It was designed with comfort and elegance in mind, so attention to detail is unsurpassed, whether a gathering is an intimate one or for groups of up to 125.

For example, rather than a traditional lobby, guests can gather in intimate and inviting public rooms. The parlor, which resembles an English sitting room, features a carved fireplace and furnishings that encourage guests to curl up with a good book or share intimate conversation.

Guest rooms feature elegant Queen Anne and Chippendale furnishings, including four-poster beds, marble vanities, and gold-plated fixtures. Luxurious private suites and two-story penthouses include wet bars and adjoining sitting

Steeped in old-world tradition and charm, the Canterbury Hotel welcomes all of its visitors in style, and enjoys a reputation as hotel of choice for dignitaries and celebrities.

rooms. Some also have whirl-pool baths.

Special amenities abound: valet parking, 24-hour room service, full concierge service, turndown service with chocolate truffles, nonsmoking rooms, private minibar, hair dryers, telephone and television in each bathroom, and hand-milled soaps. Complimentary services include overnight shoeshine, continental breakfast, morning newspaper, and plush terry robes.

Although traditional in its charm, the Canterbury offers the latest in technology for business travelers. Each room is equipped with a dataport and voice mail, and a variety of office services are readily available, including audiovisual service and equipment, telex and secretarial services, interpreters, and fax machines. Limousine, butler, baby-sitting, and dry-cleaning services, as well as sight-seeing and shopping tours, can be arranged by request.

Outstanding reviews of the Canterbury's delicious American and continental cuisine prepared by award-winning Chef Volker Rudolph lure discriminating diners from around the state. The hotel's quiet, wood-paneled dining room, replete with upholstered chairs and banquettes, offers a peaceful haven for enjoying expertly

prepared meals. The Canterbury has won the coveted DiRoNa (Distinguished Restaurants of North America) Award for its breakfasts, lunches, and dinners.

In the spirit of an English gentlemen's club, the Canterbury cocktail lounge features fine ports and cognacs, as well as a stock of fine cigars. Reservations are suggested for afternoon tea in the atrium or parlor, a favorite among locals throughout the year.

The hotel provides a private entrance to Circle Centre, the upscale shopping, dining, and entertainment mall at the heart of downtown Indianapolis. The Indianapolis Convention Center and RCA Dome can be reached via an enclosed skywalk. The hotel is also within a few blocks

of the Conseco Fieldhouse, Monument Circle, Indiana Repertory Theatre, Union Station, and Market Square Arena.

Hotel of Choice

Steeped in old-world tradition and charm, the Canterbury welcomes all of its visitors in style, and enjoys a reputation as hotel of choice for dignitaries and celebrities. "Our hotel staff is trained to assist our guests during their stay with us," says Letitia Moscrip, general manager. "We cater to their individual needs and make sure every detail is well organized. When actor Ted Danson was here for the National Collegiate Athletic Association championship in 1997 and couldn't find a taxi to take him on a tour of the city, one of our bellmen used my car and gave him a personalized tour."

The Canterbury staff have also become security experts, and on more than one occasion have discreetly whisked a celebrity out of the hotel's back entrance to a waiting limousine. The hotel's VIP list is an impressive read, including the Gorbachevs, Tipper Gore, Janet Jackson, the Rolling Stones, and Cher.

Mark Twain once remarked, "All saints can do miracles, but few of them can keep a hotel." Considered a wonderful home away from home by many of its guests, the Canterbury Hotel takes pride in performing miracles every day.

In the spirit of an English gentlemen's club, the Canterbury cocktail lounge features fine ports and cognacs, as well as a stock of fine cigars.

The hotel's quiet, wood-paneled dining room, replete with upholstered chairs and banquettes, offers a peaceful haven for enjoying expertly prepared meals.

Top Notch

OR MORE THAN 15 YEARS, THE MISSION OF TOP NOTCH HAS been to foster teamwork between labor unions and management in the union construction industry. A not-for-profit association, Top Notch provides a forum for communication between the two groups and works to promote the benefits of using union labor during construction.

The labor sector of Top Notch is comprised of 18 local unions, representing more than 20,000 skilled workers. The management sector of Top Notch is comprised of general contractors and specialty trade contractors who choose to hire union labor. Together, the two groups act as one voice for the construction industry through cooperative education efforts, advertising and promotions, and community involvement.

An Investment in Education and Training

"A union workforce is a skilled, available, and safe workforce—and the most cost-efficient workforce in the long run," says Michelle Boyd, executive director of Top Notch. "By far, it is the training of our workforce that sets us apart from any competition. No group outside of the union construction industry invests as much in education as we do in our apprenticeship programs. Quite honestly, it is this level of training that reinforces our contractors' choice to employ union labor."

Statewide, through regional organizations like Top Notch, labor and management work together to fund approximately $15 million in apprenticeship programs every year. Apprenticeship programs are available in a variety of trades, with an average of five years of course work and on-the-job training required to earn the status of journeyman.

At program completion, many tradesmen can receive associate's degrees from Ivy Tech State College and are trained to embark on careers that pay good wages and promise a bright future. More than 5,000 Indiana students are currently enrolled

Labor and management jointly fund union apprenticeship programs each year for trades such as pipe fitters, carpenters, and electricians. More than 5,000 students are currently enrolled in these jointly funded apprenticeship programs.

◀ TOD MARTENS

in these jointly funded apprenticeship programs.

A Community of Cooperation

Top Notch also brings together labor and management on a number of projects that benefit the community. In 1998, members of both labor and management teamed up with the American Institute of Architecture to build a Habitat for Humanity home. It was a unique opportunity for contractors and tradesmen to work side by side with architects

and, together, they completed the home in just 36 hours.

In spring 1999, Top Notch joined forces with other local corporations as an integral part of the first annual Christmas in April Indianapolis, a national volunteer neighborhood rehabilitation program. Top Notch provided the labor manpower necessary to renovate 10 homes within a low-income neighborhood in Indianapolis. In addition, the management sector of Top Notch contributed necessary project management expertise to this important program.

A History of Contributing to the Growth of Indiana

The history of central Indiana is rich with marks of union construction. "The union construction industry is the workforce that built our state, from new additions such as Conseco Fieldhouse, Circle Centre Mall, Victory Field, NCAA Headquarters, and IPALCO Congressional Medal of Honor Memorial to any number of long-standing and familiar business structures," Boyd says. "Union construction has indeed sculpted the skyline of central Indiana."

THE COLOR BLUE HASN'T BEEN THE SAME SINCE THE NATIONAL Football League (NFL) Colts came to Indianapolis in 1984. The addition of the organization's rich history to the community's sports tradition has made Indianapolis a center for professional, as well as amateur, sports. Jim Irsay, owner and chief executive officer, has demon-

strated an aggressive leadership path for the Colts as the team readies to mark its 17th Indianapolis season in 2000-2001. "I'm excited about the future of the Colts," Irsay says. "We've redefined ourselves as an organization over the years, and we've demonstrated we'll take all steps necessary for the Colts to be consistent winners on and off the field."

A Rich History

The Colts franchise traces its history to 1946, when the bankrupt Miami Seahawks of the All-America Football Conference (AAFC) was purchased and relocated to Baltimore. The NFL eventually absorbed the team when it merged with the AAFC in 1950. In a prearranged deal, Robert and Harriet Irsay, Jim Irsay's parents, traded the Los Angeles Rams for the Colts in 1972, then moved to Indianapolis 12 years later.

During more than 50 years of play, the Colts have won three world championships and 11 division titles. A total of 11 Colts have been enshrined in the Pro Football Hall of Fame, including running back Eric Dickerson from the Indianapolis

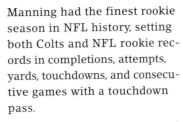

era of play. In the 1999 season, the Colts made NFL history by posting the best one-year turnaround ever, from 3-13 to 13-3. They cinched the AFC East Division championship and hosted the first-ever NFL playoff game in Indianapolis. The triple threats—Peyton Manning, Edgerrin James, and Marvin Harrison—produced recordsetting numbers with 4,000 yards passing, 1,500 yards rushing, and 1,500 yards receiving.

More recently, the club has drawn attention as the home of quarterback Manning, its number one draft pick in 1998.

Manning had the finest rookie season in NFL history, setting both Colts and NFL rookie records in completions, attempts, yards, touchdowns, and consecutive games with a touchdown pass.

A Promising Future

The Colts are committed to Indianapolis, and the team is working hard to show its dedication. In 1999, a capital improvement plan was completed at the RCA Dome. Stadium renovations included a new press box, more elevators and increased public access, and the addition of premium seating. The renovation also added two club lounges and five supersuites, and remodeling updated and enlarged existing suites to make them top-of-the-line venues for corporate entertaining.

The Colts also completed a multimillion-dollar renovation of their training complex in 1999. The state-of-the-art training and coaching facilities are among the best in the NFL. The franchise also built a Colts Pavilion available to charitable and civic organizations for meetings and special events.

Irsay and his wife, Meg, direct the Colts' extensive charitable and community involvements. Their generosity and commitment were recognized when the organization received the first Spirit of Indianapolis award as part of the Mayor's Eagle Awards program.

"The Colts have been part of the local landscape for more than 16 years, and that represents approximately one-third of our franchise's existence," Irsay adds. "We're proud to call Indianapolis home and remain committed to furthering our heritage in this all-American city."

The Indianapolis Colts' number one draft pick in 1998, quarterback Peyton Manning had the finest rookie season in NFL history, setting both Colts and NFL records in completions, attempts, yards, touchdowns, and consecutive games with a touchdown.

Owners Jim and Meg Irsay (center) direct the club's charitable and community investments. At the final game of the 1999 season, they presented a check representing $1 per ticket for the sellout game to Ellen Annala (left) and Jim Smith from United Way of Central Indiana.

EDS

OR MORE THAN 9,000 CLIENTS IN 50 COUNTRIES, EDS OFFERS solutions that harness the power of information and technology to expand horizons, productivity, and service. The company delivers information systems and technology expertise, management consulting, business process management, and E.solutions leadership through 1,200 employees in central Indiana and more than 2,000 employees across the state.

Since 1962, EDS has grown from a dream into a company of more than 125,000 employees, with annual revenues in excess of $18 billion. The firm got its start by processing client data using the idle time on other companies' computers. That novel idea gave birth to the information services industry and to new attitudes toward systems management and outsourcing.

The Leading Edge

EDS is already the market leader in end-to-end electronic business solutions, a $120 billion to $130 billion market growing at nearly 20 percent per year. Its E.solutions unit provides Internet-based consulting and applications implementation, Web-based reengineering, Web hosting and design, advanced electronic data interchange, electronic security, electronic settlement services, and consumer network services. The company expects this division will soon be handling more than 250 million clients, and will process more than 6 billion financial transactions and execute more than 100 million telephone calls for clients.

EDS' reputation for being on the leading edge of information services persists. The company can help clients develop strategies and processes to boost financial performance, envision new goods and services or enhance existing ones, and create new markets and the operations and infrastructure to support them.

EDS can also help clients generate and use information to strengthen relationships with customers and suppliers. Its Indiana clients include Allison Transmission Division, Cummins Engine, Delphi Delco Electronics Systems, the Department of Defense, the State of Indiana, and Rolls-Royce Allison.

Delphi Delco Electronics Systems, headquartered in Kokomo, is a world-class electronics manufacturer, requiring advanced information technology to retain its global competitive edge. EDS helps optimize Delco's "extended enterprise" operations, from back-office applications to wafer-fabricating production systems to supplier management tools. EDS' global deployment and management of a consistent desktop-computing environment, tightly integrated with groupware tools, give Delco unique collaboration capabilities to 9,000 employees in 36 countries on five continents.

EDS is also helping the Defense Finance and Accounting Service (DFAS), located at the

Clockwise from top:
EDS' Service Management Centers (SMCs) deliver a complete range of services supporting multiple customers from a regional geographic location. Services include print and distribution, desktop solutions, network management, and mainframe and midrange computers.

Leading EDS' teams of employees in Indiana is the company's Indiana Board of Directors, which includes (front row, from left) Rick Shaffer, Krista De Witt, Jane Bolin, Jeff Byrnes, (back row, from left) Gary Tremblay, Les Willis, and Gary Landes.

Matt O'Doherty, an education outreach volunteer, assists students with computer work.

former Fort Benjamin Harrison, to consolidate and standardize finance and accounting systems. DFAS was formed in 1991 to consolidate financial operations from the army, navy, air force, Marine Corps, Defense Logistics Agency, and other agencies into a single Department of Defense (DOD) agency. Of the original 332 DOD activities, all but 26 have been consolidated into five centers, 20 operating locations, and a headquarters activity. Through consolidation, annual savings are expected to reach $120 million. EDS performs a wide variety of services for DFAS, including business process re-engineering (BPR), software development and maintenance, E-commerce, and data mining.

As the State of Indiana's fiscal agent and information technology (IT) services provider since 1991, EDS provides the technical infrastructure and operational support for the Indiana Medicaid Program. There are more than 25,000 enrolled providers of service for approximately 525,000 recipients with more than 16 million claims processed in 1998. To support a program of this magnitude, the EDS team designed, developed, and implemented a client/server-based system known as the Indiana Advanced Information Management (IndianaAIM) System. *Computerworld, Smithsonian,* and the National Association

of State Information Resource Executives (NASIRE) awards for innovative use of technology have recognized the IndianaAIM System.

Investing in the Next Generation

Firms everywhere have been faced with a lack of employees trained in programming and information technology skills, but EDS' efforts to address this issue earned it the Indianapolis' Mayor's Award in 1998.

EDS established its own System Engineers College to develop individuals with little or no programming experience into system engineers capable of performing maintenance and development in the mainframe environment. The program consists of nine weeks of formal technical training, followed by one to two years of on-the-job experience in an application-support environment.

Corporately, EDS understands the importance of well-rounded employees and stresses the value of community involvement. Its award-winning Global Volunteer Day touches the lives of thousands worldwide with more than 360 projects. Indianapolis' volunteer day activities have involved Keep Indianapolis Beautiful, Riley Children's Hospital, Ronald McDonald House, and Concord Community Development Corporation.

Throughout EDS, more than 5,000 employees participate in

various education outreach programs that adopt area schools and provide them with mentoring, tutoring, curriculum enrichment, staff development, technical consulting, support, and training. Locally, approximately 100 EDS employees volunteer their time and talents to Mary Castle Elementary School and Indianapolis Public School 49.

EDS has also been heavily involved in the JASON Project, Dr. Robert Ballard's program to bring the wonder of undersea exploration into classrooms. For the past 10 expeditions, EDS has provided end-to-end transmission capabilities to send live JASON broadcasts to students around the world through a complex communications network. In the most recent expedition, EDS focused on the Internet component of the project, creating and managing an interactive JASON site.

"EDS has learned that community outreach adds value to business and enhances morale," says Catherine Horn, business relations manager for Indiana. "When corporate leaders encourage employees to give of themselves and to care, the employees are proud to be part of the organization. EDS customers like knowing they're dealing with a group of individuals who really want to make the world, and the community they live in, a better place."

EDS assists Indianapolis in many different ways through community outreach (left).

EDS employees work together to help clients develop strategies and processes to boost financial performance, envision new goods and services or enhance existing ones, and create new markets and the operations and infrastructure to support them.

FOX WXIN 59/Tribune Broadcasting

WHEN INDIANAPOLIS TELEVISION VIEWERS THINK OF first, fast, and fun, WXIN 59 wants them to think of FOX 59, the only local station with a solid brand identity exclusive of its station call letters. Locally, FOX 59 is number one among 10 p.m. news programs. That, along with offerings such as Major League Baseball, NFL games, and the Super Bowl, is what has made it a top television station in central Indiana.

Committed to Quality Programming

FOX 59 entered the Indianapolis market in 1984, and can be seen throughout central Indiana on 120 different cable systems by about 670,000 subscribers. The station features seven nights of prime-time FOX programming, including its highly rated 10 p.m. newscast, which debuted in 1991.

Coanchor Bob Donaldson, who joined FOX 59 that same year, is an Emmy-nominated writer and documentary producer. Cheryl Adams, the other half of the anchor team, joined FOX 59 in 1994. She has also received Emmy nominations, as well as recognition from the Associated Press, the Society for Professional Journalists, and many other broadcast awards for her ongoing coverage of family issues.

The FOX morning show, *FOX 59 a.m.*, was launched in 1999. Its energetic anchor team, graphics, music, and local emphasis provide fun for morning viewers. The quirky, relaxed nature of the show sets it apart from the other, more traditional morning newscasts. Frequent road trips to places and events around the country make *FOX 59 a.m.* an entertaining and informative morning newscast.

FOX 59's award-winning first-run programming has included favorites such as *The X-Files, Beverly Hills 90210, Ally McBeal, The Simpsons*, and *Star Trek: The Next Generation*. Locally, FOX 59 produces not only its morning and evening newscasts, but a weekly, 30-minute sports program called *59 Overtime*. The station looks for other local production opportunities such as the New Year's Eve celebration called the Downtown Countdown, which is simulcast on-air, and on the station's Web site.

FOX 59 is the only FOX station to be named FOX Affiliate

FOX 59 has established an important local presence with its highly rated 10 p.m. newscast, which debuted in 1991. The program is anchored by (from left) Eric Richey, Bob Donaldson, Cheryl Adams, and Brian Wilkes.

of the Year twice—in 1991 and 1997. Linda Gray, the station's vice president and general manager, serves on the FOX Board of Governors, a board of general managers elected from among approximately 200 FOX affiliates.

Part of Tribune Broadcasting

In addition to its association with the FOX Network, FOX 59 is one of 19 major-market television and four radio stations owned by Tribune Broadcasting of Chicago. Five of those stations besides Indianapolis are FOX affiliates, serving viewers in Seattle, Harrisburg, Grand Rapids, Hartford, and Sacramento.

Other Tribune Broadcasting properties are in 15 of the nation's top 30 markets and nine of the top 12, including Chicago, New York, and Los Angeles. All told, the firm's TV holdings reach 36 percent of the nation's households. Taking into consideration the Tribune's WGN superstation, which reaches 48 million households outside of Chicago through cable, that percentage rises to more than 75 percent. Four additional station acquisitions are pending Federal Communications Commission approval.

Tribune TV stations are news and sports leaders as well, broadcasting a combined 148 hours of news programming every week. Tribune Broadcasting also owns the Chicago Cubs, a 25 percent stake in WB Network, and 29 percent of the TV Food Network. In 1998, the company posted $317 million in profit on operating revenues of $1.2 billion.

Tribune Broadcasting is a subsidiary of media giant Tribune, which also owns publishing, interactive, and education subsidiaries, and maintains investments in a number of new-media companies such as iVillage, Excite@Home, and America Online. This interest in new technologies and evolving

channels for content delivery is consistent across the Tribune system. FOX 59 uses its Web site —www.FOX59.com—to gather news tips, recruit traffic watchers, and build sites and topics for its various on-camera features.

Committed to Community

The FOX 59 Community Fund is a fund of the Robert R. McCormick Tribune Foundation, a charitable trust established in 1955 in memory of Colonel Robert R. McCormick, the long-time editor and publisher of the *Chicago Tribune*. Through the FOX 59 Community Fund, central Indiana not-for-profits can partner with the station to add dollars to existing fund-raising efforts.

More than 40 percent of the community fund's efforts are directed toward programs and activities that foster positive youth development. The fund defines positive youth development as a process that prepares young people, ages 13 through 18, to meet the challenges of

adolescence and adulthood through a coordinated, progressive series of activities and experiences that help them become socially, morally, emotionally, physically, and cognitively competent.

This youth development approach favors organizations, programs, and activities that focus on providing opportunities for development and enhancement of youth capacity and strength, rather than a deficit-based model that focuses solely on fixing a problem or preventing a type of behavior. In its inaugural year, the FOX 59 Community Fund paid nearly $55,000 in grants to Indianapolis-based charities. In 1999, WXIN paid just over $555,000 in grants, demonstrating FOX 59's commitment to community involvement. By giving back to the community they serve, WXIN 59 and Tribune Broadcasting are securing a positive and mutually beneficial relationship with the city of Indianapolis and central Indiana.

Launched in 1999, the FOX morning show, *FOX 59 a.m.*–a production of FOX WXIN 59/Tribune Broadcasting–provides fun for morning viewers. Its energetic anchor team includes (from left) Shireen Sandoval, Jim Gavin, Cody Stark, Clarence Reynolds, Joni Michels, and Jordana Green.

Comcast Cablevision

THE INFLUENCE OF COMCAST CABLEVISION EXTENDS FAR beyond the television sets in the homes of its 150,000 central Indiana subscribers. Nationally, the company provides more than 4.5 million households in 21 states with a cable connection and a host of products and services that keep viewers on the cutting edge of information and entertainment technology. In the near future, the company will close deals that will nearly double the number of subscribers in Indiana and nationwide.

Companywide, Comcast employs about 17,000 people and posts consolidated revenues of more than $5 billion. It is the third-largest cable provider in the United States, with 80 percent of its customers situated in 10 large geographic clusters of urban and suburban areas.

The company's newest service, Comcast@Home, provides Internet access via a high-speed cable modem, with data transmission speeds hundreds of times faster than traditional dial-up phone modems and about 75 times faster than higher-speed phone lines. This faster access allows easier viewing of multimedia content such as video clips, audio clips, and three-dimensional, virtual-reality images. It also allows subscribers to access the Internet without tying up their telephone lines or adding additional dedicated lines. The system will not ring busy or disconnect users for inactivity or time-out requests.

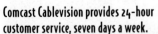

Comcast Cablevision provides 24-hour customer service, seven days a week.

Comcast also owns television and on-line retailer QVC, as well as Spectacor, which includes professional sports teams and arenas in Philadelphia, where Comcast's corporate headquarters is located. The company holds an interest in the E! Entertainment network and several advanced telephony services as well.

An Idea That Keeps Growing

In 1963, Philadelphia businessman and current Comcast Chairman Ralph J. Roberts launched the company from a Tupelo cable franchise that served 1,500 subscribers. The company name was changed to Comcast in 1969, and by 1972, when it went public, it was serving 40,000 subscribers in rural and suburban markets.

In 1986, Comcast purchased Indianapolis Cablevision, which had served most of the city's suburban areas. In 1999, the company announced a pair of swaps that doubled the number of its cable customers in central Indiana. A swap with Adelphia

Comcast employees frequently receive on-the-job training, ensuring they are knowledgeable about new products and services.

Cable allowed Comcast to serve the Muncie area. A separate deal announced in November 1999 gave Comcast ownership of Time Warner's properties in central Indiana, including Marion. Both deals were subject to regulatory approval, and were expected to close in mid-2000.

In central Indiana alone, Comcast employs about 320 people, most of whom work out of its customer call center, payment center, and administrative offices on the northeast side of Indianapolis. The company also maintains a nearby advertising sales office, as well as additional payment centers in Speedway and Plainfield.

Comcast was the first cable service provider in Indiana to launch digital cable service, completing its upgrade of the Indianapolis service area in 1998. Subscribers can now choose from more than 240 options, including 45 channels of CD-quality, commercial-free music; an on-screen, interactive programming guide; 40 channels of pay-per-view options; various sports packages; and multiplex premium channels, including 12 HBO channels. A Spanish-language package, called Canales ñ, is also available and includes 17 channels of audio and video.

Better Technology, More Choice

As technology continues to improve, Comcast predicts that options will continue to increase, making cable an even better alternative to satellite-dish service. Cable subscription rates are considerably less than most satellite services.

Comcast customers are not required to buy or lease equipment, or sign length-of-service contracts. Service can be canceled or changed at any time. A local board monitors cable service providers to ensure they meet standards for installation and service, and Comcast's local customer call center is open around the clock.

Comcast has adopted the cable industry's on-time service guarantee, through which it pays customers if its employees are not on time for installations and service calls. Comcast traditionally exceeds the National Cable Television Association's standards, with a 99.5 percent on-time service record.

A Part of the Community

Comcast gives back to the communities it serves through sponsorships and donations of television time. Locally, the company's insertion of public service announcements on 36 cable networks is valued at about $2.5 million annually.

Comcast also hosts public service programming of local origin. Its *Comcast Newsmakers,* which airs five minutes before the hour on CNN Headline News, features not-for-profit organizations, community leaders, and elected officials. Each segment airs about 50 times a month and equates to a $15,000 value for the featured organization.

Comcast also provides free cable service to all schools in its service area as part of the Cable in the Classroom program. This service, funded through a non-profit organization to which all cable companies contribute, airs educational programming late at night for taping and distribution to classroom teachers.

As an additional commitment, Comcast is making its high-speed Internet service available to libraries and elementary and secondary schools in markets where cable modem service is offered. More than 400 cable modems had already been installed in schools and libraries nationally by the end of 1998.

"We remain dedicated to the people and communities we serve," says Indianapolis Area Vice President and General Manager David Wilson, "because we know that being a good neighbor is an essential part of being a good business, and we are both. We truly want to remain a part of everything you connect with. We will be the company to look to first for the communications products and services that connect people to what's important in their lives."

The Sullivan Corporation

IN 1986, TERENCE S. SULLIVAN ESTABLISHED THE SULLIVAN CORPORATION, a general construction, construction management firm working with leading retailers, developers, architects, and owners on a national level. ◼ The Sullivan Corporation has built its untarnished reputation on the philosophy that projects are not built just of bricks and mortar—trust, confidence, teamwork, and knowledge of the business are all key elements of success in producing quality projects. Every facet of The Sullivan Corporation—from the initial idea of a project, to site selection, to construction, including the finishing touches of the architects and designers—involves the hands-on participation of the project manager, construction manager, and Terry Sullivan himself.

Building a Reputation

The Sullivan Corporation is based just north of Indianapolis, in Noblesville, with a West Coast office in Scottsdale, Arizona. The Indiana and Arizona offices house more than 35 people who work together in a turnkey concept that encompasses marketing, bidding, project coordination, construction, and finalization as each project takes shape

and comes to completion. In the field, another 70-plus individuals work in various trades to bring a project from a concept on a piece of paper to an actual building, neighborhood retail center, or award-winning landmark in the retail or commercial industry.

The Sullivan Corporation has invested much time and money on state-of-the-art technology, which enables the company to be on the cutting edge in the construction industry. In-house programs have been designed and installed to allow each department to work together and follow a project from its inception to its completion, as well as to serve as a valuable resource to clients in accessing pertinent information.

The Sullivan Corporation participates in many high-profile industry-related trade shows, such as International Conference of Shopping Centers (ICSC), SPECS, and Global Shops, a visual merchandising, store fixturing, and retail operations and construction expo. Participation in such events helps The Sullivan Corporation stay abreast of ever changing trends, which drive the construction industry both locally and abroad.

The Sullivan Corporation has also made its mark building commercial projects in historic areas where renovations and additions must adhere to architectural covenants. Experience in this area includes finishing the Eddie Bauer Store in Kansas City's Historic Plaza, the oldest shopping center in the nation, in 1993, as well as the 1998 renovation and conversion of the Indiana Oxygen Building into Dunnaway's, an upscale dining establishment in downtown Indianapolis.

The old Indiana Oxygen Building had been saved from demolition by being moved from its original location into a historic neighborhood. In order to preserve its historical significance, three of the building's four sides could not be changed. In addition, doubling the floor space had to conform to the building's exterior architecture.

Located in downtown Chicago on the Magnificent Mile of Michigan Avenue, this Eddie Bauer store was completed in the fall of 1996 and earned the Store of the Year award from *Chain Store Age* magazine.

The rooftop dining area, terrazzo floors, brushed stainless steel fixtures, and refurbished mahogany paneling are singular features that add to the ambience of the original building. With this unique project, The Sullivan Corporation won the Preservation Award, presented by the Historic Landmark Foundation of Indiana in May 2000.

Several other Sullivan Corporation projects have won recognition for their striking qualities. The Eddie Bauer store located in downtown Chicago on the Magnificent Mile of Michigan Avenue was completed in the fall of 1996. The store was named Store of the Year by *Chain Store Age* magazine. In addition, in 1998, The Sullivan Corporation built a unique local residence on Geist Reservoir, which was featured in *Indianapolis Monthly* magazine as one of the city's 50 most beautiful homes.

Good Corporate Citizenship

In the interest of good corporate citizenship, the firm is active in a number of local philanthropic organizations. The Sullivan Corporation has been very active in the Indiana Children's Wish Fund, a wish-granting organization for children who live in Indiana and have life-threatening illnesses.

Sullivan became interested in this group when his own son underwent heart surgery at

The company has a great deal of experience with retail spaces, including neighborhood retail centers (top) and high-profile retail stores like the Indianapolis 500 store (left).

Riley Hospital, and Sullivan saw firsthand that many children never have the opportunity to experience the things about which they dream. The Sullivan Corporation has since actively participated in and sponsored the organization's annual fund-raising events. In giving back to the community, The Sullivan Corporation has earned the Pacers' Mark Jackson Award for Community Service for donating 20 tickets at every Indiana Pacers home game to a nonprofit organization for use by underprivileged children.

The Sullivan Corporation may not be a household name, but its national clients—including Eddie Bauer, Abercrombie & Fitch, Gateway Computers, Toys "R" Us, and Walgreens, to name just a few—are extremely well known. Working closely with developers and architects, The Sullivan Corporation also builds neighborhood retail centers, office buildings, and warehouses that many people encounter in their daily travels. The mark that The Sullivan Corporation has made on both professional and philanthropic levels gives the community an organization that is truly one of Indiana's own.

In 1998, The Sullivan Corporation renovated and converted the Indiana Oxygen building into Dunnaway's, an upscale dining establishment in downtown Indianapolis. The restaurant earned the company the Preservation Award, presented by the Historic Landmark Foundation of Indiana in May 2000.

Covance

O BRING LIFESAVING MEDICINES TO PATIENTS WHO NEED them, pharmaceutical companies must invest millions of dollars and devote many years to research and development. Companies like Covance (NYSE: CVD) enable these companies to conduct faster, more cost-effective development of these medical products while still maintaining the highest level of quality.

The company was formed by bringing together the most respected names in drug development services under the Covance name to create broad capabilities across four areas: early development, product supply, clinical development and support services, and commercialization. The company specializes in some of the fastest-growing therapeutic areas, such as central nervous system disorders (CNS), osteoporosis, cardiovascular disease, oncology, and infectious diseases. Today, Covance is one of the world's largest and most comprehensive companies in its field, with more than 7,500 employees at 38 sites in 17 countries around the world.

"Our customers take advantage of our specialized therapeutic and regulatory knowledge to get new drugs approved and to market as rapidly as possible," says Chris Kuebler, Covance chairman and chief executive officer. "We are, in effect, the specialists' specialists in an industry that values expertise more and more."

Development of an Industry

Covance and its various divisions perform every step in the development of pharmaceuticals, including feasibility studies, clinical plan development and consulting, study design, site identification, trial monitoring, data management, patient randomization, and regulatory management.

Covance was established in Indianapolis in 1986 as SciCor Inc. by four California entrepreneurs with a vision for a centralized clinical research laboratory. Corning Inc. purchased it in 1991, combined it with a number of subsidiaries servicing the pharmaceutical industry, and spun it off as Covance, which became a publicly traded firm in 1997.

Nearly 1,000 employees working out of Covance's 264,000-square-foot Indianapolis complex provide full central laboratory testing services for clinical studies, comprehensive management of study specimens, and strategies for maintaining investigator compliance and trial protocols. The company uses specialized data management systems to track laboratory and clinical trial data, generates globally combinable data, and rapidly compiles data into one deliverable database for pharmaceutical industry clients.

Precision Partnering

In recent years, Covance has helped develop such leading-edge products as Genentech's Herceptin, one of the major breakthroughs in the treatment of breast cancer. Now, Covance is assisting Eli Lilly and Company in a landmark study of Evista, which prevents bone loss in postmenopausal women without evidence of increased risk of breast or uterine cancer. Preliminary studies have also shown that Evista favorably alters several markers of cardiovascular disease.

Covance's centralized data-tracking system streamlines processing of the vast amounts of data gathered from nearly 200 sites worldwide. Optical scanning allows rapid test transfer from clinical trial sites to a computerized data center where results can be processed in minutes. And Covance's robotic packaging technology, combined with an interactive voice-response system, handles just-in-time shipment of study medications to clinical sites and speeds packaging while minimizing inventory waste.

"We're in the business of providing our customers with innovative attention," says John Mills, president, Clinical Support Services, "It's the kind of attention only Covance can deliver because of the strength of its collective expertise, spirit of collaboration, and advanced solutions shaped to fit the customer's needs."

Nearly 1,000 employees working out of Covance's 264,000-square-foot Indianapolis complex provide full central laboratory testing services for clinical studies, comprehensive management of study specimens, and strategies for maintaining investigator compliance and trial protocols.

G.M. CONSTRUCTION, INC. PRIDES ITSELF ON BEING COMMITTED to serving its customers through the value-based approach it brings to its relationships. That pride is demonstrated in the firm's strong commitment to its customers, employees, and community. It is a strategy that has proved to breed success. ▪ The firm began in 1989 and has grown to a multimillion-dollar organization providing general contracting, construction management, and facilities management services to clientele from the Fortune 500 list. The firm maintains offices in five cities and has a growth rate of 80 percent annually for the last five years. The new headquarters opened in summer 1999, and provides 10,000 square feet of office space and 9,000 square feet of warehouse space on 1.5 acres on the city's northwest side.

A Meteoric Rise

The firm started with humble beginnings and has quickly grown to become a leader in its industry and community. Today, G.M. Construction, Inc. serves such clients as Eli Lilly & Company, Federated Department Stores, Bank One, Dow Agrosciences, Procter & Gamble, the federal government, and Coca-Cola. G.M. Construction, Inc. realizes that its greatest assets are its employees, which are referred to as associates. Its associate profile consists of 85 percent engineers and degreed managers. The focus of work has shifted from interior construction and renovation to upscale, ground-up construction through general construction and construction management. The firm excels in identifying primary and secondary client needs, and focuses on understanding client culture and building an alliance that produces repeat business.

Learning and Giving Back

As the largest minority-owned construction firm in Indiana, G.M. Construction, Inc. participated in a minority mentoring program conducted by Bovis Construction, as part of overseeing construction of the $1 billion United Airlines maintenance hub in 1993. In maintaining the spirit of this program, the company seeks out minority and low-income individuals to hire and train, in order to provide a future benefit to the community.

Thirty percent of the associates at G.M. Construction, Inc. volunteer to build housing for low-income families through the Habitat for Humanity program. G.M. Construction, Inc. President and CEO Charles Garcia dedicates himself to serving on the board of 17 different community agencies, further supporting the community values that attracted him to Indianapolis in the first place.

"Success is a matter of keeping your principles straight; everything comes after that," Garcia explains. "The people in Indianapolis embrace integrity and honesty, and that has helped G.M. Construction, Inc. to flourish."

Clockwise from top:
G.M. Construction, Inc. started in 1989 with humble beginnings and has quickly grown to become a leader in its industry and community.

Now a multimillion-dollar organization, G.M. Construction, Inc. provides services to clientele from the Fortune 500 list.

"Success is a matter of keeping your principles straight; everything comes after that," G.M. Construction, Inc. President and CEO Charles Garcia explains.

Keihin Indiana Precision Technology Inc.

GREENFIELD, INDIANA-BASED KEIHIN INDIANA PRECISION Technology Inc. (IPT), a world-class manufacturer of automotive systems for Honda, literally wears its company philosophy on its sleeve. Precision people, precision systems, and precision products are what IPT is all about, and all employees carry that message on the white uniforms they wear to work, no matter what their function or status.

The uniforms demonstrate unity, erase barriers, and symbolize quality in the manufacture of all IPT products, which include air and fuel management; electronic control; and heating, ventilation, and air-conditioning (HVAC) systems. IPT ranks as the 73th-largest automotive supplier in North America.

Everyone Is Responsible

"We have a motto of Everyone Is Responsible," explains Larry Phillippo, vice president and director. "That means everyone, from the president to the production associates, has a voice in every step of the manufacturing process and in creating the high level of teamwork that makes IPT such a great place to work."

This philosophy has met with much success. In 10 years, the plant has grown from 150,000 to 360,000 square feet, and employment has grown from 300 to 1,200. IPT has also added two child plants—one produces electronic control systems, and the other HVAC systems. One is located in Tarboro, North Carolina, and the recently completed plant is in Muncie. IPT's North American sales reached approximately $450 million in 1999.

The motto shifts employees into overdrive whenever uncontrollable difficulties threaten to delay deliveries. A few years ago, a fire on a Friday closed down a Greenfield production line, but parts shipped in from Japan had the line functioning on Monday. During the 1999 floods in North Carolina, workers could not get to the plant because of impassable roads, so the Greenfield plant picked up its production. In both cases, the company met all scheduled customer ship dates.

Committed to Quality

Lives depend on the reliability of IPT products, so Everyone Is Responsible takes on a deeper meaning. Plant workers are extremely proud of, yet are never fully satisfied with, a production rate that is more than 99.99 percent free of defects and a safety record that far exceeds the industry average. The plant is a picture of cleanliness, efficiency, and high technology— no small feat with a die-casting foundry, injector machining, electronic circuit board manufacturing, and intake-manifold and fuel-injector assembly all under one roof.

Keihin, the largest shareholder, is joined in ownership of IPT with American Honda and Honda Foundry. The Greenfield plant was built to service all of Honda's six North American plants. In this relationship, as Honda grows, so does IPT.

As Greenfield's largest employer, IPT also sets an enviable example as a corporate citizen, donating more than $200,000 in funds and in-kind services every year to charitable causes. "IPT fosters a level of respect for all people that is unique in this day and age," Phillippo adds. "We believe in serving our customers, our associates, and our community equally, with respect, honor, and the sincere dedication to helping them succeed. That's what Everyone Is Responsible is really all about."

Clockwise from top right:
Keihin Indiana Precision Technology Inc. (IPT) is a world-class manufacturer of automotive systems for Honda.

At IPT, plant workers are extremely proud of a production rate that is more than 99.99 percent free of defects and a safety record that far exceeds the industry average.

Larry Phillippo, vice president and director of Indiana Precision Technology, says "Everyone, from the president to the production associates, has a voice in every step of the manufacturing process."

LTHOUGH BOVIS LEND LEASE, INC. IS A RELATIVE NEWCOMER to Indianapolis construction, its projects tend to be high profile. Initial work locally as program/construction manager for the billion-dollar, world-class United Airlines maintenance center program at Indianapolis International Airport led to Bovis Lend Lease's opening an

office there in 1992. In 1999, the company moved its offices to expanded facilities in Park Fletcher near the airport, as growth in projects saw employee numbers double between January and July.

Bovis Lend Lease was selected to provide program management services for the state-of-the-art correctional facility located 50 miles east of Indianapolis in New Castle. The $100 million facility is the largest correctional facility undertaken by the state in recent history. In addition, the company is heading up construction of a Formula One racetrack and other site enhancements at the Indianapolis Motor Speedway, and is a player in Eli Lilly and Company's billion-dollar revitalization of the southern downtown area.

Nationwide, *Building Design & Construction* magazine has consistently rated Bovis Lend Lease the top construction manager since 1996. In addition, the firm is known for many high-profile construction management projects outside of Indiana, including the Statue of Liberty and Ellis Island restoration, the 1996 Olympic Games in Atlanta, Euro-Disneyland in Paris, and Legoland in Windsor, United Kingdom.

Although its reach is decidedly global, Bovis Lend Lease's long-standing policy of identifying with clients' goals is comfortably local in nature. In fact, the firm manages projects of all sizes, with more than 50 percent of its volume involving projects with a constructed value of less than $5 million. From commercial and retail facilities

to cutting-edge pharmaceutical and research and development campuses, it has amassed a strong portfolio across almost every market sector.

Leading Construction Manager

Bovis Lend Lease is the leading provider of fee-based program/ construction management contracts, in which the company acts as the client's representative, managing all other contractors to keep projects on time and under budget. At the heart of this process is Bovis Lend Lease's Project Quality Planning (PQP) process, which was recently incorporated into the curriculum at the University of Chicago Graduate School of Business.

The PQP process focuses on building consensus among all the stakeholders on any given project and establishing a culture based on trust and teamwork. "We've earned our reputation by taking the conflict out of construction and by producing outstanding results for our clients," says Debra Chez, senior vice president of Bovis Lend Lease Indianapolis. "In exchange, we share our expertise, enthusiasm, creativity, and understanding in a spirit of cooperation."

Although Bovis Lend Lease, Inc. is a relative newcomer to Indianapolis construction, its projects tend to be high profile, such as the billion-dollar, world-class United Airlines maintenance center program at Indianapolis International Airport (bottom), and the New Castle Correctional Facility (top).

FedEx

national hub in 1988, it paid homage to the old real estate adage "location, location, location." Because the city is the geographic center of the United States, 70 percent of the nation's major business centers are within a one-day truck run. ■ "Indianapolis has a terrific roadway system, and the people here truly live the spirit of FedEx by giving whatever it takes to get the job done," says Bob Palmer, vice president, national hub operations. "Even in a tight labor market, we're able to find good people with a strong work ethic."

Investment in the City

Indianapolis was one of the original 25 U.S. cities served by FedEx when it began operations April 17, 1973, with 186 overnight packages to deliver. No company had ever before focused on door-to-door, overnight delivery, and the way the world conducts business hasn't been the same since.

The national FedEx hub at Indianapolis has grown along with its parent company, shipping everything from business documents to Indy race cars to zoo animals. In 1994, when FedEx announced a $256 million expansion here, Indianapolis' hub capacity was already second only to Memphis.

In 1997, FedEx made Indianapolis the test site for a paperless clearance process with

In 1998, FedEx's Indianapolis hub became the point of origin for an eastbound, around-the-world delivery route through Paris, the United Arab Emirates, Bombay, the Philippines, Japan, and Anchorage.

Today, the FedEx hub in Indianapolis averages 80,000 boxes and 96,000 documents sorted every hour by 4,000 employees working in around-the-clock shifts.

U.S. Customs. Then, in 1998, it became the point of origin for an eastbound, around-the-world delivery route through Paris, the United Arab Emirates, Bombay, the Philippines, Japan, and Anchorage.

The hub expansion, completed later in 1998, more than tripled total floor space to 1.9 million square feet and added about 800 jobs. New automation features enhanced accuracy, added flexibility, and increased capacity. Box sort capacity went up 55 percent, non-conveyable sort capacity nearly doubled, and bulk-truck unload capacity shot up 162 percent. Today, the hub averages 80,000 boxes and

96,000 documents sorted every hour by 3,000 employees working in around-the-clock shifts.

With 230 acres, 69 aircraft gates, and 70 flights taking off and landing every day, FedEx is easily the largest tenant at the Indianapolis International Airport. In 1997, the company began a partnership with the Federal Aviation Administration and the U.S. Postal Service—in a program called Indy Night Partners—to maximize airport efficiency. The effort not only won a Department of Transportation award, but has also saved millions of dollars and is being modeled nationwide.

Investment in Technology

In starting the express industry, FedEx set a standard for innovation. In 1983, it was the first U.S. company to reach revenues of $1 billion without a merger or acquisition, and the firm has since expanded service offerings with the purchase of Flying Tigers in 1984 and the Caliber System in 1998.

But FedEx is today as much an information company as it is a transportation company, capturing real-time information on every package and using it to competitive advantage. It is uniquely appropriate, then, that the idea for FedEx had its origins in technology. Founder Fred Smith, observing corporate America's increasing reliance on computers, reasoned companies would need either a large inventory of parts to guard against breakdowns, or a system that could supply parts as needed overnight.

The FedEx system gave birth to a number of unique technologies that drive its business. The Customer Oriented Service and Management Operating System (COSMOS) is the information network tracking the movement of every shipment. In a typical month, customers tap into COSMOS via the Internet nearly 2 million times for update on shipment status.

SuperTracker, a handheld scanner, captures information on each package with a quick scan of the package's unique bar code. Each FedEx package receives up to 10 scans from pickup to delivery, pinpointing real-time status en route. A digitally assisted dispatch system (DADS) instantaneously transfers information in Super-Tracker to COSMOS. The wireless DADS terminals, which make up one of the largest private radio networks in the country, also alert couriers to their next pickup.

Investment in People

Fundamental to FedEx's service, quality, and innovation is its guiding corporate philosophy: People, Service, Profit (PSP). PSP maintains that when a company establishes a respectful and rewarding culture for employees, they will deliver exceptional service to customers. Delighted customers, in turn, reward a company with their business and loyalty, creating a profitable enterprise that can provide job satisfaction and job security for its employees.

Examples of PSP at work within FedEx include a promote-from-within policy, an extensive grievance procedure for employee concerns, and an annual employee critique of FedEx leadership. In addition, part-time employees have the same benefits as the CEO. In Indianapolis, FedEx partners with the University of Indianapolis to provide graduate and undergraduate classes for

employees on-site. Programs like these keep FedEx in the top 20 of *Fortune* magazine's 100 best companies to work for in America.

With more than 4,000 employees throughout the state, FedEx also strives to be a good corporate citizen. It has adopted Decatur Township schools on the city's far southwest side, where it has been involved in student mentoring, Junior Achievement, award presentations, and sports events.

Continued growth in the express-delivery industry is a given as businesses learn to manage supply chains more efficiently, and that will drive even more expansion for FedEx in Indianapolis. During the next 10 years, Palmer predicts the Indianapolis hub will continue to grow. And that should keep FedEx and Indianapolis both flying high.

Clockwise from top left:
The Indianapolis hub has grown consistently since its founding, shipping everything from business documents to Indy race cars to zoo animals.

In 1997, FedEx began a partnership with the Federal Aviation Administration and the U.S. Postal Service—in a program called Indy Night Partners—to maximize airport efficiency. The effort not only won a Department of Transportation award, but has also saved millions of dollars and is being modeled nationwide.

Because Indianapolis is the geographic center of the United States, 70 percent of the nation's major business centers are within a one-day truck run. That made the city a logical choice for a FedEx hub, which opened in 1988.

Weiss Communications Inc.

WEISS COMMUNICATIONS INC. REACHES MORE THAN A quarter of a million readers—both residents of and visitors to the Indianapolis area—each month through its two publications, *Indianapolis Woman* and *WHERE Indianapolis*. With an evolving strategy, Chief Executive Officer Mary B. Weiss has developed her company through keen recognition of opportunities for growth and by capitalizing on niche marketing trends.

An Evolving Strategy

Weiss Communications Inc. began its life in 1988 as Weiss Broadcasting, when Mary Weiss applied to the Federal Communications Commission (FCC) for a comparative hearing process for an FM frequency in central Indiana. When the hearing concluded in August 1992, a construction permit was awarded to Weiss, and the station went on the air in February 1993. The FCC granted the license six months later.

Weiss changed the name of the company to Weiss Communications Inc. when she moved into publishing in December 1994, purchasing the one-year-old *Indy's Woman*. The first Weiss-published magazine hit the newsstands in February 1995 with the new name *Indianapolis Woman*. In fall 1997, the monthly magazine began subscribing to Media Audit, and received accreditation from Audit Bureau of Circulations in May 1998.

When the FCC changed rules, allowing more radio stations under individual ownership in a market, Weiss decided to sell her radio station. With stand-alone stations in high demand, she recognized this was an excellent time to maximize the return on her investment, and began her pursuit of another niche market close to her heart.

The Emergence of *Indianapolis Woman*

The 1990s ushered in statistics showing general acceptance of women as major, emerging decision makers. The numbers finally reflected that women nationwide controlled 80 percent of household purchasing

decisions and controlled or strongly influenced most household decisions about banking and investment, health care and insurance, education, and lifestyle. Those numbers set the stage for the unique appeal of *Indianapolis Woman's* emergence on the local readers' scene.

Utilizing the proven format of a glossy magazine with editorial features and monthly departments, *Indianapolis Woman* has grown in circulation because the magazine recognizes women's achievements, whether overcoming obstacles or celebrating successes. The magazine has strong credibility with readers because it reports on issues of interest to women from a local point of view.

Weiss' mission for both readers and employees of the magazine has remained constant from the first issue. Beyond inspiring and informing Indianapolis-area women, Weiss wants to help them maximize strengths and manage weaknesses so they grow to reach their full potential at home, in the community, and in the workplace.

WHERE Indianapolis

In its ever burgeoning quest for niche markets, Weiss Commu-

With an evolving strategy, Chief Executive Officer Mary B. Weiss has developed Weiss Communications Inc. through keen recognition of opportunities for growth and by capitalizing on niche marketing trends (top).

Utilizing the proven format of a glossy magazine with editorial features and monthly departments, *Indianapolis Woman* has grown in circulation because the magazine recognizes women's achievements, whether overcoming obstacles or celebrating successes (bottom).

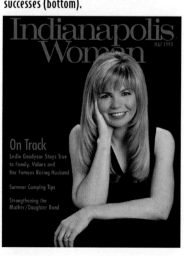

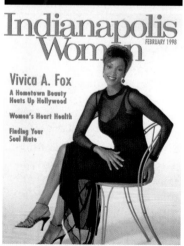

WHERE
INDIANAPOLIS

WE GOT GAME
INDIANA'S PASSION FOR BASKETBALL JUMPS IN MARCH

nications has acquired a second magazine, *WHERE Indianapolis*. In June 1999, the company purchased a four-year-old franchise that was part of the international network of *WHERE* magazines.

Recognizing the growth potential of a visitors' magazine distributed through local hotels and retail outlets, Weiss Communications sees the role of *WHERE Indianapolis* as a vehicle for promoting the city of Indianapolis as a unique destination. Issues of the magazine detail city sites, history, diversity, and culture, as well as dining, shopping, and other entertainment.

In addition to the role the magazine plays in providing important information for vacationers and business travelers, Weiss feels it has an economic development role to play. *WHERE Indianapolis* is a strong vehicle for showcasing the city to companies considering a relocation or the addition of a local branch office. Because it shows off the city to its best advantage, *WHERE Indianapolis* also can be used by local companies expanding their workforces. In essence, the magazine can help Indianapolis grow by creating new jobs and the need for more services. In turn, it also can help companies attract the best talent.

Making the Most of Opportunity

Weiss Communications' mission includes giving back to the Indianapolis community, particularly in philanthropic and volunteer efforts that benefit

WHERE
INDIANAPOLIS

PLAY BY THE BOOK:
A DOWNTOWN GUIDE

SPORTY SPOTS:
DINING IN INDY

FOR THE RECORD:
B-BALL STATS

ROARING ATTRACTIONS
TOP TEN SITES IN INDY THAT KEEP 'EM HUNGRY FOR MORE

women, with an emphasis on education, health, and women in the workplace.

Looking to the future, Weiss sees an opportunity to expand women's publications in other geographic markets. While maintaining corporate headquarters in Indianapolis, Weiss is planning corporate and franchise operations throughout the Midwest to increase national and regional advertising, and to garner

local business directed toward women. With industry downsizing and more companies outsourcing their publishing needs, opportunities also abound for growth of Weiss Communications' custom publishing division.

At Weiss Communications, one thing is certain. Its founder and CEO's keen eye for opportunity in niche markets will continue to hold her and her company in good stead.

WHERE Indianapolis highlights city attractions such as the Indianapolis Zoo (right) and the 2000 NCAA Basketball Final Four (left).

GSC Industries

AS A COMPANY, GSC INDUSTRIES REPRESENTS ONE FATHER'S dream for his sons to own and operate a successful business together. As a tribute to their father, the four Gonzalez brothers have collaborated to fulfill his lifelong wish. ■ While they were growing up, the Gonzalez brothers were constantly reminded of the importance of working together. Their father, Robert Gonzalez, told them he was helping them learn to get along so they could be in the business someday. An owner of a landscaping company in Houston, he familiarized them with his work.

If the company's success today is any indication, his work ethic and determination set a strong example. Since founding their company in 1989, the brothers have built GSC Manufacturing, their core business, into an advanced-technology manufacturer of machined automotive parts with more than $26 million in annual sales. They started a second subsidiary, GSC Leasing, in 1997.

Quality-Conscious Growth

In 1994, the firm moved to its current facility on Indianapolis' northwest side, where it has since expanded to 48,000 square feet. That same year, GSC was selected to take part in General Motors' mentor-protégé program, and in 1995, it received its first big break in the form of a $30 million contract from the automaker. The Gonzalez brothers were also named Ernst & Young Entrepreneurs of the Year in 1995.

More honors ensued, including Chrysler's Gold Pentastar Award and the National Minority Supplier Development Council's Supplier of the Year award in 1996. The firm became one of Chrysler's preferred suppliers in 1997 and entered Caterpillar's mentor-protégé program in 1998. QS 9000 and ISO 9002 quality certifications followed, topped off by a $24 million contract award from Caterpillar and a $30 million contract award from DaimlerChrysler.

GSC also received the 1999 State of Indiana Quality Improvement Award. Its recent certification by the Small Business Administration as an 8(a) company makes the firm eligible for federal contracting set-asides and business-development assistance. And the Department of Defense recently selected the firm as its first mentor-protégé in the state.

High-Tech Precision

GSC's precision-machined components for the automotive industry include a variety of goods produced from bar stock, casting, forgings, and tubing. With strong, fully integrated engineering and technical teams, the company's information systems provide drawings on demand with design parameters linked to dimensional control plans. Prototyping and redesign services are also in demand, and more than once the

GSC Industries has received numerous industry awards, including the National Minority Supplier Development Council's Supplier of the Year award in 1996 (top).

In 1994, GSC Industries, an advanced-technology manufacturer of machined automotive parts with more than $26 million in annual sales, moved to its current facility on Indianapolis' northwest side, where it has since expanded to 48,000 square feet (bottom).

company has helped to improve a part that is causing problems.

Because it truly values its workforce, the company uses cross training as a way to broaden employees' skills and to evaluate their potential as well. Shop employees get experience working in quality control and in engineering, while machine operators rotate. Cell manufacturing centers enhance workflow with a group of machines that work on similar projects. The company's high-tech machinery makes it possible for it to produce 20,000 to 30,000 parts per day.

In 1997, GSC Industries branched out by starting GSC Leasing to lease out manufacturing, hospital and medical, and office equipment, in addition to trucks and buses. The division's main focus is on serving the Michigan and Indiana areas, but it also has customers in the southeastern and southwestern United States.

Core values of quality work and customer dedication—values the brothers also inherited from their father—have added to GSC's success, attracting such blue-chip customers as New Venture Gear, DaimlerChrysler, Caterpillar, General Motors, and Borg-Warner Automotive.

Family Matters

Today, GSC employs not only the four Gonzalez brothers, but also two sisters, three brothers-in-law, a sister-in-law, and a son of one of the founding brothers. Manuel Gonzalez heads up the holding company, while Martin

is president of GSC Manufacturing, Robert is president of GSC Leasing, and Benedict is a manufacturing engineer.

Through its 80 percent minority workforce, the firm maintains its commitment to the community by helping other people of minority heritage realize their dreams. More than half of its 185 workers are of Hispanic heritage, but the workforce also represents those of Russian, Laotian, Vietnamese, and African-American backgrounds. Grants from the Indiana Department of Commerce have helped with training and expansions.

As a concerned corporate citizen, GSC Industries anticipates expansion of its community involvement in the coming years. The firm has always earmarked a percentage of corporate profits

for community giving; however, 1999 marked the first year when contributions were a budgeted item. The firm donated approximately $80,000 during the year for scholarships, churches, and community activities. One project in particular involves sponsorship of *Americanos: Latino Life in the United States,* a photographic exhibit at the Eiteljorg Museum of American Indians and Western Art.

The Gonzalez brothers' father died in 1986, just a few years before his sons established GSC. Based on their upbringing and training, they are convinced that the company's success is attributable to his vision. And from the laudatory response within the industry, the company's success should continue for generations to come.

GSC's precision-machined components for the automotive industry include a variety of goods produced from bar stock, casting, forgings, and tubing.

As a tribute to their father, the four Gonzalez brothers have collaborated to fulfill his lifelong wish for his sons to own and operate a successful business together. Manuel Gonzalez heads up the holding company, while Martin is president of GSC Manufacturing, Robert is president of GSC Leasing, and Benedict is a manufacturing engineer.

Standard Management Corporation

"**F**OND MEMORIES FROM CHILDHOOD—A FAVORITE TOY, GAME, OR TV show—stay with us because of something extra, something special about them," says Ronald D. Hunter, CEO of Standard Management Corporation (SMC). "What we remember tells us something about who we are and where we're headed. At SMC, we believe these memories translate to lessons that can be used to enhance our future."

It is not typical rhetoric for a life insurance holding company, but then SMC isn't run-of-the-mill. Through its subsidiaries, SMC provides insurance, annuities, and tax-advantaged investment products to clients in 48 states and 98 countries. Since purchasing Standard Life Insurance Co. of Indiana in 1989, total assets have grown from $2.8 million to $1.2 billion.

The company's success can be attributed to setting ambitious goals, then following through with superior results. Record operating earnings in 1999 included net income of $5.27 million on revenues of $73 million, with a 51 percent increase in recurring operating earnings per share. Sales soared to $220 million with U.S. sales up 102 percent and international sales up 30 percent over 1998 figures. There is little wonder the firm ranked number 11 on the *Indianapolis Business Journal*'s 1999 list of the area's fastest-growing public companies.

An Eye toward Growth

SMC considers itself both young and established, global and local, a life insurance holding company and more. It began operations in Indianapolis in June 1989; the same year, it purchased Standard Life, which was founded in Indianapolis in 1934. Standard Life provided SMC with a nationwide license base and has remained the firm's flagship company.

After an initial public offering of 2.3 million shares in February 1993, which raised $30 million, SMC expanded globally by purchasing Premier Life SA, headquartered in Luxembourg, and Premier Life Ltd., headquartered in Bermuda. The companies offer tax-advantaged life assurance products worldwide. Six other acquisitions have followed, bringing the firm's total assets to $1.2 billion, placing it among the 200 largest insurance conglomerates in Europe and North America.

"One way we've been able to grow is by participating in the consolidation of small to medium-sized insurance and financial services companies," Hunter says. "Now we want to grow from within by integrating our acquisitions, taking advantage of operational economies, and capitalizing on marketing and distribution—something few companies have done."

Innovation in Product Design

SMC plans to outperform competitors in product design and customer service. If past results are any indication, investors can rely on success. "Rather than introduce a product every year or so that is a plain-vanilla annuity, we have begun offering an equity-index annuity line, tied to indices such as the Standard & Poor's 500 and Dow Jones Industrial Average. These prod-

Leading Standard Management Corporation (SMC) in success are executive officers (from left) Raymond J. Ohlson, Ronald D. Hunter, Edward T. Stahl, Stephen M. Coons, and Paul "Pete" B. Pheffer (top).

In 1993, SMC expanded globally by purchasing Premier Life SA, headquartered in Luxembourg (bottom).

In spring 2000, SMC broke ground on its 58,000-square-foot headquarters in Carmel. Scheduled to open in spring 2001, the facility will include generous classroom space for ongoing training and development, along with a more open floor plan to promote teamwork.

ucts let customers participate in equity markets and generate income for both the client and the agent," Hunter says.

Such products have driven the company's record-setting sales, accounting for 37 percent of annuity sales in just one year. The line holds particular appeal for baby boomers seeking less risky companions to stock-heavy investments in 401(k) plans and individual retirement accounts. Also appealing to this burgeoning market is Critical Choice Plus, a 15-year term product that guarantees income in the face of serious illness. Introduced in 1998, it pays a 100 percent lump sum benefit if the insured suffers health threats such as heart attack, stroke, cancer, paralysis, or Alzheimer's disease.

Building Intellectual Capital

SMC has increased its overall management depth in recent years with about 150 employees supporting a network of more

than 4,000 active agents. Employees are known for good customer and agent service, maintaining a cost for processing insurance/ annuity policy applications that is lower than the industry average, and turning around commissions for annuity sales in 24 hours. Their devotion and responsiveness have helped to increase agent productivity 30 percent in just one year.

In spring 2000, the firm broke ground on the next phase of its growth and a significant investment in its talent pool— a 58,000-square-foot corporate headquarters in Carmel, Indiana. Scheduled to open in spring 2001, the facility will include generous classroom space for ongoing training and development, along with a more open floor plan to promote teamwork.

Community Involvement

With a philosophy that states, "We believe in our people. We believe in our community. We believe in helping others," SMC is dedicated to investing in the central Indiana community by supporting programs and activities that make the community a better place to live and work. SMC has provided financial and other support to more than 60 organizations during a recent three-year period. In 1998, it started the Standard Management Open Golf Tournament,

which raises money for charitable and community endeavors.

Then, in 1999, the company established the Standard Management Corporation Charitable Trust, a nonprofit trust designed to distribute even more funds to local causes. A recent gift to Ball State University of $100,000 will establish the Center for Actuarial Science, Insurance, and Risk Management to offer specialized training for business students.

"Our record performance in all arenas is proof that our philosophy of returning the industry to the people it belongs to—the agent, the consumer, and the employees that make it happen—is working," Hunter says. "It's a move that can only enhance the future of our company, our employees, our investors, and our customers."

SMC is dedicated to investing in the central Indiana community by supporting programs and activities that make the community a better place to live and work (right).

At SMC, team building is a top priority (left).

Lockwood Greene

CCORDING TO THOMAS EDISON, "A PROMISE WITHOUT A process is just wishful thinking." Lockwood Greene, a global consulting, design, and construction firm with a thriving Indianapolis office, puts process in gear first to help create a promising future for its clients. As the oldest professional design firm in continuous operation in the United States, Lockwood Greene traces its roots to 1832, when its engineers traveled to New England on horseback, providing their services to mills. In 1882, this engineering firm became Lockwood, Greene & Company, and was known for its consulting and engineering work in the textile industry. The company became Lockwood Greene Engineers, Inc. in 1928, and prospered by securing several World War II-related contracts and from the burgeoning economy that followed the war. Thereafter, Lockwood Greene began to diversify its services by adapting to the emergence of technology-based industries in which the firm is a leader today.

As part of its recent global strategy, J.A. Jones, Inc. designated Lockwood Greene as its global industrial engineering and construction leader.

Lockwood Greene opened its Indianapolis office in 1990 as an outgrowth of its Midwest business unit. The business unit employs more than 250 people, with 100 in the Indianapolis office. The constructed value of design for Lockwood Greene exceeds $4 billion annually through a network of 44 international offices throughout the Americas, Europe, and Asia.

A Full-Service Consulting, Design, and Construction Firm

As a global business partner for consulting, design, and construction, Lockwood Greene serves manufacturing, process, power, and institutional clients.

The company's Indianapolis office and Midwest business unit serve a wide variety of these clients, including those in the general manufacturing, chemicals, pharmaceuticals, food and beverages, and consumer products industries.

In addition to providing full-service engineering, procurement, and construction for various industries, the Indianapolis office specializes in chemicals and pharmaceutical process design, and has completed a wide variety of grassroots and retrofit projects ranging in size from $5 million to more than $100 million. Lockwood Greene has serviced many of the largest chemical, pharmaceutical, and food and beverage companies in the world. For instance, the Midwest busi-

An example of the work performed by Lockwood Greene's Indianapolis office is the chemical-processing plant in Memphis, Tennessee.

ness unit has performed extensive work for chemical and pharmaceutical projects globally.

Outcomes by Design®

The company's reputation for excellence today is bolstered by its trademarked Outcomes by Design®, a quality-based partnering model implemented in 1993. The program provides a foundation for continually improving performance, relationships, and results for clients. Outcomes by Design® incorporates a proprietary, three-phase client relationship development cycle that includes relationship management, process management, and project management phases. The relationship management phase seeks to align agendas by focusing on client expectations and by establishing a common mission. The process management phase identifies the accountabilities of all

parties, establishes performance criteria, and allocates and commits the required resources for the project. The project management phase then focuses on producing expected project outcomes and leveraging greater expertise on each client's behalf.

"A good example of the success of Outcomes by Design is a retrofit project with a division of a major international pharmaceutical firm," explains Hank Salzberg, vice president and head of the Midwest business unit. "In initial conversations, the client had defined its project goals around cost, schedule, and start-up date. However, through further discussion, we helped identify 12 key goals, including the need to keep the existing facility operating, clean, and safe during construction. We tracked our progress on the 12 goals in monthly client reports, and met all objectives because

we took the time at the outset to make sure all the key client objectives had been identified and agreed upon."

The Midwest business unit has performed engineering, procurement, and construction on a wide number of finishing/ compounding projects and material-handling projects all over the globe.

"Results like these are largely why most of our work comes from repeat customers," Salzberg adds. "We take the most pride in the relationships we are able to build through our alignment with client business objectives."

Finally, Lockwood Greene's client focus and multiple office locations throughout the world allow the firm to leverage its talent and resources at the local level. Its Indianapolis presence is established with key area clients that will position the firm to grow along with Indianapolis' continuing business expansion.

Protection Plus Inc.

WHEN CLIENTS HIRE PROTECTION PLUS INC. FOR THEIR security needs, the big plus they get is Marie Stanley, its founder and president. She'll be working with the same good sense and zeal that built her firm into the largest woman-owned business in Indianapolis to protect their facilities,

job sites, and special events.

Protection Plus began as a two-person, home-based security business to provide Stanley and her husband, Ray, with part-time work. She incorporated in 1990 with 10 full-time workers, and now employs 135 security guards and traffic-control officers for construction security, traffic control, and site security.

Revenues exceeded $3 million in 1999, with a client roster that includes the RCA Dome and Convention Center, the Federal Aviation Administration (FAA) at Indianapolis International Airport, and a variety of construction companies, stores, and apartment complexes.

Training Makes the Difference

According to Stanley, what sets her security officers apart from the competition is the expert training they receive. She relies on her own 25 years of experience as a security officer, 20 years as a Marion County special deputy, and several years of working security at the City-County Building. Ray Stanley, a retired Indianapolis Police Department (IPD) officer, brings additional expertise to the business, as well as a network of contacts.

Together, their backgrounds help the Stanleys cast a keen eye on applicants in a tight labor market. "We may hire 10 and only keep two," Marie Stanley explains. "If our standards weren't so high, we could have grown the business faster. But we'll turn down work if we don't have the staff, rather than put out cattle calls for anyone and everyone."

Stanley says she looks for potential employees with security

Marie Stanley, founder and president of Protection Plus Inc., has made the firm into the largest woman-owned business in Indianapolis, protecting clients' facilities, job sites, and special events.

experience, examines their job histories closely, and runs criminal background checks before hiring anyone. Applicants then receive on-the-job training with experienced officers before being sent out on their own.

Protection Plus offers both armed and unarmed security officers, uniformed or in plain clothes. All are certified in first aid, cardiopulmonary resuscitation, and use of a tactical baton, and they receive ongoing training in areas such as public relations, report writing, and firearms and pepper spray use. All traffic officers take an Indiana Department of Transportation test, those who carry guns must qualify at the Marion County Sheriff's Department (MCSD) range, and many take advan-

tage of other training programs administered by MCSD. For example, those who complete the special deputy program have arrest powers as well.

Taking It Personally

The Stanleys have a genuine interest in their employees, and they feel in the long run, this focused approach also sets apart the service they provide clients. For example, they both work at events alongside their officers. They work to get to know their people and learn their needs. Those employees who perform well have many opportunities for overtime and often receive special help.

"We've had good luck employing women with children who only want to work a few days a week," Stanley explains.

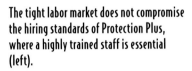

The tight labor market does not compromise the hiring standards of Protection Plus, where a highly trained staff is essential (left).

With 135 security guards and traffic-control officers, Protection Plus provides construction security, traffic control, and site security (right).

"Those we see who have potential, we try to help. For instance, we have an employee who never finished high school doing dispatches out of her home. We're paying her to complete her general equivalency degree [GED] so she can move up to FAA work at the airport. We want our employees to know we're committed to providing career paths for them."

After completing a probationary period, Protection Plus security officers also receive benefits almost unheard of in the industry—paid vacation and sick days, company-furnished uniforms, take-home radios, health insurance, and a pension plan. Stanley believes that she has higher-quality officers because Protection Plus offers better pay, and that the 35 women officers she currently employs are especially attracted by the benefits. She takes pride in the fact that several former Protection Plus employees have gone on to become IPD officers.

"Law enforcement has fascinated me my whole life," Stanley explains. "I think it was because I wanted to make a difference. As employers, Ray and I both look for opportunities to make a difference in the lives of our employees as well."

A Woman in a "Man's" Business

Stanley is proud of the success she's achieved in a traditionally male-oriented business, but points out that not all clients are comfortable communicating with a woman business owner. "We get a lot of contracts where some guys don't want to talk to a woman," she says. "That's when it's good to have Ray to fall back on."

Ray is quick to credit Marie with superior handling of employees. "She'll call the officers up about different things," he says, "and somehow they just seem to respond better to her."

But sitting behind a desk all day is not Stanley's style, and she can break up a fight or make arrests with the best of them. Following a 1998 Indianapolis Colts home game, she was on ground-patrol duty when a fan broke through the perimeter and ran onto the playing field. In front of thousands, including the local Fox affiliate's cameras, Stanley—in skirt, hose, and heels—chased the fan, tackled him, and sat on him until additional help arrived.

She got a standing ovation from the crowd and a feature on the evening news. "It was good exposure for the business, but it cured me from ever wearing a dress to work again," she laughs.

Revenues of Protection Plus exceeded $3 million in 1999, with a client roster that includes the RCA Dome and Convention Center and the Federal Aviation Administration (FAA) at Indianapolis International Airport.

Star Environmental Inc.

STAR ENVIRONMENTAL INC. APPROACHES EVERY ENVIRONmental cleanup or consultation task with a winning attitude. Although the firm will tackle almost any project, its focus has been legally mandated asbestos abatement since it was founded in 1990. "We eliminate liability for our customers," says Todd Strader, company founder and president. "Since the cleanup has to be done, our goal is to do it safely, do it right, and do it efficiently." Strader uses that philosophy as the text and his business as the classroom for teaching skills and developing attitudes that will help employees get along better in work and in life.

The Clean Air Act gives the Environmental Protection Agency and the Occupational Safety and Health Administration responsibility over exposure to asbestos, a naturally occurring, fibrous mineral that can cause cancer if ingested in large enough quantities over time. Because of its strength and resistance to fire and corrosion, asbestos has been used in hundreds of commercial products, such as brake linings, floor tile, and insulation. Its presence there harms no one unless the product is disturbed and the asbestos fibers escape into the air, where people can inhale them. Companies consult with environmental contractors such as Star prior to extensive remodeling or demolition to test for and encapsulate or remove asbestos.

A Firm Foundation

Both Strader and his general manager, Chris Zumbaugh, have the educational backgrounds and experience to meet the exacting task of environmental cleanup. Both worked as general managers for one of Indiana's largest asbestos abatement contractors and both have relevant educational backgrounds—Strader in biology and Zumbaugh in architectural engineering.

The firm operates out of a 5,000-square-foot warehouse on the city's near southwest side, from which the two partners have diligently worked to develop the business. Their goal has been to build a foundation of positive relationships with local environmental consultants, regulatory agencies, corporate clients, and employees.

Based on company numbers, they have been successful. Since its founding, Star has become the second-largest asbestos contractor in the city and the eighth-largest overall environmental contractor. Annual revenues almost doubled in 1999, exceeding $4.3 million.

Star acts as a general contractor on demolition work or as a subcontractor. Customers run the gamut from home owners getting a furnace replaced to Fortune 500 companies, developers, and other environmental contractors. The company's team has worked for city, state, and federal government entities, every major university in the state, and Indianapolis Public Schools, and has even traveled out of state for clients. What speaks even more highly of the work done by Star Environmental is that every client—past and present—has given the company permission to use them as a reference. Satisfaction, created client by client, is paramount to progress for this forward-thinking company.

Safety policies are written with implementation in mind and reviewed at tailgate safety meetings every day before work begins. Employees wear state-of-the-art protective gear and strictly adhere to industry standards to ensure zero contamination or exposure.

Star provides all clients with a detailed proposal of all available options prior to the start of the work, followed by thorough, post-removal sanitization and air sampling by an independent laboratory to ensure credibility. A final report to clients contains all

Star Environmental acts as a general contractor on demolition work or as a subcontractor. Customers run the gamut from home owners getting a furnace replaced to Fortune 500 companies, developers, and other environmental contractors.

necessary sampling, removal, and management information.

Building up Employees

The nature of environmental cleanup, and particularly asbestos abatement, involves tearing structures down and often leaving them looking worse than before. "That, coupled with the fact that we work tough hours—nights and weekends— with carcinogens, makes it difficult to find and motivate employees in this tight labor market," Strader says.

He addresses this issue by treating his employees well and creating positive experiences for them, including volunteer opportunities with Star Missions, a nonprofit arm of Star Environmental that sponsors construction and medical projects in developing countries. By providing employees with opportunities to assist underprivileged communities, Strader hopes to instill a sense of understanding and compassion that will carry over into the workplace.

Overseas projects have included building a four-room elementary school in Ecuador, constructing a health center and medical clinics in Guatemala, and constructing a community center in Guatemala. Locally, Star has also assisted Habitat for Humanity, the American

Cancer Society, the Breast Health Awareness League, Traders Point Christian Church, and the International School of Indiana with volunteers, in-kind services, and donations.

"Our employees will do a better job for our customers if they have opportunities to give to others less fortunate and to build something up rather than just tearing things down," Strader says. He developed an interest in overseas missions during trips to Kenya and Nicaragua while a student at DePauw University. A friend in the Peace Corps now helps

him find projects, and Strader recruits volunteers from his business, church, and schools.

He hopes employees use the experience to help develop their careers. "Most of the people we encounter in these missions trips have little opportunity to improve their circumstances," he says. "I hope my employees, by comparison, see how many opportunities they have to improve their lives and take advantage of some. If the job Star provides them with becomes a stepping-stone to something better, then we have done our duty as an employer."

Star approaches every environmental cleanup or consultation task with a winning attitude.

Trinity Homes

TRINITY HOMES HAS BEEN HELPING PEOPLE BUILD THEIR DREAM homes in the Greater Indianapolis community since 1991. From its association with the best communities, to its solid house plans in every price range, to its flexibility of design and opportunities for customization, Trinity has a reputation for attention to detail and solid construction.

As a true champion of well-designed living spaces, Trinity works to stay at the forefront of national building trends in materials and design. The firm has won numerous industry awards not only for its designs, but also for its merchandising, as well as in recognition of its quality, professional sales staff.

The Trinity Difference

For Trinity, a philosophy of proper engineering is the first construction step. Its homes are engineered to last, with guaranteed dry basements, high-quality construction specifications, and expertly finished trim.

Trinity homes are designed to please as well, with open, flowing floor plans, stunning paint jobs, and countless custom options that come standard. "Trinity consistently builds the most the customer's budget allows—customization included," says Jim McKenzie, president. "That philosophy is the same regardless of whether the home is $120,000 or $500,000."

Standard features include wood-burning fireplaces, hardwood cabinetry with adjustable shelving, cultured marble bathroom vanities, and lighted walk-in closets. Outside, patios, generous landscaping, energy-efficient windows and doors, and weatherizing are standard. Quality building features include sturdy two-by-four, 16-inch-on-center stud construction; an engineered floor system; copper plumbing water supply; and energy-efficient ventilation and water-treatment systems.

About 95 percent of Trinity buyers take advantage of their options to customize, culling ideas from the decorated models the firm maintains in about 25 new home communities city-wide. These homes help define the personalities of the neighborhoods where they're built, making a Trinity home one that holds its value longer in the resale market.

All home buyers receive blueprints for their homes and are encouraged to visit the building sites during construction. Trinity maintains long-term relationships with the tradesmen who build its homes, and it has confidence in their work. Trinity feels home buyers will be equally convinced of the value they're receiving as they see their homes take shape.

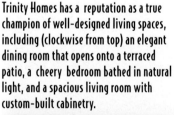

Trinity Homes has a reputation as a true champion of well-designed living spaces, including (clockwise from top) an elegant dining room that opens onto a terraced patio, a cheery bedroom bathed in natural light, and a spacious living room with custom-built cabinetry.

From the beginning, Trinity encourages home buyers to be part of the building process by holding a preconstruction meeting with the superintendent, as well as a midconstruction overview prior to installing drywall. Then, in addition to making some 600 quality checks on each home, Trinity and its subcontractors assure two preclosing walk-throughs, a third walk-through after closing, and a 10-year home owner's warranty.

Convenience Marks Sale

Trinity's spacious new headquarters in Carmel combines all its many services to home buyers under one roof. Eventually, the large, modern facility will include a design center to help new home buyers in selecting options such as lighting, flooring, and finishes.

Pyramid Mortgage Company, a Trinity subsidiary, maintains offices at Trinity's headquarters as a convenience for home buyers shopping for financing.

If home buyers select Pyramid, Trinity pays points and closing costs. Having its own mortgage company also makes Trinity more flexible to the needs of its customers and gives it an even greater incentive to get homes finished and buyers moved in.

Pyramid is a full-service mortgage company that can provide financing for qualified buyers of any new or existing homes. The company provides a full range of mortgage financing options and participates in a nationwide network of mortgage loan brokers, providing access to the most competitive programs and interest rates on the market.

If prospective home buyers have existing homes to sell, Trinity can help there, too, putting the equity in the existing homes to work in building new homes. If an existing home meets the terms of Trinity's Guaranteed Sale Program and it hasn't sold by the time the new home is finished, Trinity will buy it.

Building Homes and Communities

Trinity builds more than homes. It builds communities, participating in a variety of related services that give something back to the central Indiana region. The firm recently built and sold a house for the benefit of the STAR Alliance for Drug-Free Youth, an Indianapolis organization. In addition, every year since Trinity was founded in 1991 it has also built a Habit for Humanity home.

"Building a home is one of the most important investments any person makes, both financially and emotionally," McKenzie says. "At Trinity, we begin with quality workmanship, and we don't stop until our home buyers have a new home that reflects their style, taste, and expectations. Whatever the circumstances, our award-winning team is always working to make the building experience a pleasant one."

Trinity's houses are marked with open floor plans, countless custom options, and comfortable spaces such as (clockwise from top) master bedrooms truly fit for the master, a warm library evocative of fine traditional homes, and casual rooms for any gathering of family and friends.

1993 Alltrista Corporation

1993 Eris Survey Systems Inc.

1994 Guidant Corporation

1994 Indiana Health Industry Forum

1995 Manufacturing Technology Center at Indianapolis (MTC-I)

1996 Escient Technologies, LLC

1997 Clarian Health Partners, Inc.

1997 Globe Corporate Stay International

1997 ONEX, Inc.

1997 Platinum Television Group

1997 SAFECO

1998 Keane, Inc.

1999 Telstreet.com

2000 ImagineX Radiology Alliance, L.L.C.

Leading the Way

Alltrista Corporation

ALLTRISTA CORPORATION MAY BE NEW TO THE LIST OF corporate headquarters located in Indianapolis, but the firm has roots that go back more than a century. Alltrista's metal and plastic products range from home canning supplies and coins to refrigerator door liners, and from components for heavy-duty trucks to plastic pallets and cathodic protection systems for bridges.

The production of coin blanks is a huge business for Alltrista Corporation. Approximately 10 billion blanks are produced each year for the U.S. Mint. The company is also the sole supplier of one-cent blanks to the Royal Canadian Mint, and produces blanks for many other countries as well (top).

Alltrista's management committee includes (from left) Kevin D. Bower, senior vice president and chief financial officer; Thomas B. Clark, president and chief executive officer; Jerry T. McDowell, group vice president, metal products; and John F. Zappala, group vice president, plastic products (bottom).

From A to Zinc

Alltrista's history goes back to 1880, when two brothers borrowed $200 from an uncle and founded the Ball Brothers Glass Manufacturing Company in Buffalo, New York. By the early 1900s, their small company had become a leading manufacturer of glass home canning jars and had expanded to include a zinc mill, a paper packaging facility, and a rubber goods manufacturing plant, all of which then contributed to the production of the famous jars.

Canning jars and lids remain an important part of Alltrista's metals group, and with the 1993 spin-off from what had evolved into Ball Corporation, exclusive rights to use the Ball® brand were retained. Alltrista subsequently acquired Kerr in the United States and Bernardin in Canada, both prominent home canning brands. The firm also markets dry-mix food preservation products used in the canning process, as well as a growing line of glassware and housewares.

Zinc is still an important product line for Alltrista, although zinc lids have not been used on home canning jars for more than a quarter-century. The product line shares responsibility for the growth in the metals portion of the business. The company pioneered the use of copper-plated zinc blanks for the production of pennies in the early 1980s, and today is the sole supplier of those coin blanks to the U. S. and Canadian mints, as well as for other countries. In addition, Alltrista manufactures fabricated zinc products, such as battery cans for zinc/carbon batteries, and zinc strip used by markets as diverse as automotive electronics, plumbing, and architecture.

Zinc's durability and unique anticorrosion properties have made it an ideal successor to less capable or more expensive metals. Because it inhibits rusting, zinc is used on ships, bridges, and coastal structures.

One use of zinc pioneered by Alltrista involves protecting the columns that support bridges from the corrosion caused by salt water. An Alltrista product called Lifejacket® can be used to encapsulate the column with zinc mesh and prevent rusting of metal reinforcements that would otherwise lead to destruction of the column. Lifejackets cost about $2,000 per bridge column, eliminating the cost of replacement, which is usually $30,000 per column. Perhaps more important, the bridge doesn't need to be taken out of service if Lifejackets are used. Lifejacket was developed from Alltrista's studies of zinc and its unique electrochemical properties, and the metal will likely play a role in product offerings in the future.

Impact in Plastics

Forty-seven percent of Alltrista's 1999 sales resulted from the company's plastics group, and its April 1999 acquisition of Triangle Plastics will put Alltrista on track for increasing its overall sales to $500 million by 2002. In fact, much of the company's

growth potential is tied to its increasing involvement in the plastics industry. The acquisition also made Alltrista the largest industrial thermoformer in North America, manufacturing heavy-gauge parts for trucking, agriculture, portable-toilet, recreational, construction, and materials-handling markets.

The company's other plastics activities use processes such as injection molding and extrusion. Alltrista has long supplied the appliance industry with refrigerator door liners and is a major producer of lightweight plastic tables for use in the hospitality marketplace. Manufactured housing and recreational vehicle markets will also play a role in the company's strategy to grow in plastics.

One of Alltrista's strong suits has always been the ability of its engineers to add value for customers in need of parts design and subassembly production, and their willingness to use their expertise to solve clients' problems. For example, the company designed and engineered a surgical suture retainer especially for Johnson & Johnson. "Other manufacturers told Johnson & Johnson that this part was impossible to produce in plastic and still function as specified," says President and CEO Thomas Clark. "Our engineers took on the problem and solved it. We recently received recognition from Johnson & Johnson for shipping the billionth unit of

the part that other companies said couldn't be made."

Lean and Mean

Alltrista prides itself on maintaining a flat organizational structure. Although the firm employs about 2,000 people at 15 locations in nine states and Canada, Alltrista's corporate and group headquarters staff on the northeast side of Indianapolis has fewer than 25 people.

"Our approach to increasing our business is to emphasize marketing rather than sales," Clark says. "We have specific competitive strategies for each of our product areas, and we grow our businesses based on market segmentation. We're less focused on shipping product than we are on determining what represents value to our customers and meeting those needs. That's an advantage that customers would be hard pressed to find elsewhere."

Clockwise from top left:
Alltrista is the leading supplier of home-canning products in North America with its Ball®, Kerr®, and Bernardin® brands. The company's Fruit-Fresh fruit protector is used for canning, as well as for keeping fruits from browning.

Value-added thermoforming of plastic is a fast-growing product line at Alltrista. Products thermoformed by the company range from inner-door liners for side-by-side refrigerators and freezers to products for the agricultural, heavy truck, manufactured housing, material handling, portable rest room, and recreational vehicle markets.

Eris Survey Systems Inc.

ERIS SURVEY SYSTEMS INC. OFFERS A VARIETY OF HEALTH RISK assessment solutions and claims analysis tools to employers, insurers, and health care providers. The questionnaires and proprietary software solutions created by Eris have been used with more than 2.7 million people around the world. ■ The company name derives from Eris, the Greek goddess of chaos. "The name speaks to our goal of bringing simple solutions to chaotic health care problems," says Jeanita Schulten, president. "We want to help people accept responsibility for their own health, help them become healthier, and decrease the cost of care through simple, wellness-based solutions."

The Road to Success

Eris Associates Inc. was founded in 1983 in Scotts Valley, California. Schulten, a founding partner of Eris Survey Systems, bought the firm's assets in 1993 and moved its headquarters to Indianapolis; however, the firm is very much a virtual organization. The company's employees— located throughout the United States— serve clients around the globe.

In 1987, the Centers for Disease Control selected Eris to develop and manage the first public domain health risk assessment as part of a joint project with the Carter Presidential Center of Emory University. From that partnership emerged a more functional survey product that uses a validated science base and has evolved into a trusted industry standard.

Indiana University School of Business listed Eris as a Growth 100 company in 1996, 1997, and 1999, highlighting its annual sales growth in excess of 50 percent. Ernst & Young also recognized the firm's accomplishments by naming Schulten its 1998 Entrepreneur of the Year among women-owned businesses.

Eris has provided more than 400 custom health risk assessments to clients that include Kaiser Permanente, Monsanto, the U.S. Army, and the U.S. Department of Health and Human Services. Its surveys have been translated into several languages, and the company created the only survey specific to Native Americans for use at reservations by Indian Health Services.

In fall 1998, Eris took another step forward by becoming a subsidiary of Gordian Health Solutions, a national health improvement company based in Nashville. The two firms fit together well, since Gordian provides intervention programs based on Eris' risk assessments.

Data-Driven, Results-Oriented Products

Eris survey products call attention to personal lifestyle choices that may directly or indirectly cause or aggravate disease. Individuals receive confidential, personalized reports; comparative graphs; and individual scores superimposed on national averages. The software program analyzing survey responses automatically includes appropriate suggestions for altering behaviors and statements of recognition for good scores.

Eris has products geared toward specific health concerns, such as cardiac disease and nutrition, and can aggregate results to provide an organization with an analysis of its unique risk concerns. Eris also offers targeted intervention programs through Gordian, work site health promotion, and tracking. Assessments can easily be administered on paper, through the Internet, or through an interactive system for the convenience of the client.

"We don't take a cookie-cutter approach, and that's the key," Schulten says. "We work with each organization to find out what they want to accomplish, and gear our products and services to meet that goal."

Jeanita Schulten, president of Eris Survey Systems Inc., says, "We want to help people accept responsibility for their own health, help them become healthier, and decrease the cost of care through simple, wellness-based solutions"(left).

Ernst & Young recognized the firm's accomplishments by naming Schulten its 1998 Entrepreneur of the Year among women-owned businesses (right).

THE INDIANA HEALTH INDUSTRY FORUM (IHIF), A STATE-
wide economic development organization headquartered
in Indianapolis, is building Indiana's reputation as a
leading center of economic vitality and innovation for
health-related business and industry. Since it was
formed as a private sector initiative in 1994, IHIF has

profiled the state's needs and resources, set up entrepreneurial partnering mechanisms, and sponsored high-technology research legislation.

IHIF is the only alliance bringing together health care providers; pharmaceutical, medical device, and equipment manufacturers; suppliers; academic institutions; public sector partners; and other professional service providers. IHIF currently has more than 75 corporate members statewide working to encourage health-related business development, and has established a strong presence on the Internet at www.ihif.org.

Framing the Vision

The founders of IHIF recognized the health industry as a significant growth sector that had been neither targeted nor leveraged as a development opportunity for the state. The health industry currently employs one in eight Hoosiers, adding 50,000 jobs to Indiana's economy and growing about 21 percent between 1989 and 1999. Overall, the state's health industry base encompasses nearly 12,000 businesses, 485,000 employees, and an $8.7 billion payroll. Accounting for 14 percent of Indiana's total payroll, the industry's average annual wage of $31,000 is a full 16 percent higher than Indiana's overall average wage and higher than the national average for health sector jobs, exceeding those in cities such as Chicago; Cleveland, Ohio; Louisville; and Minneapolis.

"The health industry is a tremendous economic engine for the State of Indiana, and it is rapidly expanding," says Jody Peloza Bentz, IHIF's executive vice president. "IHIF has developed and is implementing a

comprehensive strategic plan to help Indiana leverage its health industry strengths and resources for continued growth."

Charting the Course

Since the mid-1990s, IHIF has defined critical success factors affecting the strength and growth of the health industry: development of new technology, movement of technology into the marketplace, and development of a supportive culture. By establishing programmatic models to enhance these factors, IHIF seeks to grow the state's health industry assets.

IHIF has established and administered an innovative program called IHIFConnect© to link health industry entrepreneurs and companies in Indiana with resources to grow their businesses."Whether it's access to capital, suitable research partnerships, or links to professional services, IHIFConnect has been a valuable asset to many entrepreneurs with an idea to develop a product and take it to market," says Steve Bryant, IHIF's director of business and community development.

IHIF has been a catalyst for promoting the development of new and emerging technology by leading the way to establish the $50 million 21st Century Research & Technology Fund, which awards grants to help Indiana researchers leverage federal and private foundation dollars. Commercial by-products will bring high-wage, high-technology jobs to Indiana and retain top professional and technical talent. IHIF sponsored initial legislation to establish the fund, which was passed unanimously by

the Indiana General Assembly in May 1999.

"Business formation has been one of our fundamental goals from the beginning," Bentz adds. "Toward that end, we act as catalyst, coordinator, and convener, frequently matching technical, business, regulatory expertise, and funding sources with health industry companies looking to take advantage of all that Indiana has to offer."

Indiana Health Industry Forum (IHIF) maintains active partnerships with statewide academic institutions, such as Rose-Hulman Institute of Technology (top). Representing IHIF are Brad Thompson (left), and Jody Bentz (right), and representing Rose-Hulman is James Eifert, Ph.D. (center).

IHIF executive committee members include (from left) Bill Loveday, president; Jody Bentz, executive vice president; Steve Bryant, director of business and community development; Kathy Arnold, office manager; Brad Thompson, secretary and legal counsel; and Robert Holden, M.D., vice president, as well as (not pictured) Ron Dollens and Steve Ferguson, both of whom are past presidents, and Vince Caponi, treasurer (bottom).

Guidant Corporation

UIDANT CORPORATION PIONEERS TECHNOLOGIES THAT MAKE a difference in the way people live. Its more than 8,000 employees worldwide develop, manufacture, and market a broad array of cardiovascular-related medical solutions designed to help patients return to active and productive lives. ■ A Fortune 1,000 company headquartered in Indianapolis, Guidant was split off from Eli Lilly and Company in 1994. Since then, it has become one of the most successful medical device companies ever, delivering a 15-fold return on shareholder investment. *Smart Money* magazine named Guidant one of the best investments of 1999, placing it first in the medical devices category. The company, in February 2000, was valued at more than $20 billion, with 1999 sales outpacing 1998 by 25 percent.

Strategic Growth, Innovative Divisions

Guidant uses acquisitions for emerging proprietary technologies as part of its growth strategy, acquiring another company every five months and incorporating it into one of three major divisions—cardiac rhythm management, cardiac and vascular surgery, and vascular intervention. Guidant serves customers from sales offices in North America, Latin America, Europe, Asia, and Japan, and from manufacturing facilities in Puerto Rico, Europe, and the United States.

The cardiac rhythm management group launched the world's first implantable defibrillator in 1985 as part of Eli Lilly and Company, and remains a market leader with its automatic implantable defibrillator systems to treat life-threatening rapid heart rhythms. This division, based in St. Paul, also produces the Pulsar, Discovery, and Meridian pacemaker families, as well as a full line of endovascular leads.

The cardiac and vascular surgery group develops innovative medical instruments that help surgeons perform minimally invasive cardiovascular surgical procedures and avoid standard open surgery. Often, these procedures reduce patient recovery time, postsurgery discomfort, and treatment costs.

The vascular intervention group, based in Santa Clara, California, is a leader in interventional cardiovascular products. This division pioneered the development of balloon angioplasty, and provides a full line of coronary dilation catheters, guiding catheters, and guide wires. Its ACS Multi-Link Coronary Stent System, introduced in 1997, quickly became a market leader, providing the basis for other innovative products using tiny, mesh tubes implanted into blood vessels to prevent blockages.

Proven Product Success

Chairman Jim Cornelius and CEO Ron Dollens say the secret of Guidant's success is at once simple and demanding: relentless development and marketing of new products that include the latest in coronary stents, pacing systems, cath-

Chairman Jim Cornelius (top left) and CEO Ron Dollens (top right) say the secret of Guidant Corporation's success is at once simple and demanding: relentless development and marketing of new products that include the latest in coronary stents, pacing systems, catheters, defibrillators, and lead systems.

The company's worldwide headquarters is located in downtown Indianapolis.

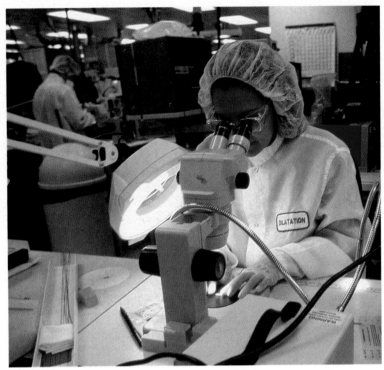

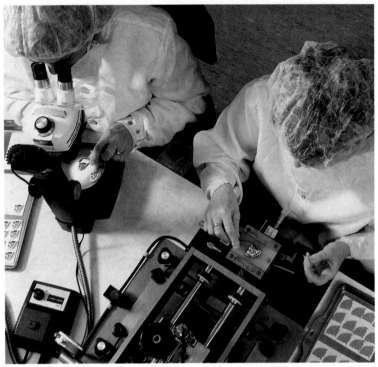

eters, defibrillators, and lead systems. In any earnings period, 60 percent of sales revenue comes from products that are fewer than 12 months old. Most recently, those products extend technological advances in coronary intervention to non-coronary applications.

In fall 1999, Guidant announced approval by the U.S. Food and Drug Administration (FDA) for market release of its Ancure System for minimally invasive treatment of abdominal aortic aneurysms, the nation's 13th-leading cause of death. Patients implanted with Guidant's device experience significantly fewer complications than those undergoing conventional surgery, and are hospitalized an average of two to three days, compared to six days with conventional surgery.

The FDA also recently approved Guidant's Rx Herculink 14 Biliary Stent System, which represents the firm's first premounted stent system for treatment of malignant obstructions of the biliary duct. The design is based on the clinically proven corrugated-ring design of Guidant's ACS Multi-Link Coronary Stent System. The biliary stent system incorporates a number of innovative features, including greater strength, flexibility, and trackability.

An Innovative Employer

Guidant prides itself on being an innovative employer and product developer. The company was listed as 31st on *Fortune* magazine's 1999 list of the 100 best companies to work for in America. The magazine lauded Guidant for being one of only 28 companies among the 66 publicly traded organizations on the list offering stock options to every category of employee. Guidant also brings patients to its annual meetings, where employees can hear stories about the positive impacts specific products are having on the patients' health.

The Guidant Foundation, through grant-making activities and employee involvement, focuses company resources outside the corporation to make a difference in the communities where employees live and work. In 1998, the foundation awarded 15 fellowships to educational institutions and hospitals that demonstrated excellence in cardiovascular research and training, while in 1999, fellowship awards focused on commitment to health care education.

Responding rapidly to customer needs and forming strong working relationships with the health care community are also essential to Guidant's success. The firm is a leading sponsor of clinical studies that enable decision making based on improved data, in addition to providing educational materials to help patients understand the procedures for their own health conditions.

Dollens, who was named to *Worth* magazine's 1999 list of the 50 best CEOs in America, credits the Guidant "team of exceptional individuals" committed to saving and improving the lives of millions of patients around the world. Dollen says, "As we approach the challenges of a new century, we're confident that we have built the capabilities— through our people, technology, and processes—to strengthen our leadership in the medical device market. We will continue to grow by strategically pursuing novel opportunities that leverage our core technologies and strong distribution systems, and by actively promoting health care delivery systems that encourage optimal patient care through innovative medical technology."

Guidant's more than 8,000 employees worldwide develop, manufacture, and market a broad array of cardiovascular-related medical solutions that have saved and improved the lives of more than 6 million patients around the world.

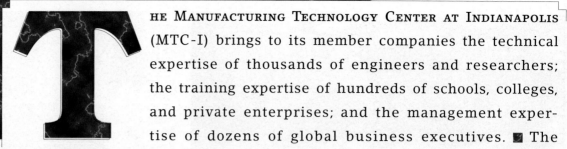

Manufacturing Technology Center at Indianapolis (MTC-I)

Clockwise from top:
Manufacturing Technology Center at Indianapolis' (MTC-I) investigation of new and innovative technologies, such as heat-treating metal components, gives its members an edge over their competition, both nationally and globally.

MTC-I's workforce assessment and development programs improve employee retention and productivity.

Building working relationships among MTC-I member companies contributes to a strong economic base in Indianapolis.

THE MANUFACTURING TECHNOLOGY CENTER AT INDIANAPOLIS (MTC-I) brings to its member companies the technical expertise of thousands of engineers and researchers; the training expertise of hundreds of schools, colleges, and private enterprises; and the management expertise of dozens of global business executives. ■ The Indianapolis-based facility is the only center among 60 in the United States that eschews federal funding to be totally self-supporting. Although this is a hefty claim for any not-for-profit organization, MTC-I remains true to its mission. Member company fees cover no more than 20 percent of MTC-I's annual expenses, while fees for services cover at least 80 percent.

Forging Partnerships

Several central Indiana corporations founded MTC-I in 1995, as part of an ongoing partnership with the City of Indianapolis to establish workforce training programs. The organization was charged with identifying advanced manufacturing practices, encouraging implementation at Indiana companies, and responding to industry requests for unique technical and training resources.

Today, MTC-I represents more than 130 companies, research and development universities, and federal laboratories in central Indiana and across the Midwest. The group has earned a reputation for delivering high-quality services at not-for-profit costs through the more than 40 educational, training, technological, and management projects it tackles each year.

For example, work with Ivy Tech State College yielded a 12-week machinist training program that meets specifications of the National Tooling & Machining Association and has graduated more than 300 skilled machinists in three years. As a result, Indianapolis has a strong precision machinist pool from which to draw.

MTC-I also plays a key role in the Indiana Advanced Manufacturing Initiative, a program of the Indiana Economic Development Corporation's regional technology partnership that benefits Indiana manufacturers attempting to upgrade technological capabilities. As part of this initiative, MTC-I evaluates a company's manufacturing technology, benchmarks it against the best in the industry, and develops an implementation plan to improve operating ratios and profitability.

Award-Winning Ventures

In fall 1999, MTC-I received the City of Indianapolis' Eagle Award for Commitment/Vision for the Future of Indianapolis as a result of its work on the MedAmerica Research Corridor, north of Indiana University-Purdue University at Indianapolis (IUPUI). Less than a year after IUPUI contracted with MTC-I to champion its development, a large, multinational biomed company had committed to the park and talks were under way with 15 additional companies.

One of MTC-I's most valuable developments has been an offering called Kaizen© Atara-Shii. The concept of Kaizen, developed by Toyota, simply means improvement, while Atara-Shii means newest. The MTC-I offering involves special consultation to help member companies eliminate duplication and unnecessary costs without laying off workers.

MTC-I adds member companies only as resources are available to expand services to meet both new and old members' needs. Even so, the group never declines a request for help. It bases selection of new members' companies on potential for unique contributions to the existing network. "In 1999 alone, our member companies identified more than $14 million MTC-I had helped them save," says President T.R. Jacks. "We're the catalyst to foster innovation and training that strengthens the economic base."

**E**SCIENT TECHNOLOGIES, LLC IS A COMPANY MAKING ITS mark in the consumer electronics industry by making technology behave. The company's innovative home entertainment convergence products combine Internet-based technologies with consumer electronics to provide compelling entertainment solutions. Through

groundbreaking technology, Escient delivers products that simplify use of home electronics, allowing consumers to instantly access and purchase entertainment in previously unheard-of ways.

Founded in 1996, Escient derives its name from the convergence of science, entertainment, and technology. In its first three years of operation, sales quadrupled, earning its cofounders Ernst & Young Entrepreneur of the Year awards and designation by the *Indianapolis Business Journal* as the fourth-fastest-growing company in Indianapolis in 1999.

With four subsidiaries, nine acquisitions, and about 150 employees, the firm moved into its new, 35,000-square-foot headquarters in 1999. This was the first building to open in the prestigious InTech Park.

A Twist of Fate

This unique company began to unfold as a result of luck and circumstance. Escient's success started with a vehicle running out of gas, which placed a voice mail pioneer and a custom audio/visual designer together on the Indianapolis roadside.

In 1995, Scott Jones moved back to Indianapolis after having founded his first venture, Boston Technology Inc. (BTI), a successful voice mail enterprise. Jones was chairman and founding scientist of BTI, which went public in 1987. By its third year under Jones' direction, BTI's revenues topped $25 million and included multimillion-dollar contracts with Bell Operating companies. By 1990, BTI owned 50 percent of the telephone voice mail market. In 1998, it merged with a

similarly sized company, Converse Technologies, resulting in a multibillion-dollar company.

The Indianapolis house Jones bought had a whole-house audio system originally installed by Tom Doherty, a local, nationally recognized audio/video designer. Doherty was taking Jones to view a client's home theater, when their vehicle suddenly ran out of gas. While waiting for assistance, Doherty described his ideas for making accessing music simpler for consumers. Jones immediately saw a voice mail parallel. They began a business partnership along with other Doherty family members.

These entrepreneurs founded Escient Technologies, LLC. By its third year, Escient had acquired nine technology companies, opened two West Coast offices, and won nine awards. Escient is now integrated into four divisions, and has introduced a new generation of home entertainment products through its Convergence Group.

Technology-Taming Products

Escient first introduced TuneBase in 1996 to help consumers manage large audio CD collections. The newest addition to the line is TuneBase 100, a Java-enabled controller that provides complete mastery of music. TuneBase 100 dials into Escient's server and retrieves information from sister company CDDB's database of 5 million songs. TuneBase automatically recognizes and displays CD covers, styles, and more on a TV screen. TuneBase has won multiple awards, including *Audio Video International*'s prestigious technology award.

In 1999, Escient introduced

a similar product for DVD collections called PowerPlay, which leverages the Internet to read discs, identify digital signatures, and provide instant access to movies. PowerPlay was named the industry's Best Video Product 1999, and has accelerated sales to the highest in Escient's history.

"We see infinite possibilities for Escient technology as we further meld the Internet with consumer electronics," Jones says. "We look forward to being a key part of this revolution that is changing the way we interact with entertainment. Escient will continue to bring powerful capabilities to people worldwide, and aid Indiana in being a significant player in the world of technology."

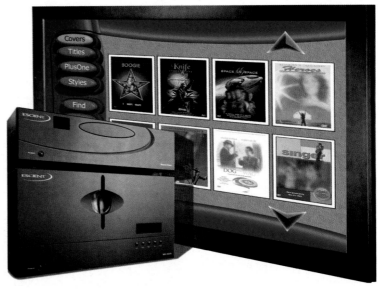

TuneBase 100 is a Java-enabled controller that provides complete mastery of music. It dials into Escient Technologies, LLC's server and retrieves information from a database of 5 million songs (top).

In 1999, Escient introduced PowerPlay, a product that leverages the Internet to read discs, identify digital signatures, and provide instant access to movies (bottom).

Clarian Health Partners, Inc.

CLARIAN HEALTH IS A CONSOLIDATED HEALTH CARE ORGANIZA-tion that includes Methodist Hospital, Indiana University Hospital, and Riley Hospital for Children. Although it has only been in existence since 1997, its hospitals share a history that dates to the early 1900s and a reputation for excellence in care, education, research, and service that is timeless.

These three strong, premier medical facilities provide highly technical clinical care and high-caliber medical education and research, and help improve the health of the central Indiana community. In a typical year, the combined Clarian system treats 60,000 people on an inpatient basis and handles 1 million outpatient visits, making it the second-busiest health care facility in the nation.

A History of Premier Care

Clarian's three hospitals have been caring for central Indiana residents since Methodist Hospital first opened its doors in 1908. Indiana University opened its first hospital in 1914, followed by Riley Hospital for Children in 1924.

Each of the partner organizations takes pride in its rich history of care. Methodist Hospital was the first local facility with a motorized ambulance as early as 1910 and a helicopter as early as 1970. Both were initially used to transport drivers

and spectators injured at the Indianapolis 500.

In 1922, Methodist worked with local pharmaceutical giant Eli Lilly and Company to develop insulin for the treatment of diabetes. Indiana's first open-heart surgery took place at Methodist in 1965, followed by its first heart transplant in 1982, and its first artificial heart implant in 1987. The state's first lung and heart-lung transplants were done at Methodist two years later, followed in 1991 by the first double-lung transplant.

Indiana University Hospital performed the state's first kidney transplant in 1964, its first bone marrow transplant in 1985, its first liver and pancreas transplants in 1988, and its first pancreatic islet cell transplant in 1996.

Riley Hospital captured the nation's attention when, in 1935, President Franklin D. Roosevelt, himself crippled by polio, visited the hospital's hydrotherapeutic pool for polio patients. Riley physicians have always been at the forefront of care for

children, performing the state's first pediatric cochlear implant in 1983 and its first infant and newborn heart transplants in 1989. Riley also opened the state's only pediatric burn unit in 1971 and its only children's cancer center in 1994.

A National Reputation

Clarian's strength of experience is easily reflected in its numbers. Annually, Clarian hospitals deliver nearly 5,000 babies, log nearly 80,000 critical care patient days, complete more than 500 solid organ and bone marrow transplants, and perform more than 800 coronary bypass operations. In addition, the system handles more than 100,000 emergency care visits, including the 1,330 patients transported by its Life Line helicopter.

Specialty services offered are pediatric heart disorder treatment, comprehensive cardiac care, cancer care, specialty obstetrics, and world-class trauma service.

Clarian also makes use of the latest leading-edge technology, such as Indiana's only Gamma Knife—a noninvasive, non-scalpel surgical treatment for brain tumors and vascular malfunctions. Established in 1964,

More than 1,700 physicians are affiliated with Clarian Health. In addition, Clarian houses one of the state's leading residency programs through its affiliation with Indiana University School of Medicine.

A young patient's day is a little brighter because of a special volunteer. Clarian is proud to have more than 700 individuals who volunteer at several departments in the hospital.

its Krannert Institute of Cardiology at the Indiana University (IU) School of Medicine is respected worldwide for its development of innovative approaches to diagnosing and treating the most difficult cardiac conditions. Additionally, Clarian is a recognized national center for heart, kidney, and heart-lung transplantation.

The IU Cancer Center is recognized as a premier national center for the study of cancer and development of cancer treatments by the National Cancer Institute (NCI). A five-year, $6.3 million support grant from NCI bolsters the $33.3 million annual funding currently received for cancer research projects. Physicians affiliated with the center are recognized for developing gene therapies for bone marrow diseases such as leukemia, the use of umbilical cord stem cells for bone marrow transplantation, and a 95 percent cure rate for testicular cancer in young men.

U.S. News & World Report consistently places Clarian hospitals among the top in the nation. Its 1999 *America's Best Hospitals Guide* ranked 11 Clarian Health specialties among the top 50 clinical programs nationwide. Specialties ranking in the top 20 included gastroenterology, cancer, urology, respiratory disorders, and neurology and neurosurgery.

Giving the Best

The Clarian Health network employs approximately 9,000 people, including nearly 1,700 physicians, 90 percent of whom are board certified. Clarian's three hospitals altogether house nearly 1,300 beds, are supported by 22 outpatient facilities throughout the area, and generate more than $1 billion in gross patient revenues.

Outreach programs serve more than 1.24 million people annually through such efforts as the Older Adult Service and Information System (OASIS), crisis intervention and counseling, injury prevention programs, low-income community health

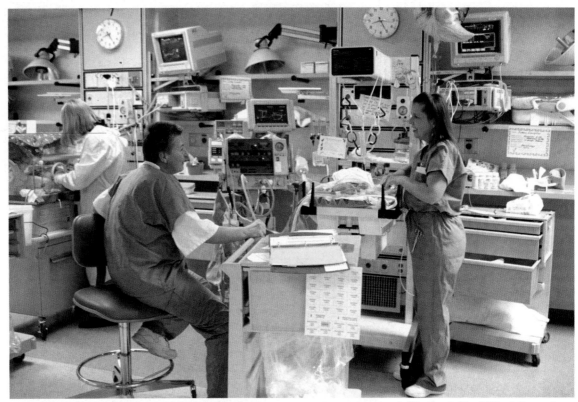

At Riley Hospital for Children's Neonatal Intensive Care Unit, some of Indiana's youngest infants are treated, giving them hope for the future (top).

A hospital waiting room can turn into playtime for a curious infant (bottom).

centers, and the Indiana Poison Center.

"Still, every day, we look at our employees, our facilities, our programs, and our costs with the same eye, asking the same question: 'Is this the best we can possibly do?'" says Bill Loveday, Clarian president and CEO. "The very nature of the question means we never stop seeking a better answer.

"It's a question that's been asked throughout the history of our participating hospitals, our partner IU School of Medicine, and all our physicians, and it has led to breakthrough clinical solutions in heart and cancer care and to the development of technology not available elsewhere. There is nothing simple about this simple question, but we'll continue to ask it to make sure we remain one of the finest health care institutions and leading organizations in the country."

Globe Corporate Stay International

THE BUSINESS OF TEMPORARY CORPORATE HOUSING IS MORE THAN square feet and furniture. It's about anticipating needs, following through, and tying up loose ends. Globe Corporate Stay International handles all the details for its clients, providing them with the comforts of home, wherever their business takes them. ■ Globe Corporate Stay International is a division of Globe Business Resources, Inc., headquartered in Cincinnati. Fifty of the company's more than 850 employees work out of the Indianapolis Globe office.

A Good Business Move

Globe Furniture Rentals was founded in 1989 by two friends, David D. Hoguet and Blair D. Neller. They took the business public in 1996, changed the name to Globe Business Resources, Inc., and today serve as its chairman and president, respectively.

Four months after the initial public offering, Globe's largest customer, a corporate housing provider, shared plans to stop renting and buy its own furniture for its properties. As a result of this threat to its furniture rental business, Globe saw an opportunity to expand its own business into the corporate housing industry. Today, Globe is one of the leaders in temporary relocation.

It turned out to be a good business decision. Corporate housing revenues, which were nonexistent before 1996, accounted for nearly 60 percent of Globe's total revenues, which were just shy of $150 million at the end of Globe's 1999 fiscal year.

The Single Source Solution®

The beauty of Globe's system lies in its vertical integration. To provide a complete solution for temporary corporate housing, Globe acquires leading corporate housing providers throughout the country that are recognized in their local markets for their commitment to customer service.

Globe then controls all aspects of the temporary relocation process. First, the company selects premier properties, and then it

guarantees the quality and consistency of furniture and housewares. Apartments include cable television, telephones, and basic housewares package, and can be customized to include specialty items such as large-screen televisions.

Owning the furniture and housewares provides Globe with a cost advantage over its competitors. By maintaining control over all aspects of the service, from the initial location request to the lamp on the nightstand, Globe ensures client satisfaction.

One toll-free call to 1-800-FOR-RENT® provides a Single Source Solution® as well. The caller can arrange for temporary housing in 80 of the largest U.S. cities, process multiple requests, and even arrange for temporary or permanent office furnishings through Globe Instant Office.

A 30-day stay in one of Globe's corporate apartments amounts to half the cost of the same stay in an average hotel. With more space, a fully appointed kitchen, and in most cases, washer and dryer hookups, a Globe Corporate Stay International apartment makes for a comfortable business decision.

Globe Corporate Stay International can arrange temporary housing in more than 80 cities nationwide (top).

A 30-day stay in one of Globe's corporate apartments amounts to half the cost of the same stay in an average hotel. With more space, a fully appointed kitchen, and in most cases, washer and dryer hookups, a Globe Corporate Stay International apartment makes for a comfortable business decision (bottom left and right).

WIRELESS TELEPHONES ARE SUPPOSED TO MAKE PEOPLE'S lives easier, so buying one should not be difficult. That is the philosophy behind Telstreet.com, one of the nation's newest e-commerce sites reselling wireless telephones phones, accessories, and service via the Internet. Scott Flanders, the company's current chairman, and Bob Laikin, a Telstreet.com board member who also serves as chairman and CEO of Brightpoint Inc., formed Telstreet.com in January 1999.

The Telstreet.com Web site launched the following September, offering name brand phones and accessories from leading global wireless manufacturers and service from leading wireless carriers.

A Better Approach

By serving as a national agent for wireless carriers such as AT&T Wireless Services, Sprint PCS, and Nextel, Telstreet.com offers a seamless shopping experience. Interested buyers can use the site's customer-friendly interface to point and click on selections they want, or they can take a needs survey to help them narrow and compare their options instantaneously.

The Telstreet.com Web site also includes information to help consumers learn more about wireless technology, with articles on topics such as digital versus analog phones, phone features, using wireless phones while driving, and wireless phone health concerns.

Telstreet.com's commitment to providing customers with the best wireless retail experience available is evident in its partnership with Brightpoint Inc., a leading wireless distribution and fulfillment com-pany also headquartered in Indianapolis.

Phones are preprogrammed for use and delivered to customers within three days. A live, in-house customer service team, fully trained by all carrier partners, is available 15 hours a day to answer customer questions.

"Telstreet.com takes responsibility for the entire customer experience," says President and CEO Terry Dwyer, "from buying to fulfillment to delivery. Customers are guaranteed to find the wireless package that best meets their needs or they get their money back."

Partnership Opportunities

Consumers will find products at Telstreet.com that are not available elsewhere. For example, Qualcomm selected Telstreet.com as the first online retailer for the pdQ smartphone, a handset that combines a Palm-Computing platform with a Web browser and a digital wireless phone.

Leading software developer Phone.com, in anticipation of consumer demand for Web-enabled phones, has turned to Telstreet.com to develop and maintain a co-branded Web site for the sale of Internet-enabled equipment and services. Through Web-based marketing partnerships, Telstreet.com also offers a simplified opportunity to enter wireless retailing.

For co-brand partners, such as Egghead.com and Hello Direct, it has developed retail Web sites that integrate the existing look of retailer-established sites with the information and technology of Telstreet.com's on-line superstore.

Additionally, Strategy.com™, the world's first personal intelligent network, has partnered with Telstreet.com to deliver personalized financial information to consumers via the Internet, telephone, and wireless devices. This partnership means Telstreet.com can offer its customers Strategy.com's personalized alerts about stock market updates, individual portfolio performance, and changes in analyst recommendations.

"Anybody can offer products for sale, but it takes a little more effort to help people find exactly what they need," Dwyer says. "We make that effort and will continue to take the extra time needed to provide customers with wireless options that fit their needs."

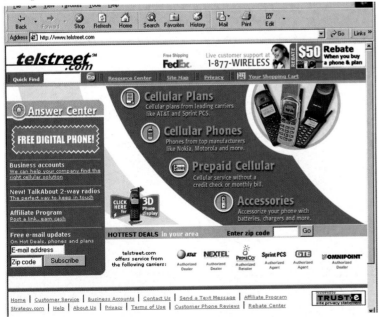

The Telstreet.com Web site includes information to help consumers learn more about wireless technology, with articles on topics such as digital versus analog phones, phone features, using wireless phones while driving, and wireless phone health concerns.

ONEX, Inc.

AT ONEX, INC., HAPPY ON MONDAY IS MORE THAN AN expression. It's a key business strategy that has helped the high-tech consulting company specializing in e-business expand its employee base from 12 people to more than 200 in fewer than three years. ◼ The growth in human resources mirrors the firm's financial resource

growth as well. It has operated at a profit from day one, posting more than $1 million in sales at the end of its first year and $15 million in sales at the end of 1999. In fewer than three years, it doubled the size of its Monument Circle offices, opened a north side annex, and set up branches in Cincinnati and Detroit. Expansion to several other cities is planned, and the total number of employees is expected to exceed 300 in 2000.

The *Indianapolis Business Journal* already lists ONEX as the area's sixth-largest computer-consulting services company, and its professional search arm as the third largest. The firm was an Indiana University Business School Growth 100 recipient and a finalist in the Emerging Growth category of Ernst & Young's Entrepreneur of the Year competition in 1999.

Winning the Talent War

ONEX is the brainchild of Joe Huffine and Sally Huffine Breen, a brother-sister team with a different idea about how to run a company and the depth of experience necessary to make it work. From the start, they knew the key would be finding and retaining the right people in an ever tightening technology hiring market.

According to the Information Technology Association of America, nearly 350,000 information technology (IT) jobs nationwide went unfilled in 1998 because of worker shortages. The U.S. Bureau of Labor Statistics estimates that nearly 1 million more jobs will be created by 2006. Still, universities are turning out a mere 26,000 computer science graduates each year. To beat those odds, Huffine and Breen knew they needed more than a business plan—they needed a battle plan.

"We wanted to build a company that made employees and clients wake up Happy on Mondays," says Huffine, president. "We also knew we wanted a company based on excellence, ethics, and fun, where employees would think like owners. Developing an ideal culture became a way to set ourselves apart in a competitive market, build a strategic store of intellectual capital, and win the talent war."

Breen, who worked in IT management and recruiting be-

fore starting ONEX as executive vice president, knows they're on the right track. "For 10 years, I listened to the marketplace and learned that technical people want an environment where they feel like they have a real impact on what they do," she says. "They also want to learn more about business as well as technology."

At ONEX, they get that chance, and the enthusiasm for the result extends beyond the employees to the clients. The firm serves more than 90 of Indianapolis' and Cincinnati's most prominent Fortune 1,000, not-for-profit, and emerging companies.

Process, People, Recruiting

ONEX is dedicated to improving client operating performance through integrated consulting, technology, and people solutions, primarily in the emerging world of e-business. The firm's talented professionals provide integrated methodologies that drive a full life-cycle approach to assessment, design, and implementation in the areas of technology, business process, and people.

Whether a company needs e-business, infrastructure man-

At ONEX, Inc., a fast-paced environment and colorful contemporary design create a remarkably different, energetic corporate culture.

people—specifically, its employees. The company pledges to listen, inform, and respond to clients in a timely manner. It asks clients to join employees in building a long-term, fun relationship and in treating each other according to the Golden Rule. A Walker Information employee survey in 1999 indicated an unusually high level of employee loyalty, one of the highest ever registered by the renowned research firm.

ONEX employees demonstrate their commitment not only professionally, but in their service to local communities as well. Collectively, they are involved in more than 250 professional and community organizations. Each year, the company pays employees back by giving them $200 to pass along to the organization of their choice. In 1999, employees made the company proud by reaching a doubled United Way goal of $30,000 in fewer than two weeks.

"In a word, we're about people," Huffine says. "In essence, we're about values, service, and innovation. In effect, we're about excellence, performance, and results."

Having created a corporate culture that values enthusiasm and dedication, ONEX has set a new standard in the fast-paced IT consulting and recruiting market. More growth for ONEX and its satisfied clients is sure to come.

Cofounders Joe Huffine and Sally Breen opened the company's Monument Circle office in 1997. A second Indianapolis office and a Cincinnati branch opened two years later.

agement, enterprise resource planning, business transformation, financial consulting, information management, or project help, ONEX has answers. Its program management group can assess the strategic value of consolidating or outsourcing overall management of a client's multiple vendors, processes, and pricing.

ONEX also provides supplemental staffing to help with both project management and functional skills in information technology and finance under the client's direction. Or if a more permanent staffing solution is needed, ONEX is experienced in executive searches and recruiting for technical, finance, and accounting industries. Using a project approach, the company matches clients with an experienced project manager, recruiter, and researcher to result in faster hiring cycles, higher-quality hires, and better retention.

Think Fast. Go Further.

The ONEX slogan, Think Fast. Go Further., highlights the company's focus as a full-

service, e-business enabler. E-business is more than a set of tools and technologies. It is a complex development environment driven by strategy. Speed and quality service are essential as ONEX takes its clients to the next level—increased revenues and decreased costs using the Web as a new business and sales channel.

ONEX is not just about business. The company is focused on

ONEXites are actively involved in more than 250 professional, community, and civic organizations. The company provides $200 per employee to be used toward supporting that involvement.

SAFECO

OR MORE THAN 75 YEARS, SAFECO HAS BEEN KEEPING PROMISES with an unparalleled reputation for integrity, financial responsibility, innovative financial products, and top-quality services at competitive rates. Largely a West Coast company until its acquisition of the Indianapolis-based American States Financial Corporation in 1997, SAFECO boasts offices across the country and claim services that cover America from coast to coast.

The SAFECO of today came from one man's challenge of the conventional insurance wisdom of his day. Hawthorne K. Dent launched SAFECO's predecessor, General Insurance Company of America, in 1923 in Seattle, combining the financial stability and responsibility of an investor-owned company with the preferred-risk underwriting and lower prices of a mutual or policyholder-owned company. In 1953, General launched the Selective Auto and Fire Insurance Company of America (SAFECO), which used computer-based automation tools to help independent agents compete with direct insurance writers. The board of directors recognized the success of this venture by changing the corporation name to SAFECO in 1968.

In 1997, SAFECO increased its presence nationally with its $2.8 billion acquisition of American States Financial Corporation. The deal effectively doubled the firm's independent agency distribution force and increased its presence east of the Rocky Mountains. Through its SAFECO American States Business Insurance product line, the company became a leading writer in business insurance for small to medium-sized companies.

The firm further increased its national presence in 1998, when it purchased naming rights to the Seattle Mariners' ballpark. SAFECO Field now helps increase recognition of the SAFECO brand to hometown and visiting baseball fans, as well as to television viewers tuning in worldwide.

With more than $30 billion in assets and $6.6 billion in annual revenues, SAFECO is the premier company selling insurance and financial products through independent agents. The company employs more than 12,000 people nationwide, 1,300 of whom work in Indianapolis.

SAFECO has always distributed its products through independent agents, knowing consumers value the expertise and individual attention an independent agent can provide. Today, the firm is represented by more than 8,000 independent agencies throughout the United States.

Extensive Product Lines

SAFECO products include property and casualty insurance, life insurance, annuities, surety bonds, commercial credit, and other financial products. The firm's personal lines—auto, homeowners, and many miscellaneous products—represent 61 percent of its business. With nearly 2.6 million insured vehicles, SAFECO is one of the largest auto insurers writing through independent agents.

Formed in 1969, SAFECO Credit Company provides financing and leasing for barges, computers, construction, forklifts, mining and production equipment, tugboats, truck/trailers, and more. The company tailor-made financial services fund construction, manufacturing, and transportation equipment, as well as specialty niches that include corporate aircraft, marine vessels, and restaurant franchises.

Through its Safeline Leasing Division, SAFECO Credit customers can secure leasing financing for office equipment ranging in cost from $10,000 to more than $500,000.

SAFECO Life, started in 1957, ranks in the top 100 life insurance companies in the United States based on its assets and in-force policies. The company provides a comprehensive array of individual and group life insurance programs, retirement services, and annuity products backed by skilled investment management and world-class customer care. SAFECO Life's excess loss program continues to be the core product in the group life category, providing reinsurance to self-insured plans. Additional plans include term, universal life, variable universal life, and disability income products.

Retirement services include a complete line of investment

The premier company selling insurance and financial products through independent agents, SAFECO employs more than 12,000 people nationwide, 1,300 of whom work in Indianapolis.

With the acquisition of American States Financial Corporation in 1997, SAFECO established a major presence in Indianapolis. The company now maintains offices across the country and claim services that cover America from coast to coast.

SAFECO products include property and casualty insurance, life insurance, annuities, surety bonds, commercial credit, and other financial products. The firm's personal lines—auto, home owners, and many miscellaneous products—represent 61 percent of its business.

opportunities targeting individual and business planning with 401(k), tax-sheltered annuities, individual retirement accounts, and pension plans. SAFECO offers a complete range of fixed, indexed, and variable annuities, and is a leading provider of settlement annuities, which provide immediate income for victims of personal injury accidents.

Nineteen SAFECO Mutual Funds are sold directly and by agents, making SAFECO one of the largest full-service financial providers in the nation. The firm also manages and distributes personal and institutional financial products and services, marketed through a variety of channels.

The company is one of the nation's leading writers of contract and commercial surety bonds as well. Product lines cover emerging small contractors, large corporations, and individuals. Through its contract surety line, SAFECO handles bonds for construction contractors, ranging from emerging to well-established companies. SAFECO's commercial surety handles the domestic and international bonding needs of more

than 30 percent of the Fortune 500 companies. Industries served include energy, financial services, food services, health care, technology, manufacturing, retail, transportation, utilities, and service.

The Community Connection

SAFECO believes success in business has a direct correlation to strong and healthy communities. That's why the firm has positioned its giving program—Strengthening America's Neighborhoods—to target and support the social concerns of communities nationwide that align with SAFECO's business goals and enhance its reputation as an active community partner.

Investments, which include matching gift programs for employee volunteers, are targeted to creating neighborhoods that are safe and vigorous, as well as economically secure and stable.

"SAFECO keeps its promises to its policyholders, its agents, and the communities where employees live and work," says President and Chief Operating Officer Boh A. Dickey. "In the end, that's what insurance is all about—a promise to be there when you need us. Our record

of assisting people in need is unparalleled. We've built our reputation on that promise, and customers from coast to coast know the comfort of being protected by a SAFECO promise kept."

Keane, Inc.

THE SLOGAN WE GET IT DONE MAY BE A BRAVE CLAIM FOR any consulting firm, but Keane, Inc. makes that claim and stakes its reputation on it. The IT is information technology, and the firm relies on its proven ability to complete projects—rather than merely bill hours—as a way to keep customers coming back. ■ Keane's successful move to the

Indiana market proves the strategy works. The Boston-based firm opened its Indianapolis office in 1998 to support a state contract to manage a multifaceted program management office. In less than a year, local Keane employees numbered more than 150, and Keane had a client list that included many notable local companies.

Modest Beginnings Meet Success

Keane, Inc. started above a doughnut shop in suburban Massachusetts in 1965. Founder John F. Keane, who had worked for IBM and Arthur D. Little Inc., launched the company to provide computer consulting long before anyone was talking about PCs and Y2K.

In the 1980s, Keane branched out to offer project management, systems management, and computer programmer staffing on a temporary basis. As the technology industry hit its stride, this strategy helped the firm grow. Soon, Keane was running technical-service help desks, and designing and supporting software.

Net income in 1998 exceeded $96 million on total revenue of more than $1 billion. The *Wall Street Journal* named Keane Best 10-Year Performer in 1998, and *Investor's Business Daily* listed it number one among Amex stocks during 1990-1997 because of its 2,713 percent increase in value. *Computerworld*

magazine listed the firm as one of the 20 best information technology companies to work for, and *Business Week* named Keane to its Information Technology 100 list of top technology firms, ranking it 28th. Keane's client list reads like a who's who of technology giants, including Microsoft, Gateway, AT&T, IBM, and Bell Atlantic.

Keane also made several key acquisitions in 1998 to expand its influence in the electronic commerce and customer relationship management markets. It entered the European marketplace through acquisition as well, and sees the opening of its United Kingdom office as a firm foothold for

"Producing solid results for our clients is the only way to provide meaningful, long-term employment and growth for our employees," says Ray Calloway (left), managing director, who, along with James Ison (right), director of staffing and employment development, is helping Keane, Inc. become an industry leader in Indiana.

LISA TYNER

Established locally in 1998, Keane strives to be a thought leader in the Indianapolis community.

Strategic Solutions

According to industry analysts, one of Keane's strengths is its decentralized approach. With offices in more than 50 North American cities and the United Kingdom, and some 12,000 employees, the company often wins big accounts.

Services are geared toward aligning operations with business strategy, enabling strategy through technology, and optimizing technology to meet evolving business needs. Evident in all of Keane's solutions is the application of rigorous processes and management disciplines, backed by a culture of individual accountability.

"We set up clear communications with the client from the start," says Ray Calloway, Indianapolis managing director. "We call it the 80-hour rule, and it means we never work more than two weeks on a task without reporting back to the client whether we're on schedule." Employees define the parameters of the job in detail up front, including budget, schedule, and a clear-cut set of procedures for approving changes.

With a repeat business rate of 90 percent—one of the highest in the industry—Keane's clients must appreciate the firm's approach. Even the first client in

1965 remains with Keane today. The company has been very successful at leveraging its most recent success in the 2000 market, while expanding its reputation for delivering large, mission-critical projects.

A growing part of Keane's business involves development of program management and E-business solutions that encompass strategic planning and tactical execution to help companies leverage the Web for maximum business results. Keane's proprietary Internet E-scorecard analyzes a business' maturity, presence, and visibility on the Web to determine return on investment the company is currently receiving.

A Partnership with Indiana

Keane's initial Indiana client, the State of Indiana, provides perhaps the best example of the firm's accomplishments locally. In 1997, Keane started working on a large-scale program management office to assure that systems supporting critical services such as the Indiana State Police, Health and Human Services and the Bureau of Motor Vehicles would operate effectively in 2000 and beyond.

As the partnership grew, Keane collaborated with the Department of Fire and Building Services and the Public Safety Training Institute to re-

place all mission-critical systems. Keane developed and tested the new client/server-based system, which supports divisions such as code enforcement and elevator inspections.

The application development and systems integration project enabled the state to operate more efficiently by eliminating repetition of stored information. It also allowed management access to more comprehensive and updated files on public safety and code-related issues.

Beyond service to any particular client, Keane strives to be a thought leader in the Indianapolis community. To that end, the firm sponsors events for local CEOs where industry experts discuss how technology is impacting business, and issue reports on various aspects of business and technology development. For example, an Indiana E-scorecard released in fall 1999 indicated only 1 percent of the top 100 companies in the state had fully optimized, interactive Internet strategies, so the report explained what could be gained from them.

"This office sells only to Indiana, so we view ourselves as a stakeholder in the community," Calloway says. "Producing solid results for our clients is the only way to provide meaningful, long-term employment and growth for our employees."

ImagineX Radiology Alliance, L.L.C.

THE FORMATION OF A NEW RADIOLOGY PRACTICE BY INDIANA University Radiology Associates (IURA) and Radiologic Specialists of Indiana (RSI) is setting a new standard of radiology care in Indiana under the name ImagineX Radiology Alliance, L.L.C. The July 2000 merger brought together two premier radiology practices, creating the largest radiology group in the state and one of the 10 largest in the nation. The 90 radiologists and other imaging specialists at ImagineX interpret more than 1 million radiology images annually.

Although the new practice is based in Indianapolis, it serves hospitals throughout the state with on-site radiologists. In addition, all hospitals are equipped with electronic image transmission capabilities (teleradiology), permitting high-resolution images to be interpreted by ImagineX subspecialists in other facilities. Currently served are 14 Indiana hospitals, in addition to Clarian Health Partners hospitals and clinics in Indianapolis. The merged practice plans to link with additional health care facilities in underserved parts of the state to provide a higher standard of readily available radiologic care. Mobile services, imaging service partnerships, and new satellite offices will all be established.

The ImagineX Radiology Alliance, L.L.C. Board of Directors includes (standing, from left) Mervyn D. Cohen, M.B.,Ch.B., M.D.; James M. Pearce, M.D.; Benjamin B. Kuzma, M.D.; Kenneth A. Buckwalter, M.D.; Donald R. Hawes, M.D.; (seated, from left) Handel E. Reynolds, M.D.; Kenneth E. Marnocha, M.D.; and Bryan T. Burney, M.D.

A Tradition of Service and Innovation

IURA traces its history to 1915, when it was established at Long Hospital, the first of the IURA facilities to open. RSI was founded in 1969 to provide professional radiology service to Methodist Hospital in Indianapolis. The two practices began contemplating a common organization in 1995, following the announcement of plans for Indiana University Hospital, Methodist Hospital, and Riley Children's Hospital to merge into Clarian Health Partners, a project completed in 1997.

The ImagineX parent companies and the hospitals they serve have long been innovators in the field of radiology. Methodist Hospital and Indiana University Hospital have often been the first in Indiana—and in many cases, among the first in the United States—to begin using new radiology modalities and technologies. For each new advancement made, both groups have been committed to training and employing subspecialists who are experts in the new technologies.

For many people, radiology still means X ray, but the field encompasses many other technological advances. IURA, RSI, and their respective hospitals have led the way in providing state-of-the-art diagnostic equipment for Indiana citizens, as well as for patients from across the United States. Methodist Hospital installed the state's first computed tomography (CT) scanner in 1974, while Indiana University Hospital installed the state's first magnetic resonance imaging (MRI) machine in 1982 and its only positron-emission tomography (PET) scanner in 1993. Methodist Hospital was the first hospital in the state to have 24-hour, on-site coverage by board-certified radiologists and 24-hour, seven-day-a-week teleradiology coverage. In 1986, Riley Children's Hospital, for which IURA provides radiology service, became

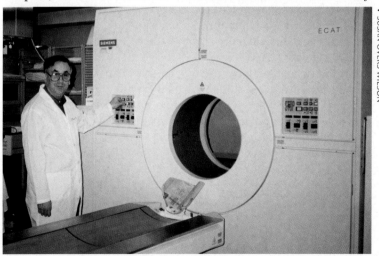

Alex M. Aisen, M.D., calibrates the state's first positron-emission tomography (PET) scanner at Indiana University Hospital.

the first children's hospital in the world to offer electronic imaging, with one objective being to reduce the radiation dosage of multiple or duplicate radiology exams on the hospital's young patients. The application of each new technology has helped to raise the standard of radiologic care in Indiana.

In addition to the technology utilized by the highly subspecialized radiologists of ImagineX, medical education is an important responsibility of the group. With 60 residency positions, the four-year Indiana University School of Medicine (IUSM) residency program in radiology is the second-largest program in the country, and offers training in a full range of radiology subspecialties. Following completion of their residency, IUSM radiologists practice in areas throughout the world.

Better Care for More People

ImagineX physicians are board-certified radiologists representing a range of subspecialties, including breast imaging, abdominal radiology, pulmonary radiology, musculoskeletal radiology, interventional radiology, neuroradiology, nuclear medicine, pediatric radiology, emergency radiology, and general radiology. Through electronic image transmission, this sub-specialized radiology care is available to patients throughout the state on a 24-hour basis. Electronic linkage provides for quick access to the subspecialty radiologists, allowing radiology examinations to be interpreted without the necessity of patients having to travel from their hometowns.

Use of more exacting radiological procedures continues to contribute to earlier diagnosis and improvement in a patient's chances of recovery. Access to the latest in radiological care also can eliminate the need for exploratory surgery, thus reducing risk and decreasing expense for the patient. ImagineX interventional radiologists perform various closed operative procedures, which greatly aid patients in more rapid recoveries.

ImagineX makes radiological expertise more accessible through the link it creates between IUSM, the second-largest medical school in the nation, and Methodist Hospital, the largest hospital in Indiana. Research conducted by ImagineX physicians provides assistance to radiologists throughout the state.

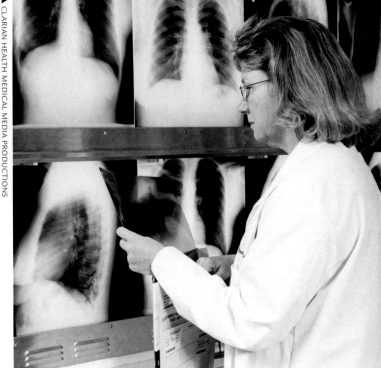

The combined practice also emphasizes the development of new methodologies for service delivery, such as flexible patient scheduling. Such scheduling facilitates more rapid radiology examination reports to referring physicians and more rapid follow-up care. Insurance providers also benefit from improved patient scheduling by getting more timely access to information they require.

"The developments that have transformed patient care and revolutionized modern medicine make radiology a complex field," says Dr. Mervyn D. Cohen, chairman of Indiana University's Department of Radiology. "Combining the expertise of the two top radiology practices in the state shows a dedication to continuing leadership in developing and applying new radiological imaging and therapeutic techniques."

"The new ImagineX organization also adds to our national reputation," says James S. Cairney, ImagineX chief operating officer. "As always, our primary goal will be to render the best clinical care possible to all patients through the use of advanced radiological techniques and services."

Susan J.F. Meyer, M.D., reviews and interprets a radiology exam (top).

A state-of-the-art computer network enables neuroradiologist Benjamin B. Kuzma, M.D. to interpret MRI exams from multiple imaging facilities (bottom).

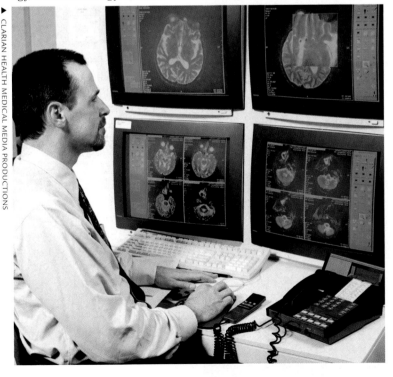

Towery Publishing, Inc.

BEGINNING AS A SMALL PUBLISHER OF LOCAL NEWSPAPERS IN the 1930s, Towery Publishing, Inc. today produces a wide range of community-oriented materials, including books (Urban Tapestry Series), business directories, magazines, and Internet publications. Building on its long heritage of excellence, the company has become global in scope, with cities from San Diego to Sydney represented by Towery products. In all its endeavors, this Memphis-based company strives to be synonymous with service, utility, and quality.

A Diversity of Community-Based Products

Over the years, Towery has become the largest producer of published materials for North American chambers of commerce. From membership directories that enhance business-to-business communication to visitor and relocation guides tailored to reflect the unique qualities of the communities they cover, the company's chamber-oriented materials offer comprehensive information on dozens of topics, including housing, education, leisure activities, health care, and local government.

In 1998, the company acquired Cincinnati-based Target Marketing, an established provider of detailed city street maps to more than 200 chambers of commerce throughout the United States and Canada. Now a division of Towery, Target offers full-color maps that include local landmarks and points of interest, such as recreational parks, shopping centers, golf courses, schools, industrial parks, city and county limits, subdivision names, public buildings, and even block numbers on most streets.

In 1990, Towery launched the Urban Tapestry Series, an award-winning collection of oversized, hardbound photo-journals detailing the people, history, culture, environment, and commerce of various metropolitan areas. These coffee-table books highlight a community through three basic elements: an introductory essay by a noted local individual, an exquisite collection of four-color photographs, and profiles of the companies and organizations that animate the area's business life.

To date, more than 80 Urban Tapestry Series editions have been published in cities around the world, from New York to Vancouver to Sydney. Authors of the books' introductory essays include former U.S. President Gerald Ford (Grand Rapids), former Alberta Premier Peter Lougheed (Calgary), CBS anchor Dan Rather (Austin), ABC anchor Hugh Downs (Phoenix), best-selling mystery author Robert B. Parker (Boston), American Movie Classics host Nick Clooney (Cincinnati), and Challenger Center founder June Scobee Rodgers (Chattanooga).

To maintain hands-on quality in all of its periodicals and books, Towery has long used the latest production methods available. The company was the first production environment in the United States to combine desktop publishing with color separations and image scanning to produce finished film suitable for burning plates for four-color printing. Today, Towery relies on state-of-the-art digital prepress services to produce more than 8,000 pages each year, containing more than 30,000 high-quality color images.

An Internet Pioneer

By combining its expertise in community-oriented published materials with advanced production capabilities, a global sales force, and extensive data management capabilities, Towery has emerged as a significant provider of Internet-based city information. In keeping with its overall focus on community resources, the company's Internet efforts represent a natural step in the evolution of the business.

The primary product lines within the Internet division are

Towery Publishing President and CEO J. Robert Towery has expanded the business his parents started in the 1930s to include a growing array of traditional and electronic published materials, as well as Internet and multimedia services, that are marketed locally, nationally, and internationally.

the introCity™ sites. Towery's introCity sites introduce newcomers, visitors, and longtime residents to every facet of a particular community, while simultaneously placing the local chamber of commerce at the forefront of the city's Internet activity. The sites include newcomer information, calendars, photos, citywide business listings with everything from nightlife to shopping to family fun, and on-line maps pinpointing the exact location of businesses, schools, attractions, and much more.

Decades of Publishing Expertise

In 1972, current President and CEO J. Robert Towery succeeded his parents in managing the printing and publishing business they had founded nearly four decades earlier. Soon thereafter, he expanded the scope of the company's published materials to include *Memphis* magazine and other successful regional and national publications. In 1985, after selling its locally focused assets, Towery began the trajectory on which it continues today, creating community-oriented materials that are often produced in conjunction with chambers of commerce and other business organizations.

Despite the decades of change, Towery himself follows a long-standing family philosophy of unmatched service and unflinching quality. That approach extends throughout the entire organization to include more than 120 employees at the Memphis headquarters, another 80 located in Northern Kentucky outside Cincinnati, and more than 40 sales, marketing, and editorial staff traveling to and working in a growing list of client cities. All of its products, and more information about the company, are featured on the Internet at www.towery.com.

In summing up his company's steady growth, Towery restates the essential formula that has driven the business since its first pages were published: "The creative energies of our staff drive us toward innovation and invention. Our people make the highest possible demands on themselves, so I know that our future is secure if the ingredients for success remain a focus on service and quality."

Towery Publishing was the first production environment in the United States to combine desktop publishing with color separations and image scanning to produce finished film suitable for burning plates for four-color printing. Today, the company's state-of-the-art network of Macintosh and Windows workstations allows it to produce more than 8,000 pages each year, containing more than 30,000 high-quality color images (top).

The Towery family's publishing roots can be traced to 1935, when R.W. Towery (far left) began producing a series of community histories in Tennessee, Mississippi, and Texas. Throughout the company's history, the founding family has consistently exhibited a commitment to clarity, precision, innovation, and vision (bottom).

Allsport was founded the moment
freelance photographer Tony
Duffy captured the now-famous
picture of Bob Beamon breaking
the world long-jump record at
the Mexico City Olympics in
1968. Originally headquartered
in London, Allsport has expanded
to include offices in New York
and Los Angeles. Its pictures
have appeared in every major
publication in the world, and
the best images from its portfolio have been displayed at elite
photographic exhibitions at the
Royal Photographic Society
and the Olympic Museum
in Lausanne.

Tim Bickel, who holds an associate
degree in electrical engineering
technology, has attended classes
at Winona School of Professional
Photography and Indiana
University-Purdue University
Indianapolis. His work has
appeared in *Light and Life*,
Touring America, *Open Wheel*,
and *Career World*, as well as
Towery Publishing's *Indianapolis: Crossroads of the American
Dream*. His client list includes
Indianapolis Mayor Stephen
Goldsmith and race car driver
Lyn St. James. Bickel is a photographer for Eastman Kodak and
the codirector of photography
for A Diverse Focus, a group
that organizes and exhibits its
photos in Indianapolis and
throughout the state of Indiana.

E.A. Boase moved to Indianapolis
in 1995 from LaGrange County.
In addition to photography, she
enjoys gardening, animals, and
sprint cars.

Kelsey Byus graduated from Indiana University, Bloomington, in
1993 with a sports marketing
degree. Originally from Fairmont,
he moved to Indianapolis in 1995.
Byus specializes in architecture
and landscape photography, but
also enjoys photographing
sporting events and festivals.

Charlene Faris, a native of Fleming
County, Kentucky, is the owner
and operator of Charlene Faris
Photos. Specializing in travel,
historic, and inspirational photography, Faris has won numerous
awards and was a 1994 Pulitzer
Prize nominee for wedding
photos of Lyle Lovett and Julia
Roberts, which have now been
published in more than 20
nations. Faris also completed an
art project for the Hoosier Salon
with a grant from the Indiana
Arts Commission and the
National Endowment for the
Arts. Faris' images have appeared
in several Towery publications,
including *Atlanta: The Right*

*Kind of Courage, Orlando: The
City Beautiful, St. Louis: For the
Record*, and *San Antonio: A
Cultural Tapestry*.

Larry Goshen is a retired professional musician who specializes
in music photography. He has
worked for the Indianapolis Jazz
Foundation and *Downbeat*
magazine, and has done photography for several compact disc
covers. An Indianapolis resident
since 1951, Goshen now works
for Face the Music, Inc.

John Kapke, an Indianapolis resident
since 1960, entered the field of
photography in 1981. He is the
chairperson for the Southport
Travel Photo Club and teaches
photography classes at Emmerich
Manual Evening School. Kapke's
photographs can also be seen in
Towery Publishing's *Indianapolis:
Crossroads of the American Dream*.

William Lesch is an Indiana native
now living in Tucson. He received
a bachelor of fine arts degree
from the University of Arizona in
1978, and did graduate work
there from 1978 to 1981. Lesch
now owns William Lesch Photography and specializes in land-
scapes, still lifes, and architecture.
His work has been featured in
the Los Angeles County Museum

of Art and the Tucson Museum of
Art, as well as exhibited in
Germany, Japan, and England.

Paul McCreary was an art and
special education teacher for
almost 30 years before focusing
on photography full-time. He
specializes in science photography and has displayed and sold
work in Michigan, Florida, Indiana,
Colorado, Arizona, and New
Mexico. McCreary also photographs weddings and does
work for several Internet-
based businesses.

Mike McDaniel specializes in
corporate, stock, and architecture photography. He is an
Indiana native and works for
Dark Star Studio.

Laurie Mullen, a student at the
University of Northern Iowa,
specializes in travel photography.
She has photographed the bound-
ary waters of Minnesota; Canada;
Central Mexico; Costa Rica; and
Nice, France.

Photophile, established in San
Diego in 1967, is owned and
operated by Nancy Likins-
Masten. An internationally
known stock photography agency,
Photophile houses more than a
million color images and repre-

sents more than 90 contributing local and international photographers. Subjects include extensive coverage of the West Coast, business/industry, people/lifestyles, health/medicine, travel, scenics, wildlife, and adventure sports, plus 200 additional categories.

Terri Quillen, a native of New Orleans, is a self-employed writer, designer, and photo stylist. A registered nurse, she specializes in family celebration and travel photography, though she also enjoys many other types of photography. Quillen's photo work has appeared in *Doll World*, *Bridal Crafts*, and Towery Publishing's *Indianapolis: Crossroads of the American Dream*, and she regularly contributes her written work to *Nursing* magazine and other nursing journals. Quillen owns her own studio, Q.C.C.

Curtis B. Stahr has photographed the migration of the American eagle from Alaska to Florida; some 20 national parks and monuments; and all 99 Iowa courthouses. He has walked with his camera across Canada from ocean to ocean and photographed life in each of the contiguous United States. Stahr has exhibited in 32 juried/invited art shows and 16 one-man shows; received 11 purchase awards; and is listed in *American Artists of Renown*, *Who's Who in Photography*, and *Who's Who in the World*. His work has also appeared in Towery Publishing's *Greater Des Moines: Iowa's Commercial Center* and *San Francisco: City for all Seasons*.

Michael Vaughn specializes in images of people for corporate advertising and editorial clients. His work features strong black-and-white photography as well as colorful portraits. An Indiana native, he has been owner and operator of Michael Vaughn Photography since 1986.

Steve Warble is the owner and operator of Mountain Magic Photography in Elgin. He specializes in stock photo sales and decor photography. Warble's work has been featured in several magazines, calendars, and books, as well as in commercial and environmental displays. He has traveled extensively across North America photographing nature scenes from the High Arctic to the Rio Grande, and from Alaska's Brooks Range to northern Georgia.

Library of Congress Cataloging-in-Publication Data

Price, Nelson.
    Indianapolis : leading the way / by Nelson Price ; art direction by Jonathan Postal.
        p.   cm. — (Urban tapestry series)
    Includes index.
    ISBN 1-881096-82-3 (alk. paper)
        1. Indianapolis (Ind.)—Civilization.   2. Indianapolis (Ind.)—Pictorial works.   3. Indianapolis (Ind.)—Economic conditions.   4. Business enterprises—Indiana—Indianapolis.
    I. Title.   II. Series.
    F534.I35 P75 2000
    977.2′52—dc21   00-033769

© JONATHAN POSTAL / TOWERY PUBLISHING INC.

[Printed in Spain]

Towery Publishing, Inc., The Towery Building
1835 Union Avenue, Memphis, TN 38104
WWW.TOWERY.COM

Publisher: J. Robert Towery Executive Publisher: Jenny McDowell National Sales Manager: Stephen Hung Marketing Director: Carol Culpepper Project Directors: Dawn Park-Donegan, Mary Hanley, Jim Tomlinson Executive Editor: David B. Dawson Managing Editor: Lynn Conlee Senior Editor: Carlisle Hacker Editor/Profile Manager: Stephen M. Deusner Editors: Jay Adkins, Brian Johnston, Ginny Reeves Editor/Caption Writer: Sunni Thompson Copy Editors: Rebecca Green, Danna Greenfield Editorial Assistant: Andrew S. Harlow Profile Writer: Susan C. Lawson Creative Director: Brian Groppe Photographic Consultant: Stephen H. Baker Profile Designers: Laurie Beck, Laura Higley Production Manager: Brenda Pattat Photography Coordinator: Robin Lankford Production Assistants: Robert Barnett, Loretta Lane Digital Color Supervisor: Darin Ipema Digital Color Technicians: Eric Friedl, Brad Long, Brent Salazar, Mark Svetz Production Resources Manager: Dave Dunlap Jr. Print Coordinator: Beverly Timmons

Indianapolis